Preparing Classroom Teachers to Succeed with Second Language Learners

This volume identifies resources, models, and specific practices for improving teacher preparation for work with second language learners. It shows how faculty positioned themselves to learn from resources, experts, preservice teachers, their own practice, and each other. The teacher education professionals leverage their experience to offer theoretical and practical insights regarding how other faculty could develop their own knowledge, improve their courses, and understand their influence on the preservice teachers they serve.

The book addresses challenges others are likely to experience while improving teacher preparation, the challenge of adding to already-packed courses, the difficulty of recruiting and retaining busy faculty members, and the question of how to best frame the larger issues. The authors also address options for integrating the work of improving teacher preparation for linguistic diversity into a variety of different teacher education program designs. Finally, the book demonstrates a data-driven approach that makes this work consistent with many institutions' mandate to produce research and to collect evidence supporting accreditation.

Thomas H. Levine is an Associate Professor in the Department of Curriculum and Instruction of the Neag School of Education at the University of Connecticut, where he teaches social studies methods courses for elementary and secondary educators at both the graduate and undergraduate levels.

Elizabeth R. Howard is an Associate Professor in the Department of Curriculum and Instruction of the Neag School of Education at the University of Connecticut, where she teaches graduate courses related to the education of English Language Learners (ELLs). Together with Julie Sugarman, she is the author of *Realizing the Vision of Two-Way Immersion: Fostering Effective Programs and Classrooms*.

David M. Moss is an Associate Professor in the Department of Curriculum and Instruction of the Neag School of Education at the University of Connecticut. His published books include *Reforming Legal Education: Law Schools at the Crossroads*; *Critical Essays on Resistance in Education*; *Interdisciplinary Education in an Age of Assessment*; *Portrait of a Profession: Teachers and Teaching in the 21st Century*; and *Beyond the Boundaries: A Transdisciplinary Approach to Learning and Teaching*.

Routledge Research in Teacher Education

The Routledge Research in Teacher Education series presents the latest research on Teacher Education and also provides a forum to discuss the latest practices and challenges in the field.

Books in the series include:

Preparing Classroom Teachers to Succeed with Second Language Learners
Lessons from a Faculty Learning Community
Edited by Thomas H. Levine, Elizabeth R. Howard, and David M. Moss

Preparing Classroom Teachers to Succeed with Second Language Learners

Lessons from a Faculty Learning Community

Edited by Thomas H. Levine, Elizabeth R. Howard, and David M. Moss

NEW YORK AND LONDON

First published 2014
by Routledge
711 Third Avenue, New York, NY 10017, USA

and by Routledge
2 Park Square, Milton Park, Abingdon, Oxfordshire OX14 4RN

First issued in paperback 2016

Routledge is an imprint of the Taylor & Francis Group, an informa business

© 2014 Taylor & Francis

The right of Thomas H. Levine, Elizabeth R. Howard, and David M. Moss to be identified as the authors of the editorial material, and of the authors for their individual chapters, has been asserted in accordance with sections 77 and 78 of the Copyright, Designs and Patents Act 1988.

All rights reserved. No part of this book may be reprinted or reproduced or utilised in any form or by any electronic, mechanical, or other means, now known or hereafter invented, including photocopying and recording, or in any information storage or retrieval system, without permission in writing from the publishers.

Trademark Notice: Product or corporate names may be trademarks or registered trademarks, and are used only for identification and explanation without intent to infringe.

Library of Congress Cataloging-in-Publication Data

Preparing classroom teachers to succeed with second language learners : lessons from a faculty learning community / edited by Thomas Levine, Elizabeth Howard, David Moss.
   pages cm. — (Routledge Research in Teacher Education ; 1)
   Includes bibliographical references and index.
 1. Language and languages—Study and teaching—Foreign speakers. 2. Second language acquisition—Study and teaching. 3. Language teachers—Training of. 4. Classroom management. 5. Communication and education. I. Levine, Thomas. II. Howard, Elizabeth R. III. Moss, David M. IV. Title: Lessons from a faculty learning community.
   P53.P693 2014
   418.0071—dc23
   2014002177

Typeset in Sabon
by IBT Global.

ISBN 13: 978-1-138-28687-0 (pbk)
ISBN 13: 978-0-415-84116-0 (hbk)

We dedicate this book to Dr. Mileidis Gort, a colleague at the University of Connecticut from 2001 to 2006. During her time at UConn, Millie kindly yet persistently urged her fellow faculty members to learn more about cultural and linguistic diversity and to infuse that knowledge into course materials, activities, and assignments. Her work began modestly with two colleagues, grew to include more of us in a reading group, and ultimately inspired Project PREPARE-ELLs. We are grateful to continue our collaborative work with Millie today.

Contents

List of Figures ix
List of Tables xi
Acknowledgments xiii

PART I
Defining the Problem Space and Possibilities

1 The Urgency of Preparing Teachers for Second Language Learners 3
   ELIZABETH R. HOWARD, THOMAS H. LEVINE, AND DAVID M. MOSS

2 Teacher Educator Capacity to Prepare Preservice Teachers for Work with Emergent Bilinguals 17
   THOMAS H. LEVINE AND ELIZABETH R. HOWARD

3 Recruiting and Organizing Learning among Busy Faculty Members 37
   THOMAS H. LEVINE, ELIZABETH R. HOWARD, AND MILEIDIS GORT

PART II
Revising Courses and Developing Practices

4 Using a Conceptual Frame to Infuse Material about Emergent Bilinguals into a Teacher Education Course 63
   MEGAN E. STAPLES AND THOMAS H. LEVINE

5 Solving Problems of Space, Time, and Knowledge: How to Fit Learning about Linguistic and Cultural Diversity into Teacher Education Courses 85
   DOUGLAS KAUFMAN, MARY P. TRUXAW, ALAN S. MARCUS, SANDRA B. BILLINGS, AND MANUELA WAGNER

viii Contents

6 Teaching Preservice Teachers How to Learn from—and about—Their Emergent Bilingual Students: The Foundation for Everything Else 105
DOUGLAS KAUFMAN

7 Leveraging Clinical Experiences to Prepare Teachers for Culturally and Linguistically Diverse Students 122
REBECCA D. ECKERT, SUSAN L. PAYNE, ROBIN E. HANDS, AND RENÉ ROSELLE

PART III
Assessing Outcomes and Learning along the Way

8 Assessing Progress Within and Across Cohorts 139
ELIZABETH R. HOWARD, MEGAN E. WELSH, THOMAS H. LEVINE, AND DAVID M. MOSS

9 Instruction in Progress: In Search of Effective Practices for Emergent Bilinguals 154
CORY WRIGHT-MALEY, THOMAS H. LEVINE, AND EILEEN M. GONZÁLEZ

10 From Professional Learning to Professional Action and Back Again 174
RACHAEL GABRIEL AND MANUELA WAGNER

11 Preservice Teachers' Evolving Knowledge and Practice toward Linguistically and Culturally Responsive Pedagogy 190
WENDY J. GLENN AND MILEIDIS GORT

PART IV
Moving Forward

12 Pathways to Success: Models of Teacher Preparation for Cultural and Linguistic Diversity 219
DAVID M. MOSS, J. ZACK, AND SUSAN L. PAYNE

13 Final Recommendations for Initiating a Faculty Learning Community 231
ELIZABETH R. HOWARD, THOMAS H. LEVINE, AND DAVID M. MOSS

Contributors 243
Index 249

Figures

2.1	Conceptualizing what preservice teachers need to work effectively with emergent bilinguals.	18
2.2	Conceptualizing what teacher educators need to prepare preservice teachers to work effectively with emergent bilinguals.	21
2.3	Conceptualizing a developmental progression: four additive models of promoting teacher educators' capacity to prepare teachers for linguistic diversity.	32
4.1	In-class activity focused on language and mathematics.	83
7.1	Structured observation and reflection task regarding literacy and language.	132
8.1	Change in IBM preservice teacher self-efficacy over time for each cohort.	148
8.2	Change in TCPCG self-efficacy over time for each cohort.	149
8.3	Mean self-efficacy at program completion by IBM cohort.	151
8.4	Mean self-efficacy at program completion by TCPCG cohort.	151

Tables

2.1	Three Models for Enhancing Teacher Educators' Ability to Prepare Teachers for Linguistic Diversity	23
2.2	Models for Teacher Educators Partnering with Others to Develop Capacity to Prepare Preservice Teachers for Linguistic Diversity	26
3.1	Critical Friends Protocol	50
4.1	What Elementary Education Students Reported Getting from an Opening Session Framing Teaching Emergent Bilinguals	74
4.2	Progression of Topics and Course Materials Related to Language in a Secondary Math Education Methods Course	80
8.1	Preservice Teachers' Second Language	143
8.2	Preservice Teachers' Second Language Oral Proficiency	145
8.3	Quantity of ELLs in Classrooms Where Preservice Teachers Taught or Interned	145
8.4	TELLSES ANOVA Results by Cohort within Program	149
9.1	Preservice Teachers' Disciplinary Backgrounds by Cohort	156
9.2	Most Frequently Enacted SIOP Features	160
9.3	Least Frequently Enacted SIOP Features	161
9.4	Student Teachers' Self-Described Strategies for Working with Emergent Bilinguals, 2011 and 2012	163

Acknowledgments

We, the editors of this book, would like to acknowledge the various funders that have greatly facilitated our work. First, we would like to express our appreciation to the Carnegie Corporation of New York, which provided a generous Teachers for a New Era (TNE) grant to the teacher education programs at the Neag School of Education at the University of Connecticut. With the critical support of the Dean's office in general and Associate Dean Marijke Kehrhahn in particular, we sought and received permission from the corporation to use some funds from the larger TNE grant to fund the project that gave rise to this book. We are also grateful for a faculty grant awarded by the University of Connecticut Research Foundation to support data collection and analysis. The content of this volume is solely the responsibility of the authors and editors and does not necessarily represent the official views of the Carnegie Corporation or the University of Connecticut.

We are grateful for the support of more individuals than we can easily name, but we want to especially highlight a few. We are grateful to Maria Brisk, Deborah Short, and Allene Grognet for wise counsel that helped us design and implement this project. Our Department Chair, Mary Anne Doyle, has valued and championed our work, encouraging and supporting us at every turn. Donalyn Maneggia, in the Office of Teacher Education, has handled all manner of logistical arrangement, budget, and catering with skill and unflappable good energy. Lisa Rasicot similarly has helped us with a bevy of logistical tasks. Mary Rinaldo-Ducat has also provided critical support by helping us with proofreading, and administrative matters. Finally, we were blessed with wonderful and dedicated graduate assistants: Cory Maley for our first two years, and then Eileen Gonzalez in our third year.

We acknowledge our colleagues' patience and professional commitment as we have embarked on a multi-year journey together to learn about linguistic and cultural diversity while improving teacher preparation for emergent bilinguals. Although three of us are credited as editors, the whole group conceived of this book and its purpose, brainstormed content, and worked together with esprit de corps while critiquing each other's work and humoring our requests for multiple revisions. We are grateful to work with peers who willingly chose to explore their own gaps in knowledge and practice in ways that have made us all better.

We are grateful to our Routledge Editor Stacy Noto, Editorial Assistant Lauren Verity, and IBT/Hamilton Page Compositor Michael Watters. Their careful work and support improved this book and helped us throughout the entire process of production. Finally, we thank our spouses and families for their encouragement and support.

Part I
Defining the Problem Space and Possibilities

1 The Urgency of Preparing Teachers for Second Language Learners

Elizabeth R. Howard, Thomas H. Levine, and David M. Moss

THE OVERARCHING CHALLENGE

Sunhee arrived from Korea in 1990 as a shy seventh grader who flashed a beautiful, bashful smile whenever she didn't understand what someone said to her. Two years later, in a Massachusetts suburb, Tom, the second author of this chapter, saw that smile much more often than he heard her voice in his ninth-grade social studies class. As Tom recalls,

> By that time, I was striving to be a great history teacher and was enjoying some measure of success. Several classes of students had chosen me to be graduation speaker. Staff had chosen me as teacher of the year. My top students were acing A.P. U.S. history exams, and a course I created integrating special education and regular education students had attracted fifty visitors from other schools. None of this helped Sunhee. My B.A. in history and M.A. in teaching hadn't ever included mention of English language learners; my preservice and in-service teacher education also never challenged my belief that it was someone else's job to provide help that addressed Sunhee's needs as an "emergent bilingual," someone still mastering English.

The school district is more diverse today. In the early 1990s, however, the rarity of students like Sunhee—together with Tom's lack of preparation and his preconceptions that teaching English language learners (ELLs) was not his responsibility—all kept Tom from devoting any appreciable time to thinking about how to teach emergent bilinguals.

Compared to other mainstream teachers, Tom was certainly not atypical in the early 1990s. Even today, especially in suburbs where there have typically been fewer ELLs, many mainstream teachers lack the required knowledge, skills, and dispositions to teach such students effectively. The first part of this chapter addresses this issue directly, responding to the question, "Why is it important for classroom teachers to be prepared to work effectively with second language learners?" Specifically, the chapter highlights the growth and diversity of ELLs in U.S. schools, the need for such students to be well educated to ensure the continued health of the nation's democracy and economy, and the lack of attention to the needs of second language learners in most mainstream teacher preparation programs. We then describe the teacher education programs at the University of Connecticut to provide readers with a context for understanding the material presented in the rest of the volume. We conclude with an overview of the contents of subsequent chapters, thus addressing how this book can help teacher educators prepare preservice teachers to work effectively with second language learners.

WHY IS IT IMPORTANT FOR ALL TEACHERS TO BE PREPARED TO WORK EFFECTIVELY WITH SECOND LANGUAGE LEARNERS?

To convey the urgency of this work, let us first start with our own nation. In the U.S., the health of our nation's democracy and the vibrancy of our economy depend on our success in equipping students like Sunhee with the language, knowledge, and skills to thrive as contributing members of society. English language learners can now be found in more than two thirds of all U.S. public schools (U.S. Department of Education, 2009). This growth reflects 158 percent increases in the population that speak a langauge other than English from home between 1980 and 2010; during the same period, the entire population grew 38 percent (Ryan, 2013). Similarly between the 1989–1990 school year and the 2005–2006 school year, the total population of students enrolled in U.S. schools increased 20.6 percent while the percentage of English language learners increased 152.1 percent (Institute of Education Sciences, 2011). By 2030, the U.S. Census Bureau estimates that 40% of U.S. students in K–12 public schools will come from homes where they will learn a first language other than English (Lucas & Grinberg, 2007). If current trends hold, in 2030, roughly half of these students will come to school with sufficient English proficiency to be able to participate in educational activities without special language supports. This fifth of our future students would still be better served by classroom teachers who understand—or know how to learn about—the differing knowledge, experiences, and values emergent bilinguals and their families bring into schools. The other fifth will arrive at school without sufficient mastery of English to thrive academically unless we proactively provide additional support, ideally through a combination of highly trained classroom teachers and specialists such as bilingual and/or English as a Second Language (ESL) teachers. Moreover, there is not only ongoing growth in the percentages of ELLs in schools across the nation, but also an increase in the geographical locations where second language learners reside (National Center for English Language Acquisition, 2012). Historically, the majority of ELLs in the U.S. resided in one of five states (California, Texas, Illinois, Florida, or New York), whereas current trends show dispersion of ELL populations into states where there have not been high concentrations in the past, particularly in the Southeast and Midwest. Similarly, within states, ELL populations are migrating from urban centers into suburbs and rural areas. In other words, regardless of which state a teacher works in or where in the state that teacher works, odds are increasing that ELLs will be part of the classroom population. Finally, attending to the needs of ELLs has become even more urgent because many states now limit the amount of time these students can spend in separate programs designed to support their mastery of English and academic content. Students are pushed more quickly into mainstream classrooms and thus need teachers skilled at helping them master content while mastering a second language.

We term this second group of students—those who are still engaged in mastering English for academic learning—"emergent bilinguals." We consider the term "second language learners" an adequate synonym for "emergent bilinguals," and we use it in our book title and chapter headings because it is more familiar, but we prefer "emergent bilinguals" for two reasons. First, depending on where these students grew up in the world, they may have already learned two or more languages, so that the language of instruction is not really their second language. More important, phrases like "second language learner" or "English language learner" emphasize what these students don't have—and reinforces a perspective emphasizing deficits and deficiencies—without crediting linguistic and cultural resources that they do have, which could facilitate learning of a second language and content.

Emergent bilinguals in the U.S. are a large, diverse group with varying strengths and challenges. While the clear majority are native Spanish speakers, more than 150 different language groups are represented (Batalova & McHugh, 2010). Some emergent bilinguals are born in the U.S., whereas others travel from another country with their families or on their own. Those who come from other countries may or may not have had the benefit of formal education prior to their arrival and therefore have highly varying levels of prior academic content mastery, English proficiency, and knowledge of school culture in general. Parent education levels of emergent bilinguals tend to be lower than those of the native English-speaking population (Ballantyne, Sanderman, & Levy, 2008); however, some emergent bilinguals have parents who have had extensive formal education themselves, including graduate-level education in the U.S. or other English-speaking countries. Likewise, while a considerably higher percentage of emergent bilinguals than native English speakers live in poverty, as indicated by participation in free/reduced lunch programs (Ballantyne, Sanderman, & Levy, 2008), other emergent bilinguals come from more affluent circumstances.

The continuous increase of emergent bilinguals presents the U.S. with great opportunities, but those opportunities can only be realized if we take the appropriate actions. If we as educators fail to create supportive instructional environments for all students, including those who are learning English in addition to another language, a generation of emergent bilinguals will be underprepared for entering the workforce and/or further education, at tremendous cost to themselves and the nation. Without efforts to respond to their needs and understand the values and resources that they bring to the classroom, many will fail to realize their potential within and beyond school, as evident in their disengagement, underperformance on standardized tests, and high dropout rates (Ballantyne, Sanderman, & Levy, 2008). In 2005, wages for high school dropouts and those with only high school diplomas were one third and one half, respectively, of the wages of those with bachelor's degrees. It is not just that tax coffers diminish and employers suffer when the workforce is underprepared; research has shown that U.S. high school dropouts are less likely to vote (McCaul, Donaldson, Coladarci, & Davis, 1992), use more publicly funded services (Rumberger, 1987), and are six times more likely to be incarcerated than students who graduate from high school but don't attend college (Sum, Khatiwada, & McLaughlin, 2009).

The great opportunity is that if we equip teachers with the knowledge, skills, and dispositions to help these learners, we can hasten the contributions we expect from the latest newcomers to the U.S. while strengthening the fabric and diversity of our society. If teachers who have spent a career learning and teaching their own subject area are also taught successful approaches to working with emergent bilinguals, then these students can continue the American tradition of cultural, economic, and social progress achieved via the hard work and talents of immigrants and their children.

The urgency of preparing teachers for work with second language learners is not limited to the U.S. Throughout the world, political, economic, and environmental forces are leading an increasing number of people to migrate. The nations of the European Union (EU) have witnessed considerable legal migration across their borders; in addition, political refugees and undocumented workers have come from beyond the borders of the 27 EU nations (European Commission, 2010; Extra & Yagmar, 2002; Strieff, 2007). Turkey has seen an upsurge in the internal migration of citizens from different language groups into its cities (Akar, 2010). In some Sub-Saharan African nations, drought, soil erosion, and desertification have led millions to relocate—sometimes permanently—away from their traditional homelands (Myers, 2002; Scheffran, Marmer, & Sow, 2011). In South Korea, a paucity of marriageable women in the countryside has seen the rate of "international marriage" triple between 2000 and 2008; one in eight marriages now involves one immigrant (Onishi, 2008), often a Chinese or Vietnamese woman, who will play a major role in childrearing. In these nations and more, students with diverse cultural and linguistic resources and needs are arriving in school systems ill prepared to serve them (e.g., Akar, 2010; Bratsberg, Oddbjørn, & Kunt, 2011; Faas, 2011). Across many nations, there is an urgent need to prepare teachers for work with second language learners.

Worryingly, those who will teach such emergent bilinguals in the coming decades may enter teaching as unaware and unprepared as Tom was in 1992. In the U.S., most teacher education programs do not require future teachers to take any course on issues related to English learners (Ballantyne, Sanderman, & Levy, 2008; Menken & Antunez, 2001). This omission is glaring because few teachers have personally experienced the challenges of growing proficient in a second language or negotiating daily tasks without the benefits of being a member of the dominant culture (Zehler et al., 2003; see also Gort & Glenn, 2009). Like preservice teachers, it seems that most teacher educators have neither the personal backgrounds nor the professional training to equip them to address issues of language and culture in their classes. Perhaps as a result of what teacher educators don't know, schools of education typically prepare teachers to teach some "amorphous, 'average' student" who, by default, is a monolingual English speaker (Commins & Miramontes, 2006, p. 240). Rather than assuming at the outset that cultural and linguistic diversity is the norm and should be a fundamental given in each course of study, teacher preparation programs may offer only one stand-alone course—or no course at all—that provides principles or theory for teaching culturally and/or linguistically diverse students. Even where preservice teachers receive such a course and it addresses emergent bilinguals, they are often left on their own to apply broad principles to the thorny dilemmas of teaching subject-specific content and skills to their students. Thus, it should be no surprise that a majority of teachers report that they do not feel prepared to teach ELLs (Ballantyne, Sanderman, & Levy, 2008; Gandara, Maxwell-Jolly, & Driscoll, 2005; National Center for Education Statistics, 1999).

We don't lack relevant knowledge or strategies for working with emergent bilinguals, but we need to help teachers—and those who teach them—to acquire new kinds of knowledge, practice, and dispositions. Many of the effective strategies for teaching emergent bilinguals will improve all students' education; thus, the work of preparing teachers to work with emergent bilinguals will often create better teachers for everyone.

GETTING TO KNOW OUR CONTEXT: TEACHER PREPARATION AT THE NEAG SCHOOL OF EDUCATION

Like the U.S.A. as a whole, the state of Connecticut has experienced dramatic growth in its population of emergent bilinguals, with more than 50% growth in the ELL student population over a 10-year period from 1997–1998 through 2007–2008, compared with less than 10% growth in the total student population over the same time period (U.S. Department of Education, 2010). The teachers graduating from the Neag School of Education at the University of Connecticut (UConn), on successive alumni surveys, provided feedback to the school indicating that they felt unprepared to work with this growing population of emergent bilinguals. Most of the faculty preparing teachers likewise felt woefully unprepared to address this issue within their various courses. We suspect that our school is similar to a great number of other teacher preparation programs. In response to our growing awareness of what both our preservice teachers and we, as teacher educators, needed to learn, we started Project PREPARE-ELLs (Preparing Responsive Educators Who Promote Access and Realize Excellence with English Language Learners). We'll tell the story of how we began in Chapter 3; at this point, we describe the two models of teacher education at the university to provide a context for understanding the project.

The Integrated Bachelor's/Master's program (known as the IBM program) and the post-baccalaureate program (known as the Teacher Certification Program for College Graduates [TCPCG]) mirror each other in program design. Both programs require early course work (including methods courses), place the student teaching experience at essentially the midpoint within the program, and mandate post-student teaching internships to foster reflection on the prior student teaching semester and broaden candidates' experiences in engaging with issues of school reform. They also share a number of core tenets, including the importance of a strong liberal arts background, the development of general pedagogical knowledge as well as subject-specific pedagogical knowledge, and the inclusion of high-quality clinical placements. These commonalities across program models, bounded by a culture of assessment at the Neag School, helped allow Project PREPARE-ELLs to thrive and the faculty working across these programs (often at differing physical campuses) to communicate and collaborate in mutually beneficial ways.

Integrated Bachelor's/Master's (IBM) Program

The IBM program is located on the main campus of UConn in Storrs. It offers courses of study for certification in the following areas:

- Elementary Education (Grades K–6)
- Secondary Education (Grades 7–12)
    - English
    - History/Social Studies
    - Science
    - Mathematics
    - World Languages
- Comprehensive Special Education (K–12)
- Music Education (PK–12)
- Agriculture Education (K–12)

Prior to admission into the IBM program, prospective freshman and sophomore students are generally classified as pre-education students. During these first two years of university study, students benefit from the Neag School of Education's strong partnership with the College of Liberal Arts and Sciences and its concurrent commitment to a strong liberal arts education. The admissions process begins in the spring semester of a student's sophomore year, with accepted students beginning the IBM program the following fall. Admission to the IBM program is highly competitive, keeping with the program goals of preparing outstanding educators to be decision makers, leaders, and innovators. It includes an extensive application process (written expression, teaching-related experience, letters of recommendation) and interview, as faculty seek candidates for whom teaching is a clear calling.

On admission into the program, students become members of cohort groups. The program is organized around three themes—student as learner, student as teacher, teacher as leader—that require progressively more complex and demanding coursework and clinic placements. Each cohort takes three years to complete their program; during each of six semesters, students complete course work, clinic placements, and a seminar that fosters reflection on and learning from clinic placements. The full-time student teaching occurs in the senior year (second year in the program as they are admitted as juniors). The final year of study (often referred to as the fifth year because it adds one year to the typical four-year undergraduate experience) is when students engage in graduate-level course work and a year-long internship. This internship is co-developed with partner schools and designed to go beyond student teaching and leverage the teacher as leader theme of this final year of the program. Students earn a bachelor's degree (at the conclusion of their senior year) and a master's degree (at the conclusion of their fifth year), and they are ultimately recommended for certification in their area of study only after they successfully complete all program requirements at the conclusion of the program.

Teacher Certification Program for College Graduates (TCPCG)

The TCPCG operates out of three regional UConn campuses: Avery Point, Greater Hartford, and Waterbury.

- Candidates in the program earn Connecticut Teacher Certification and an MA in Education.
- TCPCG is a full-time 11-month accelerated program.
- The program involves four consecutive semesters of coursework: Summer Session I, Summer Session II, Fall Semester, and Spring Semester.

TCPCG Certification Areas

Avery Point Campus: Mathematics Education, Science Education (STEM focus)
Greater Hartford and Waterbury Campuses: Agriculture Education, English Education, Mathematics Education, Science Education, Social Studies Education, Special Education, World Languages Education

Like the IBM program, the TCPCG has competitive admissions. Successful candidates are frequently career changers or students matriculating directly from a non-education undergraduate degree program (including UConn). This cohort-based program demands intensive full-time study, including course work across the two summer sessions, student teaching in the fall, and a semester-long internship in the final semester of this program. The student teaching experience and internship are pivotal components of the TCPCG and serve as the core experiences in which students apply learning from the intensive summer sessions and reflective seminar courses that complement both school placements over the full academic year.

The internship experience in both the IBM program and the TCPCG unfolds in conjunction with an inquiry project. This teacher-as-researcher requirement fosters candidate engagement above and beyond classroom teaching and invites pre-professionals to explore larger issues of teaching, learning, and school reform. Additionally, both programs culminate with a portfolio requirement designed to serve as a catalyst for program reflection while considering next steps as an early career professional.

HOW WILL THIS BOOK HELP TEACHER EDUCATORS PREPARE PRESERVICE TEACHERS TO WORK EFFECTIVELY WITH SECOND LANGUAGE LEARNERS?

This book addresses a pressing national and international need: to prepare future teachers for work with emergent bilingual students by improving what teacher education professors know and what they do, both in individual courses and across teacher education programs. To accomplish this goal, the book is organized into four parts, each addressing a different aspect of the work that teacher educators must to do: (a) defining the problem space and possibilities, (b) revising courses and developing practices, (c) assessing outcomes and learning along the way, and (d) moving forward.

The first part of the book—this introductory chapter and the two subsequent ones—help readers understand the problems and possibilities of preparing teachers for emergent bilinguals. This chapter has introduced contextual information to argue for the urgency of addressing emergent bilinguals and to help readers understand the setting in which Project PRE-PARE-ELLs takes place.

The second chapter of the book develops conceptual tools for understanding and addressing teacher preparation for emergent bilinguals. It asks, "To prepare preservice teachers for work with second language learners, what do teacher educators need? How might they get what they need?" The chapter develops a conceptual framework calling for both teacher educators and preservice teachers to develop knowledge, practice, dispositions, and vision. The chapter then presents four conceptual models for faculty development to foster these characteristics. Drawing on a small body of published work, we identify three extant models for enhancing teacher educators' ability to prepare teachers for work with learners of additional languages. We also introduce a fourth model: a faculty learning community that we have created for preparing both preservice teachers and teacher educators for this important work. The chapter closes with an annotated bibliography of readings that will support educators as they begin to develop knowledge about emergent bilinguals and second language acquisition.

Chapter 3 addresses the questions, "How is it possible to attract busy faculty to participate in collective efforts to improve teacher preparation for emergent bilinguals? What kinds of recruitment strategies and activities are more likely to maintain participation and to result in changes in what preservice teachers learn and can do?" Where Chapter 2 developed broad conceptual models for faculty professional development, here we draw on our experiences to offer practical recommendations for those seeking to engage faculty in work that will improve teacher preparation for work with emergent bilinguals. We describe, for instance, ways of organizing book clubs, ways of working with peer coaches to revise courses, and ways of using protocols to reflect on colleagues' practices and student work within a faculty learning community. This chapter also shares the perspective of the project facilitators regarding the work of initiating and sustaining various activities focused on improving teacher preparation for emergent bilinguals. We describe the tensions that we navigated—and others will likely face—during this kind of work.

Part II of the book is about revising courses and developing practice. It aims to identify instructional practices that teacher educators can adopt, highlighting challenges that participants in our faculty learning community have faced while integrating their ongoing learning into their courses, and how they have addressed those challenges.

For example, teacher educators must decide how to introduce and frame the issue of working with emergent bilinguals. If teacher educators strategically choose a conceptual frame as they infuse new material, assignments, and readings into pre-existing courses not focused on emergent bilinguals, then they create the potential for synergy and coherence rather than making the new information an add-on. Chapter 4 asks, "How can conceptual frames help teacher educators weave new content powerfully into existing course? How can such frames promote more coherent and deep learning related to both core course content and emergent bilinguals?" The chapter uses two case studies to suggest how choosing a frame creates opportunities for learning, and it identifies a number of conceptual frames that could help other professors infuse new material in ways that go beyond just adding new topics.

Another dilemma facing many teacher educators who embark on this type of work relates to this set of questions: "How do we fit issues of linguistic and cultural diversity into our courses so that they enhance what we already do? How do we introduce such issues so that they re-contextualize what we already teach and provide a more holistic, inclusionary perspective of skills, methods, and content knowledge?" As teacher educators consider how to revise courses to address culturally and linguistically diverse learners, they face the challenges of how to sequence various materials and how to make new content and practices dovetail with other topics in the class. Instructors are also likely to struggle to add new readings and topics without facing the need to drop others. Chapter 5 shares the challenges experienced by five teacher educators in our program along with their insights about when, how, and how much to add to existing methods courses.

Chapter 6 asks how teacher educators can position preservice teachers to learn from—and about—their emergent bilingual students. Preservice teachers need more than pre-packaged strategies for work with emergent bilinguals; they need to respond to the specific needs, resources, cultures, and backgrounds that their own emergent bilinguals bring, crafting pedagogical responses to specific needs. This chapter addresses the challenge of using preservice teacher education courses to help teachers learn how to learn about their students' specific sociocultural, linguistic, and experiential backgrounds. Teaching teachers how to learn about and from students provides an essential context for successful teaching because students' backgrounds and experiences provide the foundation off of which new content and language learning becomes more efficient and effective. This chapter highlights what preservice teacher educators can do to develop and support teachers' identities as learners about students.

Finally, the clinical seminars and placements in a teacher education program can raise unique opportunities and challenges for preparing teachers to work with emergent bilinguals. Chapter 7 asks, "How can clinic placements help prepare preservice teachers to work effectively with culturally and linguistically diverse students?" Clinical seminar leaders describe the work that they do with students engaging in their first formal observations and participation in schools; they describe how field experiences and their accompanying seminars can introduce foundational knowledge and further dispositions.

Part III of the book documents outcomes of our faculty learning community for both preservice teachers and teacher educators. As our work together has grown over the years, it has become increasingly important for us to systematically document our progress and explore the impact on participating teacher educators and preservice teachers. Individual faculty members undertake this endeavor in a variety of ways in their individual courses, while the project directors have instituted a number of means to monitor changes in the knowledge, beliefs, and practices of preservice teachers and teacher educators. Drawing on these varied data sources, the chapters in Part III collectively tell the story of the impact of the faculty learning community to date and point to areas for continued work in the future.

Chapter 8 asks, "How can a faculty learning community gauge the impact on its preservice teachers at a programmatic level? Over time, what changes can be noted among preservice teachers within and across cohorts?"

This chapter lays out suggestions for data collection and analysis that serve dual purposes essential to teacher education faculty: (a) to inform ongoing improvement in teacher preparation for linguistic and cultural diversity, and (b) to advance the field through publishable research. This dual focus can make the work of a faculty learning community sustainable and valued by all stakeholders. We describe the development of a measure for assessing preservice teachers' self-efficacy with regard to teaching emergent bilinguals and share findings pointing to improved self-efficacy within and across cohorts of preservice teachers over a four-year period. We close this chapter with recommendations for other programs that may be interested in collecting systematic data for use in research and program improvement.

The greatest challenge that teacher educators face is to provide a sufficiently coherent and powerful combination of knowledge, practices, and dispositions to enable novice student teachers to adopt the recommended practices in their actual student teaching of emergent bilinguals. Chapter 9 therefore asks, "Does what we do in our teacher education coursework result in preservice teachers enacting effective practices for emergent bilinguals when they are with K–12 students? How can we collect data that tell us whether preservice teachers are able to implement effective practices for emergent bilinguals? Further, how can we learn more about preservice teachers' self-perceptions of their progress and challenges working with emergent bilinguals?" This chapter relies on observations of student teaching and follow-up interviews with student teachers. The authors explore the extent to which the student teachers were able to identify and carry out appropriate instructional practices for emergent bilinguals, and it describes their challenges as they attempted to do so. The authors also address the question of what additional strategies teacher education programs might adopt in order to better help preservice teachers successfully enact these reform-oriented pedagogies.

Whereas Chapters 8 and 9 address outcomes for preservice teachers, Chapter 10 shifts the focus to teacher educators, asking, "What inspires teacher education faculty to participate in a faculty learning community, and what actions result from their participation?" This chapter describes more broadly the different kinds of changes that faculty achieved in our courses and ourselves as a result of our participation in the faculty learning community, and it seeks to understand what conditions or factors inspired such changes. Drawing on varied data sources, including notes and transcriptions of monthly meetings, reflective memos, interviews with participating faculty, and course syllabi, the authors craft a narrative about the impact of the faculty learning community on participating faculty and share insights that may help others consider both what the work can look like and how to support it.

Chapter 11 returns the focus to the preservice teachers, this time in the context of a secondary English methods course. The chapter addresses two questions: (a) "How do preservice English teachers respond to bilingual learner-focused components of a preservice secondary English education methods course?", and (b) "How do preservice English teachers apply their developing understandings about language and cultural diversity, second language acquisition, and sheltered instruction in their own work with emergent bilinguals?" The authors offer two case studies of preservice teachers who navigate the course content in different ways. The authors share the strategies that the instructor employed to further the development of appropriate knowledge, skills, and dispositions among the preservice teachers in her class; explore the degree to which the two preservice teachers give evidence of taking up the kinds of knowledge, practice, and dispositions the teacher educator sought to develop; and offer implications for others engaged in improving teacher preparation for emergent bilinguals.

The final part of our book, "Moving Forward," addresses important program-level issues and highlights the importance of infusing linguistic and cultural diversity content into teacher education programs in ways that meet accreditation requirements and flexibly accommodate a variety of program designs. This part also summarizes key ideas presented throughout the book that are most likely to support teacher education programs at other universities that may want to initiate a faculty learning community.

The work of improving teacher preparation for linguistic diversity also needs to take program-level factors into account. Thus, Chapter 12 asks, "Regardless of the constraints of specific program models as well as common programmatic challenges such as accreditation, how can faculty improve teacher preparation for linguistic and cultural diversity?" At UConn, our project included teacher education faculty in our five-year IBM program and faculty in our one-year intensive MA program. Drawing on our implementation across these two programs, the authors argue for the importance of finding "reform points"—places where programmatic change can be leveraged most readily—such as methods courses. The chapter closes with recommendations for ways in which teacher education programs can successfully infuse preparation for linguistic and cultural diversity across courses and experiences.

Finally, in Chapter 13, we close with five key recommendations emerging from our work for other institutions that choose to engage in similar activities. With the goal of empowering others to engage in sustained collaborative learning activities, we also anticipate some questions that readers may have and provide answers to help them move forward.

CONCLUSION

There are political, economic, and moral imperatives for helping each nation's emergent bilinguals discover and realize their potential. At UConn, what we have learned from our own efforts and from what our preservice teachers show us is that it is possible to prepare teacher educators and classroom teachers for this important work. We can ensure that students like Sunhee will change their shy and bashful smiles into the confident grins of students whose gifts will benefit themselves, their families, their communities, and their nation.

REFERENCES

Akar, H. (2010). Challenges for schools in communities with internal migration flows: Evidence from Turkey. *International Journal of Educational Development, 30*(3), 263–276.

Ballantyne, K.G., Sanderman, A.R., Levy, J. (2008). *Educating English language learners: Building teacher capacity.* Washington, DC: National Clearinghouse for English Language Acquisition. Retrieved March 17, 2014 from http://files.eric.ed.gov/fulltext/ED521360.pdf

Batalova, J., & McHugh, M. (2010). *Top languages spoken by English language learners nationally and by state.* Washington, DC: Migration Policy Institute.

Bratsberg, B., Oddbjørn, R., & Kunt, R. (2011). *Educating children of immigrants: Closing the gap in Norwegian Schools.* Bonn: The Institute for the Study of Labor. Retrieved from http://ftp.iza.org/dp6138.pdf

Commins, N. L., & Miramontes, O. B. (2006). Addressing linguistic diversity from the outset. *Journal of Teacher Education, 57*(3), 240–246.

European Commission. (2010). *Report of the peer learning activity, Oslo, May 2007: How can teacher education and training policies prepare teachers to teach effectively in culturally diverse settings?* European Commission Directorate-General for Education and Culture. Retrieved March 9, 2014 from http://www.kslll.net/Documents/PLA_Teaching%20effectively%20in%20culturally%20diverse%20settings_May%2007.pdf

Extra, G., & Yagmar, K. (2002). Language diversity in multicultural Europe: Comparative perspectives on immigrant minority languages at home and at school. *United Nations Educational, Scientific and Cultural Organization.* Retrieved March 9, 2014 from http://www.unesco.org/most/dp63extra.pdf

Faas, D. (2011). Between ethnocentrism and Europeanism? An exploration of the effects of migration and European integration on curricula and policies in Greece. *Ethnicities, 11*(2) 163–183.

Gándara, P, Maxwell-Jolly, J, & Driscoll, A. (2005). *Listening to teachers of English language learners: A survey of California teachers' challenges, experiences, and professional development needs.* Santa Cruz, CA: The Center for the Future of Teaching and Learning.

Gort, M., & Glenn, W. J. (2010). Navigating tensions in the process of change: An English-educator's dilemma management in the revision and implementation of a diversity-infused methods course. *Research in the Teaching of English, 45*(1), 59–86.

Lucas, T., & Grinberg, J. (2007). Responding to the linguistic reality of the mainstream classroom: Preparing classroom teachers to teach English language learners. In M. Cochran-Smith, S. Feiman-Nemser, & J. McIntyre (Eds.), *Handbook of research on teacher education: Enduring issues in changing contexts* (606–636). Mahwah, NJ: Lawrence Erlbaum Associates.

McCaul, E. J., Donaldson, G. A., Coladarci, T., & Davis, W. E. (1992). Consequences of dropping out of school: Findings from high school and beyond. *Journal of Educational Research, 85*, 198–207.

Menken, K., & Antunez, B. (2001). *An overview of the preparation and certification of teachers working with limited English proficient students.* Washington, DC: National Clearinghouse of Bilingual Education.

Myers, N. (2002). Environmental refugees: A growing phenomenon of the 21st century. *Philosophical Transactions of the Royal Society of London Series B, 357*, 609–613.

National Center for Educational Statistics. (1999). *Teacher quality: A report on the preparation and qualifications of public school teachers.* Washington, DC: U.S. Department of Education. Retrieved March 9, 2014 from http://nces.ed.gov/surveys/frss/publications/1999080/

National Clearinghouse on English Language Acquisition (2009). How has the English language learner (ELL) population changed in recent years? Retrieved March 17, 2014 from http://www.ncela.gwu.edu/files/rcd/BE021773/How_Has_The_Limited_English.pdf

National Clearinghouse on English Language Acquisition (2012). *EL student change over 10 years, by county, 1999/2000–009/2010.* Retrieved March 17, 2014 from http://ncela.us/content/42_elgrowth00_10

Onishi, N. (2008, March 30). Wed to strangers, Vietnamese wives build Korean lives. *New York Times.* Retrieved March 9, 2014 from http://www.nytimes.com/2008/03/30/world/asia/30brides.html?pagewanted=all.

Rumberger, R. W. (1987). High school dropouts: A review of issues and evidence. *Review of Educational Research, 57*(2), 101–121.

Ryan, C. (2013). Language Use in the United States: 2011. Washington: Bureau of the Census. Retrieved March 17, 2014 from http://www.census.gov/prod/2013pubs/acs-22.pdf.

Scheffran, J., Marner, E., & Sow, P. (2011). Migration as a contribution to resilience and innovation in climate adaptation: Social networks and co-development in Northwest Africa. *Applied Geography, 33*, 119–127.

Strieff, D. (2007). Migration and the changing face of Europe: Demographic shift tops polls as the biggest issue of concern for Europeans. *MSNBC.* Retrieved March 9, 2014 from http://www.msnbc.msn.com/id/18981598/ns/world_news-frontier_europe/t/migration-changing-face-europe/#.T1P1cRxQa1Y.

Sum, A., Khatiwada, I., & McLaughlin, J. (2009). *The consequences of dropping out of high school: Joblessness and jailing for high school dropouts and the high cost for taxpayers.* Center for Labor Market Studies Publications, Paper 23. Retrieved November 30, 2013, from http://hdl.handle.net/2047/d20000596.

U.S. Department of Education. (2009). *Schools and Staffing Survey (SASS), "Public School, BIE School, and Private School Data Files," 2007–08.* Retrieved November 30, 2013, from http://nces.ed.gov/pubs2009/2009321/tables/sass0708_2009321_s12n_02.asp.

U.S. Department of Education, Office of English Language Acquisition, Language Enhancement, and Academic Achievement for English Language Learners. (2010). *Connecticut rate of EL growth 1997/1998 to 2007/2008.* Retrieved March 9, 2014 from http://www.ncela.us/files/uploads/20/Connecticut_G_0708.pdf.

Zehler, A., Fleischman, H., Hopstock, P., Stephenson, T., Pendzick, M., & Sapru, S. (2003). *Descriptive study of services to LEP students and LEP students with disabilities* (Volume I Research Report). Arlington, VA: Development Associates Inc. Retrieved July 30, 2008, from http://www.ncela.gwu.edu/rcsabout/rcscarch/descriptivestudyfiles/volI_research_fulltxt.pdf

2 Teacher Educator Capacity to Prepare Preservice Teachers for Work with Emergent Bilinguals

Thomas H. Levine and Elizabeth R. Howard

THE OVERARCHING CHALLENGE

A core notion of this book is that teacher education faculty can—and must—develop the capacity to prepare teachers for work with emergent bilinguals. This is no small challenge. Most teacher education faculty have devoted considerable time to developing various kinds of expertise that help them prepare teachers. However, it is likely that most of a program's faculty will not feel like they have sufficient expertise to prepare teachers for work with emergent bilinguals, and they will be unsure just what expertise they need to develop. In addition to identifying what they must learn, there is the challenge of imagining how they might achieve this new learning. Most colleges and universities position faculty to share their own expertise but do not have experience helping faculty work together to develop and apply new expertise, in systemic ways, to instructional and program improvement. Thus, this chapter asks, "To prepare preservice teachers for work with emergent bilinguals, what do teacher educators need? How might they get what they need?"

To answer these questions, teacher educators must first determine what elementary and secondary teachers need to work with emergent bilinguals. We then must identify what teacher educators need to know and be able to do in order to prepare K–12 teachers for work with emergent bilinguals. The first part of this chapter develops a bi-level conceptual framework identifying first what K–12 teachers need and, second, what teacher educators need to work effectively with emergent bilinguals. Specifically, we propose that both our preservice teachers and teacher educators must develop specific kinds of knowledge, pedagogical practices, and dispositions. The chapter then presents conceptual models for faculty development to promote essential knowledge, practice, dispositions, and vision. Drawing on published work, we first identify three extant models for enhancing teacher educators' ability to prepare teachers for work with second language learners. We then propose a fourth model, a faculty learning community, that we have adopted. We introduce the nature of our work, consider the relative advantages of each of the four approaches, and offer recommendations for how others might choose—or combine—these approaches.

CONCEPTUALIZING WHAT PRESERVICE TEACHERS NEED TO EFFECTIVELY TEACH EMERGENT BILINGUALS

Research in English-speaking nations has identified problems, opportunities, and best practices for teaching emergent bilinguals in K–12 classrooms. However, we know little about best practices for preparing teachers to succeed with emergent bilinguals in teacher education. Lucas and Villegas (2010, 2011) outline seven characteristics of "linguistically responsive teachers" that teacher education programs should work to promote. These characteristics relate to teachers' attitudes, knowledge, and practices, such as understanding and valuing linguistic diversity, understanding and applying principles of second language acquisition, and supporting content area learning through specific pedagogical approaches designed for emergent bilinguals.

Our framework incorporates these ideas. However, to think flexibly about faculty development and program revision, we find it useful to use the broader conceptual building blocks in the "Framework for Teacher Learning" developed by the National Academy of Education's Preparing Teachers for a Changing World project (Darling-Hammond & Bransford, 2005). This framework proposes that effective teachers must develop specific understandings, practices, and dispositions, categories that are similar to those already used by many teacher education programs to describe their broadest goals. This framework also calls for providing preservice teachers with visions of the possible to inspire their practice. (For our own purposes and the sake of simplicity, we omit a fifth category, "tools," believing that we can encompass material and mental tools within our discussion of practices.) Thus, as shown in Figure 2.1, we posit that preservice teachers' capacity to teach emergent bilinguals has four components. These components could be developed within and across teacher preparation courses if teacher education faculty were prepared to address these areas. We describe each component in turn.

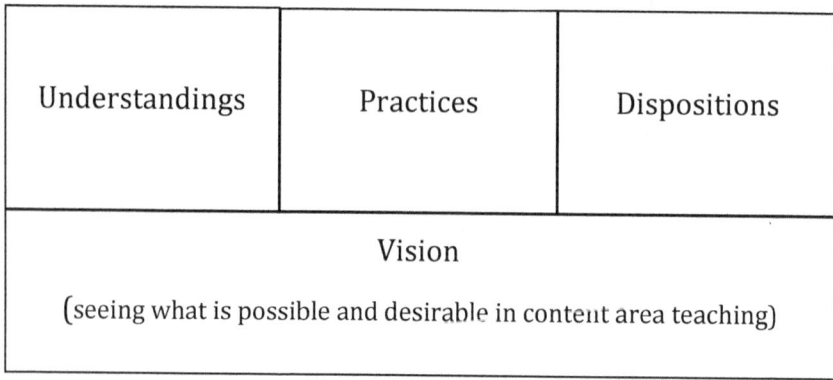

Figure 2.1 Conceptualizing what preservice teachers need to work effectively with emergent bilinguals.

Understandings

Effective teachers not only have a deep base of content knowledge, but also possess the pedagogical content knowledge (PCK) required to effectively help students learn specific subject matter. PCK is the understanding of how to make a subject area accessible to others, including both a range of pedagogical strategies and an understanding of learners' needs and misconceptions (Gudmundsdottir & Shulman, 1987; Shulman, 1994). We propose that PCK must include two kinds of understanding necessary for success with emergent bilinguals: (a) the specific aspects of a subject area that are likely to be particularly challenging for emergent bilinguals, including the role of language in texts and pedagogies (Schleppegrell, 2004); and (b) the cultural values, background knowledge, and first language skills that emergent bilinguals may bring with them, and the ways these can be leveraged to promote academic success in specific content areas (Adger, Temple, Snow, & Christian, 2002; Gonzalez, Moll, & Amanti, 2005; Valdés, Bunch, Snow, Lee, & Matos, 2005).

Practices

Beyond knowledge, teachers need practices—practical pedagogical approaches—for helping emergent bilinguals master rigorous academic content while also acquiring academic English. Existing scholarship can help to identify or adapt pedagogies for learning in specific disciplines, including the 30 desirable features of sheltered instruction listed in the Sheltered Instruction Observation Protocol (SIOP) (see Echevarria & Graves, 2003; Echevarria, Vogt, & Short, 2010); the five standards for culturally responsive pedagogy articulated by the Center for Research on Education, Diversity, and Excellence (Dalton, 1998); the Cognitive Academic Language Learning Approach (Chamot & O'Malley,1996); and the specific pedagogical strategies for emergent bilinguals identified by scholars and practitioners within specific fields (e.g., see Cruz & Thornton, 2009; Nutta, Nazan, & Butler, 2011).

Dispositions

Teacher education for linguistic and cultural diversity is insufficient if it provides knowledge and strategies without attending to what teachers feel and value. Feelings and values can create dispositions (i.e., "habits of thinking and action regarding teaching and children"), thus changing what teachers are likely to do (Hammerness, Darling-Hammond, & Bransford, 2005, p. 387). Dispositions that have been shown to affect teachers' success with students include teachers' seeking out new approaches to teaching that will allow greater success (Haberman, 1996) and believing that all children can succeed (Ladson-Billings, 1994). These broad dispositions are particularly relevant for teachers of emergent bilinguals. In addition, Lucas and Villegas (2011) propose that all teachers should come to value linguistic diversity and be disposed to advocate for students learning in additional languages. Effective teacher education for linguistic and cultural diversity must move future teachers toward these dispositions and away from deficit thinking. Deficit thinking views differences in language or culture as deficiencies that explain academic outcomes and diminish teachers' potential or responsibility to help students reach high academic standards (Valdés, 1996).

Visions of the Possible and Desirable

Visions can be understood as "images of the possible" that "inspire and guide practice" (Hammerness, Darling-Hammond, & Bransford, 2005, p. 387). Having such visions can influence what preservice teachers know, can do, and value (i.e., the first three components of teacher capacity in our framework). Indeed, respected teacher educators have argued that having a vision of possible practice helps teachers to link their beliefs and intentions with enacted classroom practice (Feiman-Nemser, 2001), to question "standard school policy and practice" (Cochran-Smith, 1991, p. 281), and to be dissatisfied with compromise while reassessing teaching (Zumwalt, 1989). Thus, in Figure 2.1, we represent such vision as a source of support that undergirds the other components of teacher capacity to teach emergent bilinguals.

In summary, we propose that teachers need understandings, practices, dispositions, and vision to be fully effective teachers for emergent bilinguals. If they lack any one of these components, our framework suggests that they will be less effective. For instance, employing appropriate practices in a rote way—without sufficient understanding—can limit teachers' impact. Similarly, teachers may possess relevant understandings and skills, but if they don't believe that they can make a difference, or that it is important to include the needs of emergent bilinguals in their pedagogical decision making, we believe that they will be less effective in helping emergent bilinguals. If teachers lack a vision of what is possible and desirable, we posit that they are not likely to continue developing—or even to maintain—the necessary understandings, practices, and dispositions.

CONCEPTUALIZING WHAT TEACHER EDUCATORS NEED TO PREPARE TEACHERS TO WORK EFFECTIVELY WITH EMERGENT BILINGUALS

Lucas and Villegas (2010), working in the context of promoting English as a second language, outline four main approaches to incorporating information about effective instruction for ELLs into preservice teacher education: (a) requiring a separate course related to the instruction of ELLs, (b) infusing all courses with information about ELLs, (c) requiring prerequisite courses such as linguistics or a foreign language, and (d) providing additional courses leading to a supplemental certificate in ELL instruction. As Lucas and Villegas point out, the effectiveness of any of these approaches can only be as good as the preparation of teacher education faculty to carry them out. Without sufficient faculty preparation and support, it is unlikely that any of these strategies will result in a teacher workforce capable of working effectively with emergent bilinguals.

For teacher educators to support a program-wide effort to prepare teachers for linguistic and cultural diversity, they will need to improve what they know and can do. As shown in the upper left box of Figure 2.2, we propose that teacher educators' capacity to teach future teachers about emergent bilinguals requires them to understand the first three elements of K–12 teachers' capacity as we described in the last section: teacher educators must identify understandings, practices, and dispositions that they want their future teachers to acquire, and they must grasp these elements with sufficient depth to teach them. Looking ahead, Chapter 3 identifies specific kinds of activities that teacher educators might engage in to develop these resources.

Teacher educators also must develop specific practices or practical approaches for infusing questions, readings, or discussion about emergent bilinguals into already packed courses, as well as the disposition that these sorts of modifications are important. To this end, teacher educators, like K–12 teachers, can be guided or inspired by an undergirding vision. In other words, teacher educators' understandings and their practices would improve by seeing how others address linguistic and cultural diversity in

Teacher Educators' Understandings • K-12 teacher understandings • K-12 teacher practices • K-12 teacher dispositions	Teacher Educators' Practices	Teacher Educators' Dispositions
Vision (seeing what is possible and desirable in teacher preparation courses, i.e., content area methods courses, clinical seminars, assessment, etc.)		

Figure 2.2 Conceptualizing what teacher educators need to prepare preservice teachers to work effectively with emergent bilinguals.

specific courses and across teacher preparation programs, including what seems to work and what struggles or dilemmas others have experienced. Thus, it would be helpful to have depictions of the processes, progress, and problems teacher educators encounter as they develop their own capacity and modify their individual courses. Such case studies could yield visions of the possible and desirable, and they could create what Shulman (1987) called "wisdom of practice" (i.e., the kinds of insight that can only emerge from living out tensions and dilemmas in practice). In this book, Chapters 4 through 6 illuminate tensions that are likely to accompany the work of teacher preparation for work with emergent bilinguals and offer a vision of how instructors have addressed these challenges. However, we believe that the field would benefit from even more work to develop wisdom of practice in teaching specific courses. We encourage readers of this book, and especially instructors of learning theory courses, subject-specific methods courses, and clinical seminars, to build on this work to craft further visions of the possible.

For teacher educators who have expertise in a specific subset of courses—methods courses for social studies, for instance, or student development and learning theory—the prospect of developing the understandings, practices, and dispositions outlined earlier is daunting. The understandings alone include first and second language acquisition, the ways in which first language abilities can support second language development, cultural knowledge and its use as an affordance to learning, and the linguistic demands of specific disciplines' texts and pedagogies. The relative complexity of these understandings may explain why some programs segregate teaching about emergent bilinguals into a separate course. We believe, however, that such stand-alone courses, while a valuable component of mainstream teacher preparation, do not in and of themselves help preservice teachers integrate the norms of linguistic and cultural diversity into the ways they think about subject-specific pedagogy, student learning, lesson design, assessment, classroom management, and all of the other kinds of understanding and skills we promote in teacher preparation. For example, there are really thorny issues of figuring out how to help a second language learner make sense of the decontextualized and abstract language in a typical history book; similarly, it is challenging for new history teachers to know how to modify historical primary sources to make them more accessible to emergent bilinguals. Given the appropriate background, social studies methods instructors could address these points with much more precision and nuance than instructors of diversity courses are typically able to offer. The content of diversity courses typically spans all content areas, and the instructors of these courses possess expertise in linguistic and/or cultural diversity, but not necessarily in content-specific domains. If we want linguistic and cultural diversity to be a feature of many of the experiences we offer preservice teachers, how can we infuse this concern throughout a teacher preparation program?

THREE EXTANT MODELS FOR IMPROVING THE CAPACITY OF TEACHER EDUCATION FACULTY TO ADDRESS LINGUISTIC AND CULTURAL DIVERSITY

Published works suggest three models for how teacher educators might build individual and programmatic capacity to prepare all K–12 teachers to work effectively with ELLs. In this section, we describe these three approaches. The remainder of the chapter explains a fourth approach from our own university and considers the advantages and disadvantages of each approach for instructors' learning.

Pull-in

Meskill (2005) presented research on a model we term "pull-in," where outside experts come into teacher education classrooms to impart information about teaching ELLs that is beyond a course's usual provenance. Thus, one approach for teacher educators to infuse content about emergent bilinguals into their courses is to identify colleagues with expertise in the education of second language learners and to invite them to share their expertise through a guest lecture. Presumably, the teacher educators witnessing others' guest teaching would begin to learn also. The primary target for learning, however, is preservice teachers. Key advantages of this approach include the limited demands on instructors' time and the relative ease of organizing these guest lectures. The key disadvantage of this approach, from the point of view of faculty development, is that it does not create sustained, coherent learning

Table 2.1 Three Models for Enhancing Teacher Educators' Ability to Prepare Teachers for Linguistic Diversity

Model & source	What the teacher education program did in cited article
"Pull-in" described in Meskill (2005)	A faculty member or graduate student with relevant expertise offers a guest lecture or activity in other teacher education courses to infuse relevant content about linguistic diversity
"Faculty institute" described in Costa, McPhail, Smith, & Brisk (2005) and Brisk (2008)	A scholar of bilingualism led two five-session seminars for other teacher educators and supported additional learning experiences for participants
"Individual mentoring" described in Gort, Glenn, & Settlage (2007)	A faculty member with expertise provided individualized support, reading, and feedback on syllabi and selected student work, thus supporting growth in understanding and pedagogical skill in individual teacher educators

that will help faculty to integrate the needs of emergent bilinguals into their ongoing discussions, assignments, and larger vision of their courses. For preservice teachers, the key disadvantage is similar to that of the stand-alone diversity course; that is, preservice teachers may not develop an integrated sense of how to work effectively with ELLs when the ELL-specific information is presented as separate from the other instruction rather than being woven deeply into all aspects of a course.

Faculty Institute

Brisk (2008) and her colleagues (Costa, McPhail, Smith & Brisk, 2005) have written about a second approach. At Boston College, Brisk and colleagues organized a faculty institute to spread knowledge and support course revision relevant to ELLs. This approach has the potential to promote coherent and deep learning in individual faculty over the consecutive meetings, readings, and other experiences associated with an institute. Designing an institute or a seminar can also create common understanding across teacher educators who share a commitment to improving preservice teachers' capacity to work effectively with ELLs, and thus facilitate later conversation or comparison of methods and outcomes among instructors. Brisk's institute included differentiated reading and support for subject-specific challenges and pedagogies relevant to working with ELLs. Participants achieved understandings that allowed them to revise the readings and assignments they required in their courses. Once such an institute ends, however, it is unclear whether instructors' learning and curricular revision will continue, especially if the seminar does not spur some kind of follow-up project or ongoing commitment to collective work.

Individual Mentoring

At the University of Connecticut, Mileidis Gort, a scholar of bilingual education, first created a reading group for teacher educators interested in infusing teaching about ELLs into their courses. She went a step further, however, holding individual meetings with some instructors to provide them with individual readings, feedback on syllabi, and, in two cases, support or co-authorship for research papers responding to instructors' efforts to shift their courses. According to two individuals who worked intensively with her, Dr. Gort was a "mentor and critical friend . . . challenging and supporting [two colleagues] . . . and encouraging them to rethink and reframe their practice" (Gort, Glenn, & Settlage, 179, 2010). Dr. Gort also provided focused support for the two individual instructors as they implemented changes in their courses and as their work raised new questions or problems. Such individual mentoring has the clear advantage of being responsive to the specific courses, background, and interests of individual faculty. However, given the large number of faculty who are not experts in issues of language compared with the few with relevant expertise in most programs, this approach is too time or labor intensive to effect widespread change and seems unlikely to create common language and understandings or systemic change across courses and programs unless it is combined with other approaches.

A FOURTH MODEL FOR BUILDING INDIVIDUAL AND PROGRAMMATIC CAPACITY FOR PREPARING TEACHERS FOR LINGUISTIC DIVERSITY: FACULTY LEARNING COMMUNITY

We, the authors of this chapter, co-lead Project PREPARE-ELLs (Preparing Responsive Educators Who Promote Access and Realize Excellence with English Language Learners). This project is engaging 18 tenure-line and clinical faculty at the University of Connecticut in intensive professional development, curricular revision, and ongoing research regarding preparing teachers for linguistic diversity. There were several converging forms of motivation for the project, including the documented growth in the ELL population in our state and across the U.S., the glaring ELL achievement gap in Connecticut and in the nation (National Center for Education Statistics, 2009), and survey feedback from our program's alumni conveying their sense that they were inadequately prepared to work with ELLs. The integrated bachelor's/master's teacher education program at the University of Connecticut requires a stand-alone diversity course in the fifth year (master's year). There has long been dissatisfaction with this approach, from both alumni (as evidenced by their survey responses) and faculty, who have recognized that it is too little too late, coming after the core pedagogical approaches and dispositions have already been formed. The members of this group have been working to incorporate more information about effective instruction for ELLs earlier and more systematically throughout the program by infusing all methods courses and some clinical seminars with relevant information while continuing to require the fifth-year diversity course. We consider this form of education to be particularly necessary for our teacher education candidates, many of whom were raised in suburbs with limited linguistic and cultural diversity (a detailed profile of our students' experience with second languages appears in Chapter 8).

Our work as a group was initiated in 2006 and has included "pull-in," "faculty seminar," and "individual mentoring" models as overlapping phases, all of which continue to a degree to this day. We have now evolved to a fourth stage by building a faculty learning community to study the impact of our own learning and course revision on our preservice teachers' beliefs, self-efficacy, and actual practices (see Table 2.2). Compared with other models, a faculty learning community focused on emergent bilinguals accomplishes the following objectives: (a) it provides ongoing professional development (Little, 2003), unlike a seminar, which by design covers set

Table 2.2 Models for Teacher Educators Partnering With Others to Develop Capacity to Prepare Preservice Teachers for Linguistic Diversity

Model	Bilingual/ESOL Scholars' Role	Impact and Limits
"Pull-in," described in Meskill (2005)	Guest lecturers bringing expertise methods instructors don't have	• Some preservice teachers receive one to three sporadic and unsystematic exposures to content about ELLs. • Some faculty begins to learn about ELLs; however, instructors have limited opportunities to build their own capacity. • The requirement for outside speakers raises questions of sustainability and depth of change in course readings, assignments, and objectives.
"Faculty institute," described in Brisk (2008)	Initiators, designers, and facilitators of study group and coaches for individual methods instructors' curricular revisions	• Participating faculty develop knowledge and confidence necessary to make additions to their preservice and in-service teacher education work • Methods instructors who develop a degree of expertise can provide readings, experiences, and questions on their own—without calling in experts—which may make learning more integrated throughout a course. Instructors' learning and curricular experimentation, however, may end with the seminar's end.
"Individual mentoring," described in Gort, Glenn, & Settlage (2007)	Mentors, providers of reading and feedback on syllabi and student work	• Allows for very focused, course-specific, and individualized provision of expertise, learning resources, and conversation to help individuals develop their own expertise and their courses. • Time intensive. • Requires scholars with expertise who are also willing to mentor and play the role of "critical friend." • On its own, seems unlikely to create systemic change across courses and programs.
"Faculty learning community" Began in our community in school year 2009	Facilitators and supporters, providing resources and guidance as needed while others increasingly take ownership/leadership	• Participating faculty continue developing knowledge, doing literature review, and experimenting in own courses; they add data collection regarding the nature and impact of their teaching to inform their practice and publish research. • Faculty jointly create shared mission, publications, presentations, and potential for grant writing; this makes the work sustainable, ongoing, and consistent with the mission and incentives of a research-intensive university.

material and assignments within a designated time frame; (b) it engages not only in reading but also in research that can inform instructional practice, consistent with writing about inquiry communities (see Cochran-Smith & Lytle, 1992a, 1992b; Cochran-Smith & Lytle, 1999); and (c) it makes our own practices visible as a means of improving our own and our students' capacity relevant to emergent bilinguals (see Lave & Wenger, 1996; Little, 2003; Wenger, 1998).

Our vision of what is possible in a faculty learning community is based on our understanding of "communities of practice," a concept that brings into focus how groups sustain or alter existing patterns of practice. Communities of practice (CoPs) can form wherever ongoing groups are engaged in a joint enterprise (Wenger, 1998). CoPs are sites where people jointly construct, transform, conserve, and/or negotiate the meanings of practices (Lave & Wenger, 1996; Wenger, 1998). In such communities, the key mechanism for individual and group learning comprises access to observing and then participating in the practices at the core of the community. We have sought to provide or create new understandings, dispositions, and access to specific practices for K–12 education and visions of possible practice in teacher preparation. We have also sought to help each other look at our individual practices, creating opportunities to build a sense of joint enterprise focused on common aims and more learning from the actual practices and outcomes of teacher preparation.

Learning in CoPs is facilitated when novices and experienced practitioners organize their work in ways that allow all participants the opportunity to see, discuss, and engage in shared practices. Thus, we hold monthly meetings throughout the academic year where individual faculty members come together to discuss common readings and share progress and dilemmas as they work to infuse their methods and other courses with information about effective instruction for emergent bilinguals. Participants in CoPs learn—or jointly construct—practices, which can be understood as ways of achieving desired ends in the world such as facilitating students' learning of history. We have created an ongoing CoP that supports its 18 members in the revision or creation of teacher education practices that prepare teachers for their work with emergent bilinguals.

Our approach also builds on empirical research demonstrating the effectiveness of professional communities. A professional community comprises a group of individuals in the same profession engaged in ongoing collaboration that improves their service to clients (Grossman, Wineburg, & Woolworth, 2001). The work of such communities is consistent with the work of scholars of professional development who call for "continuous professional learning" situated in the context, practices, and problems of actual workplaces (Webster-Wright, 2009).

Research has demonstrated that professional communities can improve professional practices and their impact on clients. The professional community that exists among *teachers*—the norms, collegial relationships, and collaborative activity that develop among teachers—can affect both the formative first years in the profession and the beliefs and practices of more experienced teachers (Johnson & The Project on the Next Generation of Teachers, 2004; Louis & Marks, 1998; Vescio, Ross, & Adams, 2008). Careful reviews of research on teacher professional community have also shown that certain kinds of professional community are associated with improved student learning (Bolam, McMahon, Stoll, Thomas, & Wallace, 2005; Vescio, Ross, & Adams, 2008).

While the largest body of work on professional communities has focused on in-service teachers in schools, research has also shown the potential of professional communities to improve teacher education. Cochran-Smith (2003) has shown how teacher education supervisors—those who work with student teachers in the field—engaged in ongoing collective inquiry; their joint work achieved learning and shifts in practice that would be unimaginable without inquiry conducted with colleagues. Carroll, Featherstone, Featherstone, Feiman-Nemser, and Roosevelt (2007) have described how ongoing collaboration transformed elementary teacher education at Michigan State University; a first-person account of this work makes clear how collaborative inquiry and critical colleagueship can help individuals identify problems and make progress in their practice as teacher educators (Norman, 2007).

If we conceive of teacher educators' work as professional—as requiring application of knowledge and choice of practices under conditions of uncertainty—then those who teach our future teachers will need to acquire a sufficiently deep and flexible set of understandings to make difficult choices and adaptations from year to year and from moment to moment while working directly with preservice teachers. This book proposes means of positioning various kinds of teacher educators as learners vis-à-vis colleagues, experts, and resources. The ultimate aim of this work is to create deep and lasting shifts in knowledge, practice, and dispositions in both preservice teachers and teacher educators. Research has shown that focusing on learning in professional communities helps professionals improve their work with clients. This book will show how the approach has worked as we apply it to our work preparing teachers for work with emergent bilinguals, even as we acknowledge the inherent uncertainties, contradictions, and next areas for growth that accompany efforts to promote coherent learning across time and multiple actors.

THREE CORE ELEMENTS OF A FACULTY LEARNING COMMUNITY

We propose that a faculty learning community approach should be characterized by three core elements: (a) ongoing professional development, (b) active research by participants, and (c) sharing of—and learning from—practices. These three elements work together to create a vibrant, systemic approach that furthers faculty learning and promotes engagement. Below, we describe how research related to professional communities has described these elements and their importance for professional learning. In Chapter 3, we illustrate these elements and describe practical advice for accomplishing them.

Ongoing Professional Development

Scholars of professional development have called for promoting "continuous professional learning" situated in the context, practices, and problems of actual workplaces (Webster-Wright, 2009). In other words, whereas professional development has often consisted of outsiders with expertise offering a one-shot presentation, current thinking about professional development often calls for situating the work of professional development closer to the actual practices and dilemmas of a profession and creating structures that create more ongoing and coherent learning and engagement with practice (Ball & Cohen, 1999; Brown & Duguid, 1991). Organizing workplaces for continuous learning throughout the professional lifespan may be particularly important for teacher educators. Teacher educators also come from quite a variety of professional backgrounds, leaving them with diverse strengths and gaps, and come into the professional at different career entry points (Cochran-Smith, 2003; Murray, 2008). Intentional efforts to support inclusive professional development may also be particularly important for non-tenure-line teacher educators, such as the clinical faculty, adjunct faculty, and teachers in residence who lead seminars or span universities and clinical sites in other roles. Such teacher educators typically "toil in the shadows," where they work in isolation and are offered little or no support for their work (Kosnik & Beck, 2008; see also Harrison & McKeon, 2008; Murray, 2008). Traditional professional development—with one-shot outsiders unfamiliar with individuals and their work presenting—seems unlikely to be responsive to teacher education instructors' diverse needs, gaps, and roles. Conversely, engaging faculty in the design and conduct of their own development increases the odds of identifying relevant outside resources and sharing internal expertise in ways that create powerful, coherent, and context-relevant learning.

The mechanism of learning, in this kind of professional development, involves means of mastering knowledge or practices generated from beyond the group and making sense of it in ways that prove most powerful for the individuals involved. Thus, the specific activities should help professionals consume new ideas or practices in a way that connects deeply with the lived dilemmas and daily needs and practices of professionals.

Active Research

We imagine professionals in communities engaging in action research. Action research can be understood as research that seeks to address immediate problems or needs, often in a localized context, rather than aiming to produce broadly generalizable findings. However, some groups may also design the nature of their questions and data collection in a way that allows them to address questions that will interest broader audiences with findings that are publishable.

Professionals who engage together in action research or more formal research into their practice can critique common practice, expose and examine underlying assumptions, and find other ways to make the language and conceptions they use problematic (Cochran-Smith & Lytle, 1992a). Professionals can also use inquiry to identify, implement, and assess new approaches to their practice through the collection and analysis of data (Hubbard & Power, 1999). Action researchers go through recursive stages of formulating problems, collecting data, analyzing data, reporting results, and planning for action. These cycles lend themselves well to individual or group efforts at curricular revision. In either case, the work would ideally unfold in groups because peers can provide scaffolding and encouragement for engaging in research and accomplishing more thoughtful teaching (Sagor, 1992). Groups of professionals who engage in research also create a venue for reading, writing, and talking about findings together to enlarge their sense of the possible and desirable in their work (Fairbanks & LaGrone, 2006).

The mechanism of learning in this element of a professional community is "systematic intentional inquiry" into the decisions, dilemmas, and knowledge that relate to their work (Cochran-Smith & Lytle, 1992a). As a result, rather than only consuming knowledge created by outside experts, this aspect of a professional community can make participants "agentive constructors of . . . knowledge" (Fairbanks & LaGrone, 2006, p. 10); they do this as they jointly create or revise concepts that guide and ground their work in empirical data about results. Some inquiry communities help teachers identify elements of their practice that are unexamined and portions of their professional knowledge that had previously been tacit (e.g., Cochran-Smith & Lytle, 1992b, 1999). A joint process of moving from tacit to explicit knowledge, and from unexamined to conscious assumptions and beliefs, allows for more explicit choices. This joint process of knowledge construction or revision allows individuals to learn from others who are similarly formulating explicit, public statements about what they know and believe.

Sharing—and Learning from—Practice

The third element, sharing of practices, relates to the importance of coming together on a regular basis to share artifacts such as syllabi, course projects, and samples of student work to reflect on challenges and successes in implementing new approaches to instruction. This coming together allows learning from concrete examples of others' work and more theoretical discussion of problems and progress; it also creates support and accountability for the work of becoming skilled at preparing teachers for emergent bilinguals. Whereas inquiry can start with research questions and data collection, sharing practices starts with talk about the work itself that may or may not always have a clear structure or end (Levine & Marcus, 2010).

The mechanism of learning in this element of a professional community comprises learning from talk about, examples of, and artifacts from practice. Scholars of professional communities have shown how professionals' joint talk can identify shared dilemmas (Little, 2002), create new ways of naming and understanding things (Horn, 2005, 2010), and lead to the creation of other shared resources that enable new kinds of practice and improved impact on clients (Levine, 2011). Professionals are more likely to benefit when such talk is rendered with more concrete detail and transparency regarding what was done (Little, 2003), as happens when teachers represent their classroom instruction to each other through a replay of what they did in class or a rehearsal of how they would handle a specific situation (Horn, 2005). Sharing actual artifacts or examples of practice can also promote such clarity and group learning (see McDonald, Mohr, Dichter, & McDonald, 2003). In Chapter 3, we suggest the use of protocols as one practical means of promoting detailed and clear examples of practice as a resource for shared learning.

RECOMMENDATIONS

Complex cultural, linguistic, and sociopolitical issues intersect in the instruction of emergent bilinguals, who are required to learn the language of instruction and content and skills through the language of instruction at the same time. To prepare teacher educators to work at these intersections, we recommend starting with backward design (i.e., identifying the outcomes in preservice teachers that a program wants to achieve). This chapter offers one possible framework. Programs could also consult Lucas and Villegas (2011) or Nutta, Mokhtari, and Strebel (2012) for help formulating their own vision of outcomes. After determining what preservice teachers need, programs can consider the pathways forward presented in this chapter to develop needed expertise in faculty.

We recommend that several factors guide choice of methods for developing faculty knowledge, practice, dispositions, and visions for what is possible and desirable in teacher education. Current levels of interest, available time, and support from various stakeholders may suggest a need to start with easier and smaller initial steps, such as pull-in approaches, seminars, or mentoring to begin building capacity; in other cases, where available resources, support, and motivation are high, groups might initiate more ambitious plans. As suggested in Figure 3.2, these models should not be seen as mutually exclusive. In our experience, they can be additive phases, with elements of prior stages remaining and continuing to this day as a faculty

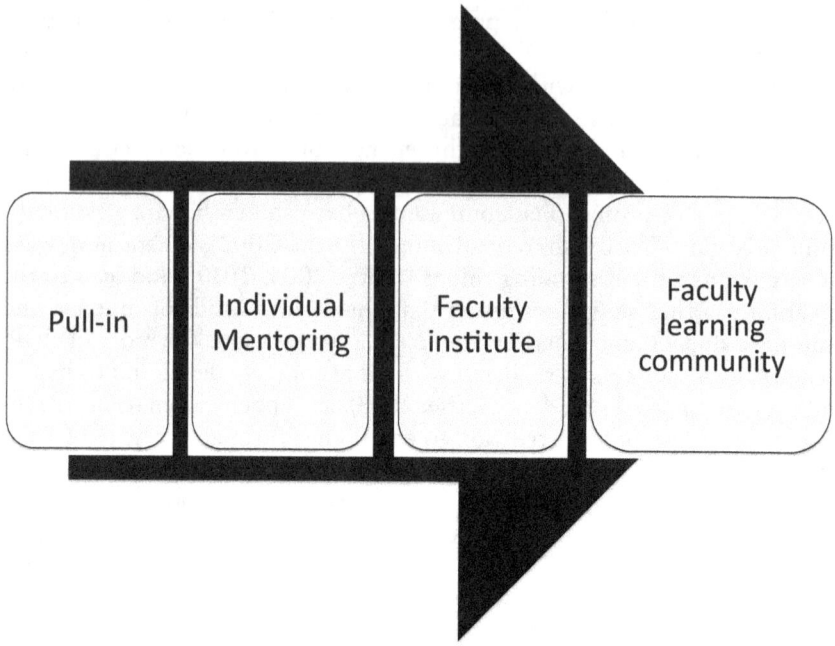

Figure 2.3 Conceptualizing a developmental progression: four additive models of promoting teacher educators' capacity to prepare teachers for linguistic diversity.

learning community develops. However a program starts, we recommend aiming for a longer term trajectory toward more widespread impact on faculty, courses, and an entire program of teacher education. The arrow in Figure 2.3 represents one such trajectory.

Finally, we recommend the development of a faculty learning community as a powerful way to accomplish both documentable and sustainable change. It positions teacher educators as change agents, using data to inform and improve their own work and to provide accountability where outcomes don't match intentions. By continuing to develop and study means of preparing teacher educators and teachers for linguistic diversity, researchers, teacher educators, program leaders, and policymakers can build a more effective and equitable teacher workforce. Indeed, the work of developing a faculty learning community focused on emergent bilinguals creates routines, group capacity, and models for professional development that can then be applied to other problems and possibilities in teacher education.

CONCLUSION

This chapter has conceptualized both K–12 teachers' and teacher education instructors' capacity related to teacher preparation for emergent bilinguals.

Both K–12 teachers and university-based teacher educators will need to develop knowledge, practices, dispositions, and vision of the possible and desirable relevant to their respective work. We have reviewed extant literature regarding models of such improvement, identifying three broad approaches to promote K–12 teacher capacity for work with emergent bilinguals, and we have proposed a fourth. We don't see the first model—pulling in guest experts—as likely to promote either deep integration of this content into other elements of courses or into teacher educators' own knowledge and vision of their preservice teachers' work. We do propose the other three models—peer coaching, faculty institute, and faculty learning community—as means that have the potential to promote sustained, coherent, and ongoing learning.

This chapter has remained fairly conceptual; the next chapter addresses more practical issues. What might programs actually do to make these last three models work? How might busy faculty be enticed to join such work? The next chapter tells the story of our own project in more detail and uses that story to offer concrete and practical suggestions for organizing learning among teacher education faculty.

REFERENCES

Adger, C. T., Snow, C. E., & Christian, D. (Eds.). (2002). *What teachers need to know about language.* Washington, DC: Center for Applied Linguistics.

Ball, D. L., & Cohen, D. K. (1999). Developing practice, developing practitioners: Toward a practice-based theory of professional development. In L. D. Hammond & G. Sykes (Eds.), *Teaching as the learning profession: Handbook of policy and practice* (pp. 3–32). San Francisco: Jossey-Bass.

Bolam, R., McMahon, A., Stoll, L., Thomas, S., & Wallace, M. (2005). *Creating and sustaining professional learning communities.* Research Report Number 637. London: General Teaching Council for England, Department for Education and Skills.

Brisk, M. E. (2008). Program and faculty transformation: Enhancing teacher preparation. In M. E. Brisk (Ed.), *Language, culture, and community in teacher education* (pp. 249–266). Mahwah, NJ: Lawrence Erlbaum Associates.

Brown, J. S. & Duguid, P. (1991). Organizational learning and communities of practice: Toward a unified view of working, learning and innovation. *Organizational Science 12*(2) 40–57.

Carroll, D., Featherstone, H., Featherstone, J., Feiman-Nemser, S., & Roosevelt D. (2007). *Transforming teacher education: Reflections from the field.* Cambridge, MA: Harvard University Press.

Chamot, A. U., & O'Malley, J. M. (1996). The Cognitive Academic Language Learning Approach (CALLA): A model for linguistically diverse classrooms. *The Elementary School Journal, 96*(3), 259–273.

Cochran-Smith, M. (1991). Learning to teach against the grain. *Harvard Educational Review, 61*(3), 279.

Cochran-Smith, M. (2003). Learning and unlearning: The education of teacher educators. *Teaching and Teacher Education, 19*(1), 5–28.

Cochran-Smith, M., & Lytle, S. (1992a). Communities for teacher research: Fringe or forefront? *American Journal of Education, 62*(4), 298–324.

Cochran-Smith, M., & Lytle, S. (1992b). Teacher research as a way of knowing. *Harvard Educational Review, 12*(4), 447–474.

Cochran-Smith, M., & Lytle, S. (1999). Relationships of knowledge and practice: Teacher learning in communities. In I. N. Ashgar & D. P. Pearson (Eds.), *Review of research in education* (Vol. 24, pp. 249–305). Washington, DC: American Educational Research Association.

Costa, J., McPhil, G., Smith, J., & Brisk, M.E. (2005). Faculty first: The challenge of infusing the teacher education curriculum with scholarship on English language learners. *Journal of Teacher Education, 56*(2), 104–118.

Cruz, B. C., & Thornton, S. J. (2009). *Teaching social studies to English language learners*. New York: Routledge.

Dalton, S. D. (1998). *Pedagogy matters: Standards for effective teaching practice.* Santa Cruz, CA: Center for Research on Education, Diversity, and Excellence. Retrieved February 6, 2009, from http://crede.berkeley.edu/pdf/rr04.pdf

Darling-Hammond, L., & Bransford, J. (Eds.). (2005). *Preparing teachers for a changing world: What teachers should learn and be able to do.* San Francisco: Jossey-Bass.

Echevarria, J., & Graves, A. (2003). *Sheltered content instruction: Teaching English language learners with diverse abilities* (2nd ed.). Boston, MA: Allyn & Bacon.

Echevarria, J., Vogt, M. & Short D. (2010). *Making content comprehensible for secondary ELLs: The SIOP model.* Boston: Allyn & Bacon.

Fairbanks, C. M., & LaGrone, D. (2006). Learning together: Constructing knowledge in a teacher research group. *Teacher Education Quarterly, 33*(3), 7–25.

Feiman-Nemser, S. (2001). From preparation to practice: Designing a continuum to strengthen and sustain teaching. *Teachers College Record, 103*(6), 1013–1055.

Gonzalez, N., Moll, L. C., & Amanti, C. (2005) *Funds of knowledge: Theorizing practices in households, communities, and classrooms.* Mahwah, NJ: Lawrence Erlbaum Associates.

Gort, M., Glenn, W. J., & Settlage, J. (2010). Toward culturally and linguistically responsive teacher education: The impact of a faculty learning community on two teacher educators. In T. Lucas (Ed.), *Preparing teachers for linguistically diverse classrooms: A resource for teacher educators* (pp. 178–194). New York: Routledge/Taylor & Francis.

Grossman, P., Wineburg, S., & Woolworth, S. (2001). Towards a theory of teacher community. *Teachers College Record, 103*(6), 942–1012.

Gudmundsdottir, S. & Shulman, L. (1987). Pedagogical content knowledge in social studies. *Scandinavian Journal of Educational Research, 31,* 59–70.

Haberman, M. (1996). Selecting and preparing culturally competent teachers for urban schools. In J. P. Sikula, T. J. Butter, & E. Guyton (Eds.), *Handbook of research on teacher education* (2nd ed., pp. 747–760). New York: Macmillan.

Hammerness, K., Darling-Hammond, L., & Bransford, J. (2005). How teachers learn and develop. In L. Darling-Hammond & J. Bransford (Eds.), *Preparing teachers for a changing world: What teachers should learn and be able to do* (pp. 390–441). San Francisco: Jossey-Bass.

Harrison, J., & McKeon, F. (2008). The formal and situated learning of beginning teacher educators in England: Identifying characteristics for successful induction in the transition from workplace in schools to workplace in higher education. *European Journal of Teacher Education, 31*(2), 151–168.

Horn, I. S. (2005). Learning on the job: A situated account of teacher learning in high school mathematics departments. *Cognition and Instruction, 23*(2), 207–236.

Horn, I.S. (2010). Teaching replays, teaching rehearsals, and re-visions of practice: Learning from colleagues in a mathematics teacher community. *Teachers College Record, 112*(1), 225–259.

Hubbard, R. S., & Power, B. M. (1999). *Living the questions: A guide for teacher-researchers*. Portland, ME: Stenhouse Publishers.

Johnson, S. M., & The Project on the Next Generation of Teachers. (2004). *Finders and keepers: Helping new teachers survive and thrive in our schools*. San Francisco: Jossey-Bass.

Kosnik, C., & Beck, B. (2008). In the shadows: Non-tenure line instructors in preservice teacher education. *European Journal of Teacher Education, 31*(2), 185–202.

Ladson-Billings, G. (1994). *The dreamkeepers: Successful teachers of African American children*. San Francisco: Jossey-Bass.

Lave, J., & Wenger, E. (1996). *Situated learning: Legitimate peripheral participation*. New York: Cambridge University Press.

Levine, T. H. (2011, April). *How teacher professional communities influence classroom practice: Two cases conceptualizing the role of power and shared resources*. Peer-reviewed, contributed paper for the American Educational Research Association conference, New Orleans, LA.

Levine, T. H., & Marcus, A. S. (2010). How the structure and focus of teachers' collaborative activities facilitate and constrain teacher learning. *Teaching and Teacher Education, 26*(3), 389–398.

Little, J. W. (2002). Locating learning in teachers' communities of practice: Opening up problems of analysis in records of everyday work. *Teaching and Teacher Education, 18*(7), 917–946.

Little, J. W. (2003). Inside teacher community: Representations of classroom practice. *Teachers College Record, 105*(6), 913–945.

Louis, K., & Marks, H. M. (1998). Does professional community affect the classroom? Teachers' work and student experiences at restructuring schools. *American Journal of Education, 107*(4), 532–575.

Lucas, T., & Villegas, A. M. (2010). The missing piece in teacher education: The preparation of linguistically responsive teachers. *National Society for the Study of Education, 109*(2), 297–318.

Lucas, T., & Villegas, A. M. (2011). A framework for preparing linguistically responsive teachers. In T. Lucas (Ed.), *Teacher preparation for linguistically diverse classrooms: A resource for teacher educators* (pp. 55–72). New York: Taylor & Francis.

McDonald, J., Mohr, N., Dichter, A., & McDonald, E. (2003). *The power of protocols: An educator's guide to better practice*. New York: Teachers College Press.

Meskill, C. (2005). Infusing English language learner issues throughout professional educator curricula: The Training All Teachers project. *Teachers College Record, 107*(4) 739–756.

Murray, J. (2008). Teacher educators' induction into higher education: Work-based learning in the micro communities of teacher education. *European Journal of Teacher Education, 31*(2), 117–133.

National Center for Education Statistics. (2009). *National assessment of education progress: The nation's report card: Results of the 2009 national and state reading assessment*. Retrieved December 1, 2011, from http://nationsreportcard.gov/reading_2009/gr12_national.asp?tab_id=tab2&subtab_id=Tab_6#tabsContainer

Norman, P. (2007). Learning the practice of field-based teacher education. In D. Carroll, H. Featherstone, J. Featherstone, S. Feiman-Nemser, & D. Roosevelt (Eds.), *Transforming teacher education: Reflections from the field* (pp. 161–179). Cambridge, MA: Harvard University Press.

Nutta, J.W., Mokhtari, K. and Strebel, C. (2012). *Preparing every teacher to reach English learners: A guide for teacher educators*. Cambridge, MA: Harvard Education Press.

Nutta, J. W., Nazan, U. B., & Butler, M. B. (2011). *Teaching science to English language learners*. New York: Routledge.

Sagor, R. (1992). *How to conduct collaborative action research*. Alexandria, VA: Association for Supervision and Curriculum Development.

Schleppegrell, M. J. (2004). *The language of schooling: A functional linguistics perspective*. Mahwah, NJ: Lawrence Erlbaum Associates.

Shulman, L. (1987). Knowledge and teaching: Foundations of the new reform. *Harvard Education Review, 57*(1), 1–22.

Shulman, L.S. (1994). Those who can: Knowledge growth in teaching. In B. Moon & A. S. Mayes (Ed.s) Teaching and Learning in the Secondary School. New York: Routlege.

Valdés, G. (1996). *Con respeto: Bridging the distances between culturally diverse families and schools: An ethnographic portrait*. New York: Teachers College Press.

Valdés, G., Bunch, G., Snow, C., Lee, C., with Matos, L. (2005). Enhancing the development of students' language. In L. Darling-Hammond & J. Bransford (Eds.), *Preparing teachers for a changing world: What teachers should learn and be able to do* (pp. 126–168). San Francisco: Jossey-Bass.

Vescio, V., Ross, D., & Adams, A. (2008). A review of research on the impact of professional learning communities on teaching practices and student learning. *Teaching & Teacher Education, 24*(1), 80–91.

Webster-Wright, A. (2009). Reframing professional development through understanding authentic professional learning. *Review of Educational Research, 79*(2), 702–739.

Wenger, E. (1998). *Communities of practice: Learning, meaning, and identity*. New York: Cambridge University Press.

Zumwalt, K. K. (1989). Beginning professional teachers: The need for a curricular vision of teaching. In M. C. Reynolds (Ed.), *Knowledge base for the beginning teacher* (pp. 173–184). New York: Pergamon Press.

3 Recruiting and Organizing Learning among Busy Faculty Members

Thomas H. Levine, Elizabeth R. Howard, and Mileidis Gort

THE OVERARCHING CHALLENGE

The previous chapter of this book argued that preparing teachers to work effectively with emergent bilinguals will require developing the capacity of teacher education faculty. Few teacher educators have already developed such capacity, which consists of emergent bilingual-related understandings, practices, and dispositions, and a vision of what is possible and desirable in teacher education.

To date, teacher education programs and research have devoted vastly more attention to methods of developing K–12 teacher capacity than to methods of developing teacher educators' capacity. Research on the professional development of teacher educators exists but is sparse. Most faculty work in institutions that don't provide a great deal of induction or professional development beyond access to generic, one-shot workshops on college teaching, and thus many faculty will not have local models and infrastructure to support them in learning together (see Harrison & McKeon, 2008; Kosnik & Beck, 2008; Murray, 2008). College faculty also face predictable obstacles to engaging in collaborative efforts to improve their knowledge and systemically infuse new teaching across courses. These obstacles include:

1. Faculty autonomy. College faculty are used to doing their work largely alone, using their own professional judgment to decide what content, methods, and values will be conveyed by their courses. Often they are the sole expert in their particular field, which makes collaborating with others on individual course content more difficult. The ideal of faculty autonomy is a longstanding cultural feature of higher education institutions, and one that continues to remain important to many professors (Gappa & Austin, 2010). The complex work of preparing teachers for emergent bilinguals, however, would ideally position multiple professors to learn together and alter course content in complementary ways.
2. Faculty role as experts. Faculty are used to being sources of expertise rather than publicly being positioned to need more expertise. The work we propose here requires faculty to shift into the mode of being

learners and identifying and addressing gaps in the company of colleagues, which may be novel and uncomfortable.

3. Limited time and scheduling challenges. Time is not structured into professors' work for either ongoing or intensive training. Work expectations emphasize output in terms of research, teaching, and service; expectations do not include the notion that higher education institutions can and should provide systemic support to improve employees' capacity. Finding time is also made hard by logistical realities. Class schedules, dedicated scholarly effort, conference presentations, service obligations, and committee meetings complicate finding common times for joint work.

4. Incentives. The incentives that institutions offer may not initially line up to reward collaborative work, which leads to program and instructional improvement. Research institutions typically find ways to recognize and reward productive researchers. Other kinds of institutions may reward work that translates more immediately into new teaching or observable service to a state or local community. Individual and program development does not typically appear as an important criterion for earning promotion, tenure, and merit pay. This can make it more difficult to recruit multiple faculty into an ongoing effort involving individual learning and instructional improvement as well as program revision.

5. Differing levels of initial understanding and commitment. Teacher education faculty come into the profession with diverse prior professional experiences and academic training in different fields (Cochran-Smith, 2003). As result, it is likely that groups of faculty who may want to work together to better prepare teachers for emergent bilinguals will start with different initial levels of understandings regarding language learning, linguistics, and culture. Their diverse values and interests may also lead them to begin with different levels of commitment to self-development. For example, whatever activities faculty develop to promote their own learning may have to work for an English teacher educator who understands much about language and has taught emergent bilinguals as a secondary teacher as well as the instructor of a learning theory course with limited prior study of language, no prior K–12 teaching experience, and a research agenda that doesn't currently line up with the nature of this work.

Given these challenges, how is it possible to attract busy faculty to participate in collective efforts to improve teacher preparation for emergent bilinguals? What kinds of recruitment strategies and activities are more likely to maintain participation and result in changes in what preservice teachers learn and can do?

This chapter addresses these questions. It provides suggestions and advice about recruitment strategies and joint learning activities while telling the story of how we engaged busy faculty in joint learning over the past seven years. We organize the sections using broad categories of learning activities identified in the last chapter: peer coaching, faculty institute, and faculty learning community. Under each heading, after clarifying what we did, we make suggestions to help others consider how they might adapt recruitment strategies and learning activities to their own setting. We close with broad recommendations for those who would initiate collaborative faculty learning experiences like the ones we discuss here.

STARTING SMALL: THE POWER OF PEER COACHING

The first collaboration that spun itself into Project PREPARE-ELLs comprised a scholar of bilingual education, Mileidis Gort, coaching a couple of interested faculty members to begin learning about and addressing emergent bilinguals. Mileidis, with a smile on her face, kept nicely but insistently asking "and what about English language learners?" when others (including faculty and students) would talk about their courses. Based on student feedback and confirmed by faculty self-reporting, it had become increasingly clear that our preservice teacher education program did not attend to the needs of linguistically and culturally diverse learners, including emergent bilinguals, and their families. Initially, two faculty colleagues representing secondary English and science education reached out to Mileidis for explicit support in rethinking and reframing their practice toward culturally and linguistically responsive pedagogy as their own concerns grew regarding the neglect of multicultural topics and the lack of ELL focus across teacher education. Focusing on the strengths of each colleague and their specific disciplines, Mileidis did several things to support faculty. She offered a series of guest lectures on their respective methods courses. She reviewed course syllabi and offered suggestions for infusing discipline-specific readings, materials, and activities. She also offered personalized support and guidance in re-envisioning each course to include ELL-specific content and relevant related course and field experiences.

As Mileidis had the chance to coach an increasing number of faculty members, she developed a set of questions that she would have faculty answer in advance of meeting with her; she learned about their courses, their objectives, their students, and their thoughts about course revision. A later modification of that protocol—used with Project PREPARE-ELLs members who attended the summer institute—appears at the very end of the appendix to this chapter.

GROWING LARGER: FACULTY INSTITUTE AS ONGOING READING GROUP

As faculty begin a journey of self-development, they will likely have differing knowledge gaps to fill and the need to grasp effective K–12 instructional practices that support emergent bilinguals. Either a more intensive, time-limited faculty institute or an open-ended reading group can help faculty learn through joint discussion of shared texts.

Initiation and Recruitment

In our university, several factors facilitated the development of a faculty reading group focused on the needs of emergent bilinguals: (a) the successes enjoyed by Mileidis, as a mentor, and the two colleagues with whom she had been engaging in peer coaching; (b) the initiation of successful teacher educator professional development on the needs of emergent bilinguals carried out by her former advisor, Dr. María Brisk, at Boston College (Brisk, 2008); and (c) a cohort of four new faculty hires, one of whom joined the Bilingual Education concentration and all of whom shared an interest in linguistic and cultural diversity. Mileidis recognized the potential for the work she had started with two colleagues to spread to a larger group, and in January 2006, she invited a new faculty member in Bilingual Education to co-facilitate a monthly reading group for interested faculty. She also reached out to other faculty in Curriculum and Instruction, asking them what they were doing relevant to emergent bilinguals in their methods courses and inviting them to learn more through the reading group. Five faculty members joined out of a mixture of interest, sense of mission, and acknowledgment that we didn't know enough to answer—or act on—Mileidis's question.

Activities

During the spring 2006 semester, the group of six faculty members met monthly to build their knowledge base by discussing brief readings provided by the group leaders (Mileidis Gort and Liz Howard, co-authors of this chapter) on "nuts and bolts" issues such as principles of second language acquisition, the demographic characteristics of emergent bilinguals in Connecticut and across the country, and effective pedagogical strategies for working with emergent bilinguals. (An annotated list of suggested initial readings for building knowledge appears in this chapter's appendix.) During the 2006–2007 academic year, the reading group took a hiatus, as Mileidis took a position at another university, and Liz was on maternity leave.

In fall 2007, the group reconvened and decided to focus on language in depth as a variety of topics had already been discussed the previous year in breadth. To this end, we decided to read *The Language of Schooling* (Schleppegrell, 2004). For many of us, prior to this reading, language was like air—something that we saw as necessary for our functioning but invisible and taken for granted. This work pushed us to see language—to explore the ways language is used differently to construct meaning in various disciplines—and to think more critically about the linguistic demands of curriculum and instruction. We began to see how language practices at the level of schools and in individual classrooms could either empower learning or complicate learning for students, including but not limited to emergent bilinguals. We also gained a clear appreciation for the challenges of academic language by reading and discussing a complex text about systemic functional linguistics, a topic about which none of us had had any prior knowledge.

Benefits

The format of a book club is familiar for academics because many in the academy are comfortable reading and talking about books. This relatively safe format also doesn't require a significant time commitment and can be modified to meet the needs and availability of different groups of faculty. We suggest meeting at least monthly to enhance the sense of ongoing conversation and build on prior discussion. Nevertheless, meeting quarterly could initiate momentum and interest while requiring little initial commitment. Finally, a benefit of this approach is the flexibility of content. Readings can be selected to target the interests and knowledge level of the group. Likewise, readings can allow for differentiation. Multiple readings can address one topic and be targeted at participants with differing responsibilities within a teacher education program or with different initial levels of understanding.

Limitations/Tensions

While we found book clubs to be a fine way to get started, it is clear that our participants varied significantly in the degree to which they did—and perhaps could—translate these initial readings into practice. Readings that are neither too long nor too challenging for newcomers make participation more manageable, but they also limit the depth of learning; group discussions may focus more on the content of the readings than application to preservice teaching. Our group tried to end most of our sessions talking about application to coursework, but we also saw value in venturing into some theoretical work on language or culture that was not immediately applicable. Another key limitation is that this kind of group is probably more beneficial when it includes participation—if not leadership—from a faculty member with expertise in ELL education and familiarity with the literature and other useful resources. The person who played that role in our group—Liz Howard—"knew a lot of the resources to bring . . . she had the connections" to specific readings and ideas and served as our "in-house SIOP person" (see Echeverria, Vogt, & Short, 2010), according to one participant. Where it is impossible to tap such in-house expertise, however, groups might pull in speakers, videos, and readings; we recommend starting places in this chapter's appendix. A final limitation is the risk that the ELL education faculty who contribute to the group bear too much of the load for leading learning (i.e., lecturing or serving as answer-giver). While faculty who may be uncomfortable identifying gaps in their courses and knowledge may be comfortable attending book clubs that turn into question-and-answer sessions, we suspect that such a pattern of dialogue would be less beneficial because it doesn't require teacher educators to articulate their emerging understandings, questions, or discomfort in ways that would ultimately be productive.

Suggestions

Based on our experience, we suggest using brainstorming or other methods of collecting input to create reading lists most likely to address a variety of participants. In tension with this suggestion, we also see the need for the active participation of a scholar with a vision of the field who can bring coherence and sequencing, increasing the odds that readings and conversations add up to more than the sum of their parts. Brainstorming regarding readings and multimedia resources could also extend to brainstorming regarding group processes, such as the frequency and duration of meetings, expectations for participation, and responsibility for beginning to apply new understandings in courses. Initial and then ongoing conversations about process can ensure that participants' needs are met, that they take increasing ownership of their individual and collective learning, and thus that they can build commitment to joint work. Where participants see their own needs met and their own learning translating into improvements in practice, they are most likely to continue participating and pulling in colleagues.

GROWING LARGER STILL: BECOMING A FACULTY LEARNING COMMUNITY

Initiation and Recruitment

In 2009, we sought to expand our efforts beyond the initial reading group because we felt that we had reached the limits of what we could accomplish within that framework and we saw value in increasing the impact of the work through greater participation and a greater emphasis on research and practice. One of the facilitators of this new effort—Tom Levine, the lead author of this chapter—had a background in learning communities, having studied them extensively (e.g., Levine, 2010; Levine, 2011a; Levine, 2011b; Levine & Marcus, 2010), and could see the relevance and potential power of this model for our faculty.

We succeeded in pulling in all four clinical faculty, all of the major subject area methods instructors except one who was transitioning out of methods instruction, and two other instructors of teacher education courses. As one participant put it, we think that "getting everyone involved was obviously really important." The importance of reaching many teacher educators and getting them onto the same page may be obvious, in retrospect, but it wasn't easy. Tom Levine, who worked with Liz Howard to start Project PREPARE-ELLs, first confirmed with the original reading group that they were interested in a project that would transcend the size and outcomes of the original group. We envisioned more accountability for moving what we were learning into instruction and engaging in research related to both our own process and preservice teachers' experiences. Tom then reached out to more faculty, beginning with those most likely to join an expanded project, hoping to create a sense of momentum, excitement, and desire to join an effort that would unite teacher educators.

Persuasive Appeals

Tom tailored his appeal to each individual, akin to how majority party whips in the U.S. Congress tailor their arguments or inducements to entice legislators to support legislation. He found that the following kinds of appeals were effective in differing combinations with different people:

- Participation will enable teaching to align with our commitment to social justice or improve education for traditionally underserved groups; moreover, joining will allow us to collectively do more than we could individually;
- Our alumni have clearly indicated through alumni surveys that we don't do enough to prepare them for emergent bilinguals; this work will help give teachers what they say they need;
- Participation will create opportunities for us to do research, make conference presentations, and publish results;
- Participation will create a rare opportunity for professional development designed explicitly for you as teacher education faculty;
- Participation will help you improve your teaching;
- Participation will allow us to work together in a deeper way than occasional committee work;
- Participation will create a model for our future professional development and improvement in other areas that we care about;
- Participation will value our teaching and make our pedagogy publicly available so that others learn from it and we can gain help with it;
- To partially compensate for the time we are asking over the summer—for training, course revision, collecting data, engaging in ongoing reading, and professional development—we can offer a $3,000 stipend (For clinical faculty, who did not engage in much of the ongoing research work and meetings, we offered a $,2000 stipend. We wrote a successful proposal to the Carnegie Foundation to use funding from the Teachers for a New Era grant for this purpose; we also received internal funding through a large faculty grant);

- We recognize that faculty time is precious. During the school year, we will only ask for time during one meeting a month, held over lunch, because faculty likely have to eat anyway . . . and lunch will be free!

Clarity Regarding Expectations and About Outcomes to Entice Participation

Clarity from the start regarding what we expected and what we would accomplish seemed to help participation. Such clarity made the project seem less open ended and threatening for faculty who face many competing time demands; lining up our expectations with our desired work products also made it more possible for us to expect the kinds of participation and input we needed. In our case, participants understood that they would be expected to do the following:

- Participate in two pre-sessions on the sociopolitical context of ELL instruction in U.S. schools taught by faculty with expertise in this topic;
- Participate in an intensive 40-hour training during the summer. Each pre-session and day of summer work would come with reading;
- Infuse new content, skills, and understanding into teacher education courses (fall 2010), and engage in further revision to curriculum and instruction (fall 2011);
- Develop new modules, assignments, and/or lessons for junior seminars and senior-year student teachers (clinical faculty);
- Collect and analyze multiple forms of data;
- Attend monthly meetings to continue professional learning and data analysis for at least two school years (tenure-line faculty); and
- Consult with an expert coach who would support individual curricular efforts.

Along with improved teacher preparation for linguistic diversity within our program, we highlighted our intention to produce conference papers and publications. Because we work in a research-intensive university, where scholarship is highly valued, designing this project with a strong research component made it more sustainable for faculty who need to produce scholarship for tenure, promotion, and other forms of professional advancement and recognition.

Building Consensus and Soliciting Input

When Tom met with individuals and presented his persuasive appeals, he required the participant to read a draft proposal for our project specifying expectations. These meetings were two-way dialogues. Tom asked everyone what we might do to increase the odds of keeping everyone at the table and help us improve what our preservice teachers can do for emergent bilinguals. In other words, we found it useful to bring persuasive appeals to individuals, and ask what would help individuals to choose participation, and increase their sense that this unprecedented (for us) joint venture would succeed. The project facilitators kept tweaking the proposal they shared with faculty to reflect the latest insights and improvements they heard from faculty; after seven revisions and additions, 16 teacher educators approved the final draft and signed on to the project.

After signing off on the agreement, those 16 faculty members attended two pre-sessions in the spring of 2010 and a weeklong summer training, as we describe later. We have proceeded to meet monthly during the school year, including a longer workday in May, over the past three years. Of the original 16 participants, one left our institution, and one has remained connected to the project but has been unable to attend monthly meetings due to competing demands; two have joined since the original 16 began our work.

Activities

The three primary activities of our faculty learning community have included our own professional development, research, and sharing of practice.

Professional Development

Because they had shown themselves to be effective for our professional development, we continued to incorporate elements of the peer coaching and reading group activities that we had initiated earlier. Specifically, peer coaching was an explicit part of the proposal, with funding allocated for experts to work with groups of faculty members to support them as they made changes in their syllabi. (The coaches were: Mileidis Gort; a postdoctoral student, Angela Lopez; and two additional colleagues in the Bilingual Education program, Eliana Rojas and Xaé Reyes).

To continue the work typical of a faculty institute and our own history of meeting as a book club, we chose one or more articles on a given topic to discuss at several of our monthly meetings during each of our first two years. As noted earlier, all participating faculty had input on the selection of topics and specific articles. Readings addressed academic language and systemic functional linguistics (e.g., Janzen, 2008; Schleppegrell & O'Hallaron, 2011; Wong Fillmore & Snow, 2000; Zwiers, 2005), funds of knowledge and the importance of building on students' cultural capital (e.g. Gutiérrez, 2008; Moll, Amanti, Neff & Gonzalez, 1992), and sheltered instruction (e.g. Echevarria, Vogt & Short, 2010; Minaya-Rowe, 2004). Our discussions of selected readings were intentionally loosely structured, with Liz or Tom typically providing a few general framing questions but allowing the conversation to evolve as the participants chose. This seemed the optimal approach given that the sharing of practice through an explicit protocol (described later) was the core activity of most meetings.

Finally, we also incorporated a number of workshops, colloquia, and presentations by experts within our department as well as from outside of the university. On their own, these activities looked like the faculty institute approach to this work described in Chapter 2. We chose to incorporate this form of professional development into our faculty learning community to avoid the risk of being insular. Readings can be sufficient as a means of bringing new ideas in; however, actually interacting with outside experts can hasten learning and allow kinds of training that are impossible without demonstration or dialogue with an author.

Leading up to our 40-hour summer institute in 2010, we designed two 3-hour crash courses to enable participants who weren't in the original reading group to develop a baseline of foundational knowledge. Colleagues with expertise in bilingual education and multicultural education—Xaé Reyes, Jason Irizarry, and Eliana Rojas—chose readings and organized discussion focused on the sociopolitical context of emergent bilingual instruction in U.S. schools. Our weeklong summer workshop was then conducted by outside experts, Dr. Deborah Short and Dr. Maria Brisk. Dr. Short is one of the creators of the Sheltered Instruction Observation Protocol (SIOP), one of the most widely implemented forms of sheltered instruction in U.S. schools (Echeverria et al., 2010). Over the course of four days, participating faculty worked with Dr. Short to learn about the SIOP model and discuss its use in methods courses for preservice teachers. Dr. Brisk is the director of the Boston College's Carnegie Foundation-funded (Teachers for a New Era initiative (TNE) to infuse education methods courses with information relevant to the instruction of ELLs, and she has also worked with K–12 teachers to use principles of functional linguistics to enhance literacy instruction. Dr. Brisk provided a day-long workshop on systemic functional linguistics, drawing on her years of work with practicing teachers in Boston.

Following this work—all in the mode of a faculty institute—we began using peer coaching and the elements of the faculty learning community described elsewhere in this chapter while continuing to provide ongoing professional development opportunities through interaction with outside experts. For two consecutive years, Manuela Wagner, a member of our group who specializes in foreign language education, together with Liz Howard organized TNE-sponsored language symposia featuring prominent scholars in the field of language education as keynote speakers. Capitalizing on this event, project facilitators invited the guest speaker each year to join Project PREPARE-ELLs's monthly meeting. In each case, we read relevant articles by each researcher in advance of her visit and also provided visiting experts with background information about our project to promote informed conversation. In 2011, we were joined by Dr. Catherine Snow, who spoke about her ongoing work to help teachers promote academic language. In 2012, Dr. Kris Gutiérrez spoke with us about her various projects promoting third space for K–12 students from immigrant backgrounds.

As noted in Chapter 2, recent research on professional development has called for "continuous professional learning" situated in the context, practices, and problems of actual workplaces (Webster-Wright, 2009). Given that recommendation and our own experience, we believe that external presentations like the ones listed earlier can be helpful but are not essential; such work should not replace activities that place more responsibility on learners to construct meanings and achieve change on their own.

Engaging in Research

In addition to ongoing professional development, we propose that active research by participants is another cornerstone of a faculty learning community. In our own case, during the first, unfunded phase of our work, when we only met as a book group, research was less systematic, was carried out by pairs or trios of faculty members rather than by the group as a whole, yet did lead to journal articles and conference papers. Regardless of audience, local inquiry can impact participating faculty, deepening both their understanding of and commitment to the issues involved.

At a minimum, research can provide data relevant to the aims of a project in order to guide the next iteration of course revision or professional development. In our case, we aimed to change preservice teachers' practices and also hoped to develop their self-efficacy for teaching emergent bilinguals. As we show in Chapters 8 and 9, our data helped us to see that students were gaining self-efficacy; they also showed us places where students were implementing some practices effective for emergent bilinguals and other areas where they needed more support.

Beyond collecting data immediately useful to assess and revise individual and collective efforts, it is possible to explore some other topic or topics of interest to the program or to create findings worth sharing in publications. In our case, we decided to focus on ourselves as teacher educators as well as on our preservice teachers, given that little had been published about the professional development of teacher educators relevant to emergent bilinguals. In other words, we sought to understand the unfolding of our own professional development and collaboration and its impact on our own teaching. We wrote out 13 research questions that we hoped we'd be able to answer related to changes in us and in our students that might occur during the time of our professional development. Our questions included: What challenges, obstacles, strategies, solutions, and insights do teacher educators experience when learning how to prepare teachers to teach specific subjects to ELLs? What supports and strategies did one group of teacher educators employ to build a community of practice engaged in critique and professional support of improved teacher educator practice?

What did one teacher education program do to develop its own—and its preservice teachers'—knowledge and skills related to teaching ELLs? What impact did this effort have on preservice teachers' self-efficacy for teaching ELLs and their observable teaching practices? To the extent that preservice teachers appear to implement strategies for teaching ELLs, how do they—and teacher educators—explain relative success in impacting practice?

Survey Instruments

Given our research foci, we created two survey instruments to help us gather data systematically: (a) the Teacher Educator Self-Assessment of Capacity for Preparing Teachers for English Language Learners (TES-CAPTELL), and (b) the Teaching English Language Learners Self-Efficacy Scales (TELLSES, described further in Chapter 8). The TELLSES has been administered repeatedly to multiple cohorts of preservice teachers over the course of the project. It provides valuable information about long-term changes in preservice teachers' sense of efficacy for effectively teaching emergent bilinguals.

Developing Qualitative Data-Collection Methods

In addition to these survey instruments, we used qualitative methods to learn more about our faculty learning community and preservice teachers' experiences. During the first two years of our project, one of the project facilitators interviewed teacher educators in order to understand how they perceived changes in themselves and their students as a result of participation in the learning community (see Chapter 10). We also asked all teacher educators to produce year-end memos, which allowed us to collect consistent project-level data over the course of our work in a format that helped us to see changes in courses, readings, assignments, and objectives across methods courses. Using a standardized electronic memo template, teacher educators also filled in specific details about changes from year to year, along with descriptions of what enabled those changes.

We recorded our monthly meetings and took detailed notes at each meeting to help us document our activities and conversations. Additionally, all participating faculty members produced written reflections about specific classes they taught, collected classroom-based evidence of their own learning as well as that of their students, and had our encouragement to engage in individual research looking at their own teaching or preservice teachers' work as they saw fit.

Finally, to better understand any changes in our students, we have purposefully selected a subgroup of student teachers from across all major disciplines (special education, elementary education, secondary math, secondary science, secondary social studies, and secondary English) and have conducted observations of one K–12 lesson per student teacher, using the SIOP instrument as an indicator of effective instructional practices for ELLs (see Chapter 9).

Suggestions

Plans for data collection must fit the expertise and resources available and the purposes that groups of faculty have. Depending on the number of participants, their institutional mission, and any available resources, research collection could be made reasonably simple. It is possible to do meaningful research looking only at products that are already being produced and assessed within teacher education courses, for instance, to gain some evidence regarding what preservice teachers can do or how preservice teacher capacity changes from year to year. Faculty or supervisors who are already observing and debriefing student teachers may be able to collect some additional data that provide guiding feedback regarding a targeted practice or set of practices. If faculty or supervisors build clear rubrics into their coursework and work together to promote inter-rater agreement and understanding of the rubrics, the work of grading assignments and observing and debriefing teachers could yield program-level data across a program without needing outside data collection. Cycles of data collection and analysis should be timed so that results are available in time to inform future action.

Learning From Practice

We foresaw that we would all likely face challenges and learn things worth sharing while infusing new objectives, readings, assignments, and activities into our courses. To promote learning from practice, we agreed to use protocols to guide joint analysis and discussion of our practical work. A protocol is a tool that structures joint talk and learning from professional practice. K–12 teachers have used protocols to give them both permission and prompting to move beyond the norms of autonomy and conflict-avoidance typical in schools (Achinstein, 2002), and to position peers to offer constructive criticism while learning from others' dilemmas or artifacts of their work.

Protocols similarly seemed to give us the permission—and impetus—to engage each other more deeply than we normally do regarding the actual work of preparing teachers for work with emergent bilinguals. Chapters 4 and 5 of this book emerged out of questions of practice that surfaced and were initially addressed in such protocol-guided discussions. Regarding protocols, one faculty member told us during an interview, "I love that we actually get to talk about our practice. I mean, here we are researchers that always talk about K–12 schools and how terrible . . . [it is that] people are isolated. We never share practice. Getting people to talk about practice is hard and we have these protocols to help them."

Critical Friends Protocol

During the three years of this most recent phase of our work together, we have held protocol-guided discussions at our fall meetings and occasionally at spring meetings also. One teacher educator would volunteer in advance to present a dilemma. A few others would volunteer to play the role of timekeeper, process checker, and facilitator; this last person would literally read instructions from the protocol, reminding us what we should be doing and for how long at each stage of the conversation. The protocol was also printed on the back of our meeting agenda so that all could refer to it. The protocol instructed the problem-presenter to present a focused question or dilemma

Table 3.1 Critical Friends Protocol

Phase	Time Limit	Description to Be Read Aloud by Facilitator to Whole Group
Volunteer for roles	2 mins	Individuals volunteer for roles: Presenter, Facilitator, Timekeeper (announces time limit if reached for each phase), Process-checker (see last phase below)
Presenter shares problem	8 mins	Main presenter: Share your course, the lesson/aspect, and a specific question or dilemma. Present so that audience members understand the nature and context of your work. Include description of students, key players, and/or key situations in order to allow peers to understand and discuss the following sections. Describe an area where you're struggling, a question you can't answer, or some other dilemma or problem that the group might help you with. Present with as many details as possible and with a clear explanation of the problem or question that you would like others to address.
Clarifying questions	2 mins	Audience asks clarifying (factual) questions.
Discuss	12 mins	Other participants discuss the problem. It is OK to ask presenter a clarifying question, but for the first 5 minutes, presenter(s) only listens. Presenter may interact after those 5 minutes. Audience considers possible courses of action, offers alternative ways of viewing a situations, and ideas about how to resolve an issue.
Extensions	5 mins	Optional: Presenter or others may raise new question/direction for group discussion.
Presenter reflections	5 mins	[optional] Presenter and/or audience may discuss "where to go from here," raising new questions, issues, or options for moving forward.
Process debrief	5 mins	Process-checker leads a debrief of the process—not the content—aiming to improve the use of the protocol next time. Group may raise questions of process.

with enough detail, context, and description of key players that colleagues could enter, learn, and offer help. As our protocols unfolded, faculty began incorporating PowerPoint presentations that explicitly identified the question or dilemma they wanted help with, and laying out key supporting details in ways that others could revisit if they needed a reminder. Our critical friends protocol was adapted from the critical incidents protocol (see Table 3.1). This protocol was inspired by work the first author observed and by the modified consultancy protocol (see National School Reform Faculty, n.d.).

Tuning Protocol

In our second year, we gave participants the option to continue gaining peer help with specific dilemmas or to begin using a tuning protocol. This sequence of steps allows peers to offer feedback on one instructors' student work, and thus to think about what is possible and desirable in preservice teachers' lesson plans or other products of university coursework. Others could also download the tuning protocol we used (National School Reform Faculty, n.d.).

Suggestions

Based on our experience, we believe that others are likely to gain from protocols if they are explicit about the potential benefits and challenges of using protocols. Teacher educators are not used to having other adults critique their work; starting with critical friends protocols is less threatening than sharing student work for peer review, but even the act of identifying an authentic challenge that one instructor cannot solve on his or her own requires being vulnerable with colleagues. Preparing colleagues to be respectful and encouraging of this kind of sharing and constructively critical help colleagues embrace the stance of vulnerability that makes this work more generative. It is also possible to modify the protocol to better support group needs and interests, as the final phrase of the protocol creates opportunities to reflect on and improve the process. We used this phase to propose and adopt minor changes to the protocol while seeking to retain its push to use our time effectively, stay focused, and hold conversations that ultimately would push our practice.

RECOMMENDATIONS FOR INITIATING AND SUSTAINING COLLECTIVE FACULTY PROFESSIONAL DEVELOPMENT

This chapter has used the unfolding story of our faculty's work organizing collective learning to suggest recruitment strategies and practical suggestions for facilitating collective professional development among busy faculty members.

The facilitators of the various stages of our work have identified three core challenges that seem likely to recur for others who seek to develop their own version of faculty development to prepare teachers for emergent bilinguals: (a) allowing enough input from participants regarding content and process while providing enough direction; (b) allowing flexibility to accommodate competing participants' commitments while creating firm enough expectations; and (c) meeting the needs of both teacher educators with limited understandings of teaching emergent bilinguals and those with more developed knowledge and experience. To the extent that other faculty groups face similar tensions—which seems likely—we close this chapter with additional recommendations to help others negotiate these tensions.

Do a Needs Assessment and Identification of Learners' Hopes

Collaborative faculty learning experiences, if they are to promote learning, should be responsive to specific needs, strengths, and motivations of the learners participating. As with any learners, responsiveness requires knowing about the learners.

Differentiate

To meet the needs of participants with diverse levels of prior knowledge, collaborative learning experiences may create differentiated options and opportunities for individuals to experiment and share their own learning. Shared experiences and texts also seem crucial, but faculty with less experience may value the chance to "catch up" via readings in advance of the shared experience, whereas more experienced or knowledgeable faculty might take on alternate assignments at times.

Balance Clear Expectations with Flexibility to Accommodate the Reality of Multiple Demands on Faculty

To accommodate the reality that some faculty will need to be at conferences or other events, set clear expectations with sufficient flexibility to allow meetings and work to get done without 100% attendance

Gather Ongoing Input

Such input from faculty can inform adjustments and increase the odds that all are gaining enough to sustain participation. Surveys, open discussion during meetings, and checking in with individuals can provide the two-way dialogue that helps an emerging community meet both its goals and the individual needs of its members.

Stay Focused on the Mission

The initial conversations and invitations for input can help to create a shared mission. We recommend keeping that mission front and center when moving forward. In our case, we opened each meeting with a short statement of our mission: We, as Project PREPARE, work together to improve teacher preparation for emergent bilinguals by changing what we know and can do in our own program, and publishing to help other programs. Given competing demands, faculty are more likely to stay involved if all stay focused on a mission they value.

Have a Planning Team Streamline the Work

When groups work, they inevitably raise questions, create the need to draft things, or engage in other work that is laborious to carry out among the larger group. Delegating tasks to a planning team that can report back to the whole group with options, draft language, or proposed direction can make faculty decision making more efficient. In our project, the facilitators and a graduate assistant met twice a month to do this kind of work and to guide data collection and analysis.

Schedule and Use Meeting Time Strategically

Again, because faculty are engaged in teaching, research, and service, it might increase participation to provide advanced notice of meeting dates, perhaps by setting meeting dates for an upcoming academic year in the preceding summer. Faculty may still face dates that they are unavailable due to other professional obligations, but providing this type of advanced notice and negotiating meeting times with participants means that meetings make it into faculty calendars before most other demands and are seen as self-selected activities rather than externally imposed ones.

In addition, some of the work of setting agendas might occur at the end of meetings, when the group might seek some consensus or input for next steps. When an agenda is published before the next meeting, it can remind participants of where they left off and of directions all agreed to; agendas that broadcast and clarify important work that is being accomplished may communicate to participants that their investment of time is yielding progress. (For quotes from our project regarding the value of monthly meetings, please see Chapter 10.)

Craft the Project to Match Some of the Institutional Incentives and Mission

In research-intensive settings, organize the work to produce research to make it more appealing and sustainable over time. Emphasize that participants will achieve measurable improvements in teaching or have an impact on local schools if either is important for potential participants and the larger institution. When recruiting participants, others might also describe how this work could dovetail with work institutions must do anyway for accreditation by responding to alumni feedback, demographic trends (see Chapter 1), and the need for data collection to demonstrate improvement in teacher education. This line of argument could help others and is developed further in Chapter 11.

REFERENCES

Achinstein, B. (2002). Conflict amid community: The micropolitics of teacher collaboration. *Teachers College Record, 104*(3), 4212–4455.
Brisk, M. E. (2008). Program and faculty transformation: Enhancing teacher preparation. In M. E. Brisk (Ed.), *Language, culture, and community in teacher education* (pp. 249–266). Mahwah, NJ: Lawrence Erlbaum Associates.
Cochran-Smith, M. (2003). Learning and unlearning: The education of teacher educators. *Teaching and Teacher Education 19*(1), 5–28.
Echevarria, J., Vogt, M. & Short, D. (2010). *Making content comprehensible for secondary English learners: The SIOP Model.* Boston: Allyn & Bacon.
Fillmore, L. W., & Snow, C. (2002). What teachers need to know about language. In C. T. Adger, C. E. Snow, & D. Christian (Eds.), *What teachers need to know about language* (pp. 7–53). McHenry, IL: Delta Systems and Center for Applied Linguistics.
Gappa, J. M., & Austin, A. E. (2010). Rethinking Academic Traditions for Twenty-First-Century Faculty. AAUP Journal of Academic Freedom, 1. Retrieved March 9, 2014 from http://www.aaup.org/sites/default/files/files/JAF/2010%20JAF/Gappa.pdf
Gort, M., Glenn, W. J., & Settlage, J. (2010). Toward culturally and linguistically responsive teacher education: The impact of a faculty learning community on two teacher educators. In T. Lucas (Ed.), *Preparing teachers for linguistically diverse classrooms: A resource for teacher educators* (pp. 178–194). New York: Routledge/Taylor & Francis.
Gutierrez, K. (2008). Developing sociocultural literacy in the third space. *Reading Research Quarterly 43*(2), 148–164.
Harrison, J., & McKeon, F. (2008). The formal and situated learning of beginning teacher educators in England: identifying characteristics for successful induction in the transition from workplace in schools to workplace in higher education. *European Journal of Teacher Education, 31*(2), 151–168.
Janzen, J. (2008). Teaching English language learners in the content areas. *Review of Educational Research, 78*(4), 1010–1038.
Kosnik, C. & Beck, B. (2008). In the shadows: Non-tenure line instructors in preservice teacher education. *European Journal of Teacher Education, 31*(2), 185–202.
Levine, T. H. (2010). Tools for the study and design of collaborative teacher learning: The affordances of different conceptions of teacher community and activity theory. *Teacher Education Quarterly, 37*(1), 109–130.
Levine, T. H. (2011a). Features and strategies of supervisor professional community as a means of improving the supervision of preservice teachers. *Teaching and Teacher Education, 27*(5), 930–941.
Levine, T. H. (2011b). Experienced teachers and school reform: Exploring how two different professional communities facilitated and complicated change. *Improving Schools, 14*(1), 30–47.
Levine, T. H., & Marcus, A. S. (2010). How the structure and focus of teachers' collaborative activities facilitate and constrain teacher learning. *Teaching and Teacher Education, 26*(3), 389–398.

Minaya-Rowe, L. (2004). Training of teachers of English language learners using their students' first language. *Journal of Latinos and Education, 3*, 3–24.

Moll, L. C., Amanti, C., Neff, D., & González, N. (1992). Funds of knowledge for teaching: Using a qualitative approach to connect homes and classrooms. *Theory into Practice, 31*(2), 132–141.

Murray, J. (2008). Teacher educators' induction into higher education: Work-based learning in the micro communities of teacher education. *European Journal of Teacher Education, 31*(2), 117–133.

National School Reform Faculty. (n.d.). *Modified consultancy protocol.* Retrieved April 22, 2014, from http://www.nsrfharmony.org/protocol/doc/smp_consultancy.pdf.

National School Reform Faculty. (n.d.). *Tuning protocol.* Retrieved November 22, 2014, from http://www.nsrfharmony.org/protocol/doc/tuning.pdf.

Schlepegrell, M. (2004) *The Language of Schooling: A Functional Linguistics Perspective.* Mahwah, NJ: Erlbaum.

Schlepegrell, M.J. & O'Hallaron, C.L. (2011). Teaching academic language in L2 secondary settings. *Annual Review of Applied Linguistics, 31*, 3–18.

Webster-Wright, A. (2009). Reframing professional development through understanding authentic professional learning. *Review of Educational Research, 79*(2), 702–739.

Zwiers, J. (2005). The third language of academic English. *Educational Leadership, 62*(4), 60–63.

APPENDIX

Suggested Readings and Web Resources for a Faculty Reading Group Seeking to Improve Teacher Preparation for Emergent Bilinguals

Readings about Language in General

Fillmore, L. W., & Snow, C. (2002). What teachers need to know about language. In C. T. Adger, C. E. Snow, & D. Christian (Eds.), *What teachers need to know about language* (pp. 7–53). McHenry, IL: Delta Systems and Center for Applied Linguistics. This chapter is a fast read and is intended to give a lay of the land rather than delve deeply into any one kind of linguistic phenomenon. It helped us start to name the understandings and skills related to language that we needed to develop in our preservice teachers.

Schleppegrell, M. (2004). *The language of schooling: A functional linguistics perspective.* Mahwah, NJ: Lawrence Erlbaum Associates. Our early reading group found this book to be complex and challenging, as it plunged us into linguistic theory. The payoff was a much clearer vision of how language works to accomplish different tasks in different subject areas, what aspects of language are challenging for some students in a given subject area, and why it would be important to help students master some of these functions/aspects of language rather than always providing modified texts or avoiding reading assignments altogether.

    An alternate choice would help readers see subject-specific uses of language: Schleppegrell & Fang's (2008) *Reading in secondary content areas: A language-based pedagogy* (Michigan Teacher Training) is an easier read, as it is intended for a wider audience.

Delpit, L., & Dowdy, J. K. (Eds.). (2008). *The skin that we speak: Thoughts on language and culture in the classroom.* New York: The New Press. Although not a book that we read as a group or one that is directly focused on emergent bilinguals, this edited collection of chapters by teachers would help others understand the intersection of home languages and local dialects with the more formal language of schooling. For example, the chapter "Some Basic Sociolinguistic Concepts" shows how vernaculars are nuanced, rule governed, and dynamic; helping preservice teachers understand this would counteract notions of "bad English." Likewise, the chapter "Trilingualism" explores how teachers can work with students whose families and communities do not speak the dominant form of English by practicing code switching, or moving among home language, work language, and school language.

Readings about Culture

Gonzalez, N., Moll, L. C., & Amanti, C. (2005). *Funds of knowledge: Theorizing practices in households, communities, and classrooms.* Mahwah, NJ: Lawrence Erlbaum Associates. This book helps readers recognize the multiple resources that ELLs' families and communities offer them, challenging some teachers' attribution of student failure to families and culture. The book suggests the ways in which schools don't capitalize on the strengths students do bring into the classroom; it proposes a scaffolded scheme of teachers making home visits to learn directly about other cultures in ways that might break rather than strengthen pre-existing notions.

Valdés, G. (1996). *Con respeto: Bridging the distances between culturally diverse families and schools: An ethnographic portrait.* New York: Teachers College Press. This book, which the whole group did not read, offers nuance and insight from a single, well-described ethnographic case. The author came to know 10 Mexican immigrant families over several years. A clear description of actual families and one school context shows how schools and Mexican-origin families can misunderstand each other's values and communication, with obvious and troubling consequences for the youth involved.

Readings about Effective Instructional Practices for Emergent Bilinguals

Echevarria, J., Vogt, M. E., & Short, D. J. (2006). *Making content comprehensible for English learners: The SIOP model* (3rd ed.). Newton, MA: Allyn & Bacon. Sheltered instruction comprises a coherent set of current best practices for making content from any discipline accessible to ELLs. The SIOP—or Sheltered Instruction Observational Protocol—is an observational tool, a checklist of 30 instructional features that serve to foster ELLs' language skills along with mastery of core academic content. While faculty in our program found the quantity of features too great to be covered in a methods course, the book gives methods instructors a vision of how it is possible to teach rigorous content to ELLs, and it provides practical approaches. Readers interested in this book should seek out the newer 2012 edition.

Janzen, J. (2008). Teaching English language learners in the content areas. *Review of Educational Research, 78*(4), 1010–1038. This fine review looks at research on teaching four core content areas to emergent bilinguals (English, math, science, and social studies). It raises issues relevant to teacher education or professional development of in-service teachers, clarifies subject-specific challenges, and offers pedagogical suggestions for content area teachers in these subject areas.

Walqui, A., & van Lier, L. (2010). *Scaffolding the academic success of English language learners: A pedagogy of promise.* San Francisco, CA: WestEd. This book describes the Quality Teaching for English Leaners (QTEL) initiative of WestEd and draws on work with secondary schools across the U.S. to provide vignettes of effective classroom practices and detailed examples of instructional activities that support and challenge second language learners.

USEFUL WEB RESOURCES

WestEd—ELL Projects and Resources

WestEd, a non-profit agency located in San Francisco, CA, focuses on research, technical assistance, and policy analysis to promote academic success for all learners. A substantial portion of their work focuses on ELLs, and there are many useful resources on their website: http://www.wested.org/area_of_work/english-language-learners/

Understanding Language: Language, Literacy and Learning in the Content Areas

Understanding Language is an initiative of the Graduate School of Education at Stanford University. It aims to help educators understand the language demands of the Common Core State Standards and Next Generation Science Standards and to support all learners, especially ELLs, in being successful in meeting those standards. Website: http://ell.stanford.edu/

Center for Applied Linguistics (CAL)

CAL, a non-profit agency located in Washington, DC, carries out research, technical assistance, and policy analysis all related to the mission of improving communication through a better understanding of language and culture. CAL has an extensive online resources, including digests, briefs, and reports that address various subtopics related to linguistic and cultural diversity, particularly in the realm of education. In particular, CAL has been a leader in developing and providing technical assistance related to the SIOP, it partners with the World-Class Instructional Design and Assessment (WIDA) Consortium and provides their primary assessment support, and it has been a partner on many large-scale research centers focused on the needs of emergent bilinguals, including the Center for Research, Education & Diversity (CREDE) and the Center for Research on the Educational Achievement and Teaching of English Language Learners (CREATE). Website: www.cal.org

National Clearinghouse for English Language Acquisition (NCELA)

The National Clearinghouse for English Language Acquisition is funded by the U.S. Department of Education's Office of English Language Acquisition, Language Enhancement, and Academic Achievement for Limited English Proficient Students (OELA). This comprehensive website provides a number of useful resources related to ELLs, including data on demographics and student achievement, as well as webinars on a variety of topics, such as assessment and instructional strategies. Website: www.ncela.us

Colorin Colorado

This Spanish-English bilingual website is sponsored by WETA/Reading Rockets and is designed to provide educators and parents with a variety of resources to help support the literacy attainment of emergent bilinguals. Resources include articles, webinars, toolkits, newsletters, and many other useful items. Website: http://www.colorincolorado.org/

ADDITIONAL RESOURCES WE FOUND USEFUL DURING INITIAL LEARNING ABOUT EMERGENT BILINGUALS (MOST REFERENCED IN GORT, GLENN, & SETTLAGE, 2010)

Brisk, M. E., Dawson, M., Hartgering, M., MacDonald, E., & Zehr, L. (2002). Teaching bilingual students in mainstream classrooms. In Z. F. Beykont (Ed.), *The power of their culture: Teaching across language difference* (pp. 89–120). Cambridge, MA: Harvard Education Publishing Group.

Bunch, G.C. (2010). Preparing mainstream secondary content-area teachers to facilitate English language learners' development of academic language. In C. Faltis & G. Valdes (Eds.), *Education, immigrant students, refugee students, and English learners.* Yearbook of the National Society for the Study of Education, 109(2), 351–383.

Commins, N. I., & Miramontes, O. B. (2006). Addressing linguistic diversity from the outset. *Journal of Teacher Education, 57*(3), 240–246.

Hadaway, N. I., Vardell, S. M., & Young, T. A. (2001). *Literature-based instruction with English language learners, K–12.* Boston, MA: Allyn & Bacon. Participants read "Our changing classrooms" and "Language acquisition and literature-based instruction."

Horan, D. A. (2006). *Supporting English language learners in mainstream classrooms.* Chestnut Hill, MA: Boston College Lynch School of Education—Title III Project ALL. Office of Professional Practice and Induction. Retrieved March 9, 2014 from http://www.google.com/url?sa=t&rct=j&q=&esrc=s&source=web&cd=1&ved=0CCsQFjAA&url=http%3A%2F%2Fwww.lesley.edu%2FWorkArea%2FDownloadAsset.aspx%3Fid%3D2011&ei=7IkcU7HCN8Ls0AHxnYHgAg&usg=AFQjCNHq_gzX2hVm5hC8j7LmvZSJZrH4sQ&bvm=bv.62578216,d.dmQ

Morahan, M. (2003). *Bilingual students in secondary classrooms: A reference for practicum students at Boston College Lynch School of Education.* Chestnut Hill, MA: Boston College Lynch School of Education—Title III Project ALL. Office of Professional Practicum Experiences. Retrieved March 9, 2014 from http://www.bc.edu/content/dam/files/schools/lsoe_sites/title-iii/pdf/fall03sec.pdf

Ramirez, A. G. (1995). Concepts of language proficiency. In A. G. Ramirez (Ed.), *Creating contexts for second language acquisition: Theory and methods* (pp. 36–57). White Plains, NY: Longman.

Reed, B., & Railsback, J. (2003). *Strategies and resources for mainstream teachers of English language learners.* Northwest Regional Educational Laboratory. Retrieved December 9, 2013, from www.nwrel.org/request/may2003/ell.pdf

Sample Text and Items to Elicit Information from Participants in Advance of Working with a Coach

This text is excerpted from a letter to our participants after their participation in a 40-hour summer training and before the following fall semester.

We have assigned _____ [name of coach] to work with you. Please contact to schedule a face to face, skype, or phone meeting at some point during July or the first half of August, at a time mutually convenient to both of you. You can email your coach at _____ .

In order for your coach to best support you, at least one week before that phone conversation, please send your coach as an electronic attachment:

- One copy of this form for each of one or two courses you'll discuss with your coach. Please type in responses to the questions below, and SAVE W/ YOUR FULL NAME and COURSE NUMBER.
- electronic versions of any supporting documents that would help you and your coach talk together; at minimum, this probably means a syllabus, and might include one more separate documents, such as assignments. For a long document—like a syllabus—please use color highlighting or some other means to focus your coach on the most relevant portions of the document.

What is the number and name of the course you'd like to revise?

1. Please describe the course briefly in terms of: who takes the course; where it falls in the course of students' teacher certification track, and—if you think this matters for talking with a coach—what experiences and courses precede your course, are concurrent with it, or follow it.
2. If you have added or revised one or more objectives of the course related to ELLs, please paste the new/revised objectives below.
3. Regardless of your answer to #3, what do you want this course to accomplish with regard to preparing teachers to work effectively with ELLs?
4. What assignments, experiences, or activities do you plan to use to achieve the objectives and outcomes you've described above? What are your questions, concerns, or thinking regarding these activities or any alternatives?
5. What assessment will help you learn about preservice teachers' progress towards your objectives?
6. How do you think you could use your assessments and any other products of your course and Project PREPARE to engage in further revision to your curriculum and instruction the year after this one?
7. What questions or concerns do you have? Is there more you'd like to read about, or wish you knew at this point? [Your coach may not have answers, but might have some guidance or suggestions for finding relevant readings or making progress with your concerns.]

Part II
Revising Courses and Developing Practices

4 Using a Conceptual Frame to Infuse Material about Emergent Bilinguals into a Teacher Education Course

Megan E. Staples and Thomas H. Levine

THE OVERARCHING CHALLENGE

Most teacher educators teach courses about important aspects of teaching that could—and should—be linked to emergent bilinguals. The work of incorporating learning about emergent bilinguals, however, should not be seen as just adding a new topic into existing courses. Rather, in courses where the primary focus is not the education of emergent bilinguals, an instructor must choose how to help preservice teachers think about emergent bilinguals in relation to the core content covered in the course. This choice has important consequences for the organization of courses as well as our preservice teachers' learning.

In this chapter, we argue that teacher educators should strategically choose a *frame* as they approach such work. We propose that choosing and using a frame offers one important mechanism by which the new material can be related to—and reinforce—core foci of existing courses. Preservice teachers are then exposed to integrated and powerful ideas rather than piecemeal ideas they must integrate on their own.

How can conceptual frames help teacher educators weave new content powerfully into existing course? How can such frames promote more coherent and deep learning related to both core course content and emergent bilinguals? Our chapter answers these questions. We explain what we mean by a frame. We examine two different frames that we—each author of this chapter—have chosen to use, explain why we chose each frame, and suggest how such frames give rise to particular opportunities for preservice teacher learning with respect to teaching emergent bilingual students. We then extend our treatment of frames by identifying additional options for frames, considering what each frame might bring into focus and what each may obscure. In our closing, we identify factors an instructor might consider when choosing frames and make other recommendations about their use.

Frames

Frames—like those in a window or around a landscape painting—can literally bring some things into focus while making other things peripheral.

Conceptual frames—as opposed to literal frames—also put ideas and concepts in relationship to one another.

So, how do conceptual frames impact preservice teachers' learning in a teacher education course? One answer is that conceptual frames can guide the conceptual models individual preservice teachers develop. Conceptual frames can act as both a structure on which to build and a filter that shapes how preservice teachers attend to and integrate new information (Grosslight, Unger, Jay, & Smith, 1991). By deliberately advancing a conceptual frame, an instructor might better help preservice teachers to weave together course themes and materials related to emergent bilinguals, making it more likely that new information develops into a coherent and flexible set of understandings. Such connected understandings are more likely to be retained when compared with learning loosely related facts and concepts. Deliberately presenting a conceptual frame can also alter existing cognitive models by bringing specific, already established models to the fore to build on, challenge, and revise as needed.

A second answer to why frames matter is suggested by sociocultural theories of learning. Sociocultural theorists have shown how concepts (conceptual tools) can be as important as physical tools to accomplish things in the world (Cole, 1996; Engeström & Miettinen, 1999; Lave & Wenger, 1991); indeed, concepts are analytic tools that are used for making sense of and thinking through situations. Conceptual framing can be akin to passing on tools developed by others in the past to enable certain kinds of noticing, thinking, and action in the present. For example, a preservice teacher is likely to see, think, and act differently in a classroom if she grasps the concept of *status* and chooses to care about it. Consistent practice using this concept may lead the preservice teacher to understand some related ideas and act accordingly; for instance, she might pay attention to how status interacts with power and identity while watching a small group work together, or when designing a subsequent learning opportunity. Thus, the choice of a specific conceptual frame in a course will likely influence the particular development of related conceptual tools, habits of thinking, and different types of activity.

CASES: HOW TWO DIFFERENT FRAMES FACILITATED DIFFERENT OPPORTUNITIES FOR LEARNING

To illuminate how different frames can give rise to different opportunities for learning, this section introduces two frames and two courses that each use one of these frames. Our examples are methods courses, but the ideas and frames can also be applied to other courses in a teacher preparation program. In the following section, we describe additional frames that others could use to help preservice teachers more powerfully connect learning about emergent bilinguals with the core content of various teacher education courses.

Subject-Specific Register Frame

One option for framing an individual teacher education course is to foreground the disciplinary or subject-specific *registers* of the school subjects students are taught, such as the scientific register or the mathematics register. A *register* is "a set of meanings that is appropriate to a particular function of language, together with the words and structure which express these meanings" (Halliday, 1975, p. 65, as cited in Pimm, 1987). A register develops to accomplish a particular purpose (such as doing mathematics or discussing baseball) in particular settings (such as among a community of mathematicians or sports enthusiasts). Registers draw from the language of the dominant culture (in the U.S., this language is most often standard English), borrowing and extending extant words and meanings, and also developing new ways of expressing ideas in response to a specific speech community's activities and its purpose(s).

The *mathematics* register is the set of vocabulary along with the particular ways of expressing ideas (such as generalizations, logical connections, or justification) that is used by the mathematics community to do mathematics together. For example, consider the phrase "Some squares are rectangles." In math class, this is a generalization, a statement that, if true, means that there exists *at least one* square that is also a rectangle. It could be that *all* squares are rectangles, *half* (or some other proportion) of all squares are rectangles, or *only one* square is a rectangle. The mathematical use of the term *some* is different from the way the term *some* is used in our everyday conversations. In everyday language, if you say, "Some birds are animals" someone might "correct" you and say, "No, *all* birds are animals." The term *some* in everyday language generally means a few, but not all, and it certainly does not mean only one. As this example suggests, one cannot understand or succeed with math unless one has some command of the math register. We illustrate the register frame in mathematics in the first case.

Using the Math Register to Frame Teaching Math to Emergent Bilinguals in a Methods Course

Megan, the first author of this chapter, teaches a secondary math methods course. To help her students think about emergent bilinguals, she frames learning the *mathematics register* as an integral part of learning math.

The Audience, Course, and Context

Megan's students are preparing to become secondary mathematics educators. They take more than 30 credits of mathematics as part of their secondary math education program, nearly completing the coursework of a pure math major. Many complete the math major in addition to their education degree. These preservice teachers love math and have developed a high degree of proficiency with the subject matter. Every year, a cohort of 9 to 16 students takes Megan's three-credit methods course during the fall of their senior year, the semester prior to student teaching.

As they begin methods class, the preservice teachers are like "fish in water"; they have become so steeped in speaking mathematically that they have forgotten what is unique, challenging, powerful, and confusing about the language of math. They love to focus on numbers, math concepts, and problem solving, and they are unlikely to see themselves as responsible for language development.

Implementing a Mathematics Register Frame

Megan first guides her preservice teachers to learn about the math register and why it matters. As a way to help her students "get" what the mathematics register is, Megan uses a short video clip, from YouTube or elsewhere on the web, with some sports analysis. Her students are fluent in the mathematics register and need to take a step back and unpack it, realizing the incredible journey individuals make to master a register. Her favorite has been the first 60 seconds of sportscaster Bonnie Bernstein discussing the Yankee manager's choice of Molina as the catcher for pitcher Burnett in one of the 2009 playoff games ("Yankees: Molina Catching Burnett," 2009).

Megan plays the clip and then asks questions about the content and meaning of the clip. To answer the questions, the students have to make sense of the baseball-ese they are hearing. To illustrate, here is an excerpt from the clip:

> Molina may have the edge as a backstop and a game caller, but at the plate his Mendoza Line-esque numbers could be a costly chink in the Yankees' locked and loaded armor. Posada on the other hand is a switch hitter with a killer slugging percentage, and, oh by the way, a few World Series rings to boot. That's all the obvious stuff. (00:32–00:51)

Students consider how every word is an English word (barring perhaps the created adjectival phrase Mendoza Line-esque) that generally can be understood in isolation, but now these words are strung together in new ways, and their meanings are sometimes different. With the idea of a register now coming into view, students reflect on how they engaged or disengaged with the short video, who appeared "smart" in this context, and how those behaviors might be recognizable in their math students.

From this point, preservice teachers begin focusing on the language of mathematics. Readings and activities help students appreciate the challenges of gaining command of the mathematics register, including a chapter from Pimm's (1987) classic *Speaking Mathematically*. Preservice teachers also think about language in terms of how it is necessary for supporting higher order thinking or how it can set up barriers to it. For example, Megan shows them an excerpt from a widely used textbook:

> In lesson 9.1, you saw that if a triangle is a right triangle, then the square of the length of its hypotenuse is equal to the sum of the squares of the lengths of the two legs. What about the converse? (Serra, 2001)

Preservice teachers realize that this two-sentence passage would make no sense to someone unfamiliar with the mathematics register.

Having preservice teachers become aware of the subject-specific register as a frame is critical for their subsequent learning about teaching mathematics and specifically teaching emergent bilinguals. If teacher candidates are not aware of the challenges and features of the language of the mathematics register, or do not recognize what language needs to be mastered beyond vocabulary, they will not think clearly about the role of language in math teaching and learning. Furthermore, without this foundational awareness, they cannot engage the next critical step: identifying language demands of each mathematical topic and lesson that they teach, and designing appropriate lessons.

After laying this foundation, preservice teachers spend a significant amount of time learning to write language objectives and developing lesson plans that support students in meeting these language objectives. This work is challenging. The focus on language objectives lets preservice teachers continue to think carefully about the language demands of mathematics and the need to explicitly target and support language development through language objectives. Subsequent course activities focus on strategies that preservice teachers can use to support language development, including some strategies from the Sheltered Instructional Observational Protocol (SIOP) (Echevarría, Vogt, & Short, 2008). The lesson planning that follows, for instance, requires preservice teachers to develop language objectives and design instructional activities to reach these objectives. Preservice teachers also identify how they will elicit information relevant to students' language use so they can gain evidence about the degree to which the language objectives have been met. See Appendix A for an overview of key course topics and corresponding instructional activities and readings related to language and mathematics. See Appendix B for two sample course activities.

This overall approach of leading with a math register frame positions the work of supporting emergent bilinguals within the larger framework of attending to learning language as part of learning mathematics. One common approach to preparing teachers for linguistic diversity is to start with emergent bilinguals and strategies that support them and then argue that what is good or critical to include for emergent bilinguals also helps others learn. Megan reverses this. She starts with language and its importance for teaching math, as math is what math preservice teachers signed up to teach and are committed to already. By leading with the mathematics register, preservice teachers consider these strategies right from the start as productive strategies for teaching mathematics to all students, as all students are math language learners. Only later does she bring instruction specifically for emergent bilinguals into focus.

Opportunities and Limitations

Based on her experimentation and work with other courses prior to pursuing this register frame, Megan has found that using the mathematics register as a conceptual framework offers several key learning opportunities and advantages for her students.

Using a discipline-focused language frame gives Megan an immediate "in" with students. For future secondary teachers, who may be highly subject affiliated, this frame starts with the subject, something about which they are passionate and curious, and builds on their strengths, including their own command of the mathematics register. Furthermore, it affords them the opportunity to reflect on the subject in a new way and appreciate some of the challenges of it that they may not have noticed before.

This approach also focuses preservice teachers on how language is critical for learning, and how learning mathematics *requires* students to master certain forms of language, ways of expressing themselves and discipline-specific vocabulary. This approach then is an imperative for their teaching of *all students*. Other arguments that Megan has advanced in the past have not had the same draw for her students. For example, she doesn't argue that they have to be prepared to teach this particular subgroup of students, as some do not envision positions where they will teach emergent bilinguals, and many preservice teacher placements have few emergent bilinguals students. A focus on the mathematics register supports a commitment to focusing on language regardless of whether preservice teachers yet experience a pressing need to learn how to teach emergent bilinguals.

In addition, this frame may help preservice teachers learn about grammatical features and specific terms needed to consume and express ideas in a discipline (see Schleppegrell, 2004; Schleppegrell & Fang, 2008). For example, when considering the phrase from the textbook passage above—"the square of the length of its hypotenuse"—preservice teachers can reflect on how one object is referenced by a dense noun phrase that includes two prepositional phrases. This type of noun phrase is common in mathematics. It aids precision but can create some barriers to initial meaning making. The frame's focus on language is also aligned well with the widely adopted Common Core State Standards, which emphasize academic language, an advantage Megan didn't foresee when she began using it to infuse new material into her course.

Megan has given an anonymous survey at the end of the semester, which includes the following two questions: How important do you think it is to attend to language in the mathematics classroom? How important do you think it is to actively teach for language development in the mathematics classroom? These questions are designed to tease apart the difference between a candidate's view that language is important and the view that it is his or her responsibility to actively teach for language development. For the 2012 cohort, for each question, eight of the nine indicated that actively teaching for language development was very important (response of 8, 9, or 10 on a scale of 1–10). These responses suggest that Megan's preservice teachers leave their math methods course seeing the importance of language in the learning and doing mathematics and feel it is their responsibility to develop it.

A focus on language also has limitations as a conceptual framework to facilitate learning about emergent bilinguals. A register frame may overshadow some specific support for and needs of emergent bilinguals. For example, preservice teachers do not learn SIOP as an integrated system with this approach. The class discusses a subset of elements, and there is a focus on those that Megan considers "high leverage," but there is not systematic attention to how particular features from SIOP are effective for emergent bilinguals. The register approach also doesn't readily lend itself to exploring *who* the emergent bilinguals in preservice teachers' classes are. Preservice teachers, for instance, don't consider that emergent bilinguals come from many varied backgrounds or may have interrupted schooling experiences, and thus teaching math to emergent bilingual students requires more than just considering language. Along with this, using a language frame doesn't lend itself to highlighting the strengths that emergent bilinguals bring to a classroom (e.g., funds of knowledge; Gonzáles, Moll, & Amanti, 2005) or how to leverage those strengths as assets in the classroom. (Megan does touch on cognates and using word roots, but not extensively.) Finally, this frame doesn't lend itself to a focus on developing language skills, such as reading and listening, although there is attention to speaking and writing. These important skills are placed in the background in service of thinking about the learning of the mathematics. Megan teaches with an awareness that her choice of frame brings some things into focus. The frame, however, does not lend itself to promoting all desirable outcomes. It is not that one *can't* attend to who our emergent bilinguals are or attend to reading. One certainly could. However, the efforts made in these areas may not be woven as powerfully into preservice teachers' emerging understandings and practices because they aren't as tightly integrated within a larger chosen frame.

Demographic Frame

A second option for a frame comprises focusing on emergent bilinguals as a particular—and an underserved—group of students. We call this the demographic frame. This framing may include attention to the characteristics of and diversity within this group, their overall educational performance, and the existence of research-based pedagogical approaches to improve their learning (e.g., the SIOP model). When teacher educators lead with this frame, they may also discuss the ways in which schools often fail to meet the needs of emergent bilinguals and/or practices that schools might use to meet this specific group of learners' needs (see e.g., Boyle-Baise & McIntyre, 2008; Gay, 2010). We illustrate this frame in the second case.

Focusing on Emergent Bilinguals to Frame Teachers' Learning in an Elementary Social Studies Methods Course

Tom, the second author of this chapter, teaches elementary social studies methods, one of five methods courses that elementary education majors take in the fall of their senior year before student teaching. Tom and his elementary methods colleagues consciously struggled with the problem of how to frame the work of preparing teachers for emergent bilinguals.

The Audience, Course, and Context

Whereas preservice secondary math teachers have a deep commitment to a specific content domain, elementary teachers must teach all content areas. Elementary teachers appear to focus more on educating whole children and identify less with teaching specific content compared with their secondary peers in our program. Where Megan could choose a frame building on the shared disciplinary training and orientations that math majors are likely to have, Tom and his colleagues decided to build on the concern for nurturing human beings that they see as a common strength of their elementary teachers. Thus, for the past two years, they have begun their semester of methods courses by introducing a specific group of learners—emergent bilinguals—and inviting preservice teachers to commit to learning a variety of strategies that will help these learners succeed across content areas.

Forty-two elementary education majors are broken into two groups, so that groups of 21 students take Tom's elementary social studies methods class during the first or second five weeks of the semester. Concurrently, elementary education majors rotate through two other intensive five-week methods blocks (science, math), take a semester-long course related to literacy methods, have another course on assessment, spend one day a week in schools, and take a campus-based clinical seminar.

Implementing a Demographic Frame

For the past two years, Tom and his colleagues have scheduled an extra meeting of the entire elementary cohort at the beginning of the semester. Preservice teachers arrived at this whole-group meeting having read the first chapter of the SIOP book introducing the Sheltered Instructional Observational Protocol (SIOP). Tom provided pre-reading questions that asked preservice teachers to grasp the existence of, nature of, and rationale for the SIOP. As elementary preservice teachers enter our meeting room, a PowerPoint slide announces the two content and one language objectives for our time together: Students will be able to (a) identify reasons that you, as a teacher, should actively seek out knowledge and practices to help emergent bilinguals; (b) explain what SIOP is and how it may help you teach emergent bilinguals; and (c) use the phrase, "I heard you say . . . " to engage in active listening and build on others' ideas. This final objective is meant to model the idea of a language objective from the SIOP model.

Tom opens with an eight-minute PowerPoint presentation titled, "Why Should You Actively Prepare for Teaching Emergent Bilinguals?" Charts and pie graphs convey information about the increasing numbers of emergent bilinguals in the nation, our state, and suburban and rural districts; Tom uses these facts to make the point that all teachers should expect that they will work with culturally and linguistically diverse students during their career. Tom presents the next set of slides to argue that our school systems currently fail to help emergent bilinguals achieve; the arguments and language in Tom's presentation locate the problem in schools' and teachers' work rather than reinforcing a deficit model. (A deficit model assumes that emergent bilinguals have deficits that account for their performance rather than also seeing what strengths they bring and observing deficits in schooling.) These slides include information about the academic performance and dropout rates among emergent bilinguals. Tom then offers what feels closer to a sermon than his typical teaching. He argues for the urgency and potential benefits—or costs—to our society and economy if teachers do—or don't—learn how to meet this group of learners' needs. There is clearly a moral pitch here; in essence, Tom urges, "It is up to us to do this . . . the problem is that, according to research, most teachers are not prepared to work with emergent bilinguals, and there are many ways in which schools disrespect—and miscommunicate with—emergent bilinguals and their families at present. We can and must turn around the patterns of underachievement."

As Tom frames the problem around a specific and underserved group of learners, he includes some visuals of students of various ethnicities in school or other relevant settings, again trying to keep the focus on a group of people. Tom closes with an unsubtle appeal to commonly shared American values of fairness, inclusion, and equal opportunity as a persuasive tactic.

This introduction is followed by a five-minute overview of the language used to engage in active listening ["I heard you say . . . "], followed by small-group conversations about the reading where our preservice teachers practice using the language of active listening. Students talk through two guiding questions that accompanied the reading; these push preservice teachers to think about the situation of one emergent bilingual presented at the beginning of the SIOP book and the kinds of instruction most likely to help him. The remaining questions help preservice teachers make sense of diversity among emergent bilinguals, their common needs, and the ways in which a SIOP model can help teachers work with emergent bilinguals. The session ends with a video example of SIOP-based instruction in an elementary classroom; the video provides preservice teachers with the opportunity to think about how grouping strategies, assessment, use of manipulative and visuals, and other elements of the teaching they saw are feasible and desirable to meet the needs of emergent bilinguals.

Thus, the issue of teaching emergent bilinguals is framed up front as one of meeting the needs and unleashing the talents of a specific group of people. After this meeting, the preservice teachers rotate through elementary science, math, and social studies methods blocks during the first, second, or third five weeks of the semester. Elementary instructors in those courses have divided up elements of the SIOP to be sure that no matter which five-week methods course preservice teachers take first or second, they experience a logical progression of SIOP features. For instance, elementary preservice teachers focus on language and content objectives during the first five weeks because this seems foundational, and then they read and practice methods for building on—and building up—background knowledge in the second five weeks regardless of which particular methods block they are taking. The instructors have developed common lesson plan assignments. Based on these common assignments, preservice teachers write units that give evidence of an increasing number of SIOP elements regardless of which particular subject-area methods course they take during the first, second, and third five-week methods block.

As Tom proceeds to teach social studies methods, he intertwines core aspects of social studies with SIOP as appropriate. Our opening frame focused our preservice teachers on the need of a particular and often underserved group of learners. For instance, preservice teachers identify the linguistic demands of two typical teaching texts used when teaching early U.S. history to fifth graders. Consistent with the opening frame, Tom creates a scenario with a specific emergent bilingual, an intermediate English language speaker who immigrated from Mexico and has some knowledge of Mexican history, to help preservice teachers think about what specific learners might bring to reading such texts, and what more they might need to gain access to their content. First, while looking at a textbook passage about events leading to the American Revolution, preservice teachers begin to see the kinds of knowledge that this specific student might need to fully access a text, and the knowledge or experience that he might possess about revolution or civil war, which would help him understand the content and vocabulary in these texts. Students apply SIOP strategies for making this typical textbook passage more accessible. Students then look at primary sources written with vocabulary and a writing style more common in colonial U.S. history. Preservice teachers practice making this primary source more accessible.

To offer one more example, Tom talks about various ways of positioning elementary students to begin talking civilly about controversial issues and thinking critically. As preservice teachers learn about various ways to help students engage with controversial issues—simulation, structured academic controversy (Johnson & Johnson, 1994), or research projects, for instance—they must become good at clarifying their expectations and instructions. Once again, SIOP offers multiple strategies for making sure that all students understand what teachers expect of them. While modeling and then having preservice teachers try such strategies, Tom refers back to meeting the needs of a specific group of underserved students or refers to what we know about emergent bilinguals while explaining why SIOP practices can be critical for emergent bilinguals learning, even if they also prove helpful to others. For example, when a teacher shows a model of a finished project or what an effective small-group discussion looks like, it often enhances learning for all students; being able to see or experience such models, however, may make the difference between understanding and not being able to do what a teacher asks for an emergent bilingual.

Opportunities and Limitations of This Frame

Opening with a demographic frame, focused on demographic facts and school achievement data about a particular group of students, is a good choice for creating or reinforcing preservice teachers' understandings about emergent bilinguals in order to support later learning of strategies. Evidence suggests that the approach Tom and his colleagues used may help preservice teachers develop an effective commitment to emergent bilinguals. In 2010 and 2012, the instructors collected exit slips after the opening session described earlier. Preservice teachers listed three things they got from the session. As shown in Table 4.1, preservice teachers left thinking about specific teaching strategies they could use, something new teachers always want. Preservice teachers also commented on the nature of SIOP, features of emergent bilinguals, and the fact that emergent bilinguals are typically underserved. Eighteen percent of the statements on the exit slips have been affective declarations about what is important, what is imperative, or what teachers feel they must do relevant to emergent bilinguals. When Tom has used exit slips at the end of other classes he teaches, he hasn't seen this kind of statement. Admittedly, exit slips may not indicate long-lasting learning and may reflect what preservice teachers think professors want to hear. Nevertheless, we think these outcomes suggest the potential strengths of this approach.

In other words, by using a demographic frame, elementary education instructors put features of emergent bilinguals, their presence in an increasing number of schools, and the fact of their being underserved in front of preservice teachers first. We believe that focusing on social and demographic facts—as opposed to subject-specific register—began fostering a moral commitment that might make future discussions of methods seem more coherent and pressing. The affective statements suggest that this frame may afford opportunities to motivate attention to the issue; depending on what follows, this frame might facilitate continuing impact on what preservice teachers deem important. Finally, showing how SIOP is appropriate to this underserved group of learners affords a practical focus on teachers acquiring and practicing some specific pedagogical tools.

One limitation of this approach is that it offers little conceptual support for understanding how language and culture can both facilitate and challenge emergent bilinguals' learning of specific subject matter. We think that our exit slips point to this. Exit slips across two years included only one statement about the nature of language or language learning: One student noted, "Academic literacy develops slower than conversation." The statements included no other broad theoretical concepts or insights that could organize thinking and practice, such as insights regarding the role of culture or language in learning. During Tom's methods teaching, he finds himself working hard to proceed to talk about the nature of developing academic language while teaching social studies content, the range of language objectives that can complement teaching of social studies content, and the nature of scaffolds appropriate to support this underserved group in accessing social studies texts. SIOP did provide practical tools that helped, and a demographic frame made clear why teachers should learn these tools. A language development frame, however, would have helped students more easily grasp the specific affordances of and need for these SIOP tools.

There is also a risk of "othering"—of talking about emergent bilinguals as others to be pitied or simply seen as "not us"—in this focus. The presence

Table 4.1 What Elementary Education Students Reported Getting from an Opening Session Framing Teaching Emergent Bilinguals

Category of Response	% of responses, 2010 (total of 143 comments across 39 exit slips)	% of responses, 2012 (total of 125 comments across 38 exit slips)
Teaching strategies I can use	50.3%	39.2%
SIOP-related (about SIOP but not strategies)	—	18.4%
Cost of not helping emergent bilinguals	—	2.4%
Affective	19.6%	16.0%
Emergent bilinguals as underserved	6.2%	5.6%
Features of emergent bilinguals	21.6%	16.8%
Other	2.0%	4.0%

of several preservice teachers in our cohorts who were emergent bilinguals helps to mitigate some of this, although Tom is careful never to single them out to serve as representatives of this group. Tom sometimes adjusts his language to address this potential risk (i.e., "those of us [or those citizens] who are emergent bilinguals" versus "emergent bilinguals... they"). When he occasionally offers case examples allowing preservice teachers to practice for a specific bilingual, he seeks to represent the diversity of emergent bilinguals, representing both second-generation students in families and communities with a first language other than English, and the children of immigrant family from all continents, for instance. Tom hopes this makes it harder to see emergent bilinguals as one kind of other.

In summary, we believe that focusing on serving a group of students matches our students' particular sense of mission; however, we can foresee the possibility that we'll revise our opening frame as our program—and the content related to emergent bilinguals that student bring in to senior year—continues to develop.

ADDITIONAL CONCEPTUAL FRAMES

We have shared, with some depth, two frames and how these frames are incorporated into two teacher education courses for preservice teachers. In doing so, we hope we have illustrated how each frame afforded different kinds of learning, and how these frames were leveraged to connect with preservice teachers' prior experiences, future selves, and course learning activities. There are many other options for frames, however. We introduce the reader to four such options here.

Language Development Frame

Language needs are vast, and there is more than one possible approach to using a language-oriented frame. Instead of focusing on developing a discipline-specific register, as shown in the first case, a teacher educator could usefully focus on more general aspects of academic language and/or literacy development. Several foci could appear, individually or in combination, in such a language development frame. This choice of frame might attune teachers to the process of developing a second language so that teachers do not inappropriately apply understandings about language learning that they have seen among monolingual English speakers to emergent bilinguals (de Jong & Harper, 2005). It could help teachers think about how all students are developing academic language in school (Scarcella, 2003), and thus how teachers should scaffold language learning for all students while also illuminating the additional needs and strategies that are relevant when working with emergent bilinguals (e.g., Scarcella, 2002). It could promote skill in analyzing the linguistic demands of common school tasks, such as participating in whole-class discussion, writing essays, or reading textbooks, and prompt attention to the kinds of scaffolds that develop language and enable participation in common school tasks (Schlepergrell, 2004; Zwiers, 2008).

Social Justice

Instead of leading with information about emergent bilinguals specifically and making them a focus, an instructor could introduce a wider social justice frame to affect how preservice teachers think about and link together their various experiences learning about emergent bilinguals. A social justice frame invites preservice teachers to consider systematic inequity in society and/or schooling. Teacher educators who lead with this frame help preservice teachers ask questions about past and present patterns of learning and policy in schools, invite preservice teachers to examine their own beliefs, and/or seek to bolster certain dispositions or commitments to practices that help traditionally underserved students, including working with their students to affect change.

Universal Design Frame

Using a universal design frame invites preservice teachers to think about how curriculum and instruction, from the outset, can be made accessible to a wide variety of students without requiring modification or adaptation later (Orkwis, 2003). The typical teacher educator prepares teachers to instruct an "amorphous, 'average' student" who—without examinations—often turns out to have no special gifts or challenges in learning material, is a monolingual English speaker in the U.S., and possesses the values and cultural knowledge of the dominant culture (Cummins & Miramontes, 2006). The emphasis of this frame is making content accessible to all learners through a variety of strategies. This frame would likely attune preservice teachers to emergent bilinguals as one of many groups whose needs must be attended to when designing all instruction. The philosophy behind a universal design approach is well aligned with the SIOP model, whose authors sometimes note that what is good for emergent bilinguals is good for all students.

Cultural Frame

Framing course content and discussions of emergent bilinguals by focusing on culture affords opportunities for teacher candidates to learn about the kinds of cultural knowledge (e.g., funds of knowledge; González, Moll, & Amanti, 2005), experiences, values, and practices that students bring from home to school, and the nature of culturally relevant pedagogy and content (e.g., Banks, 1997; Gay, 2010; Ladson-Billings, 2009; Lee, 1995).

Attention would be given to the culture of schooling and/or the ways in which teachers and schools may—or may not—work well with students, families, and communities when they reflect different cultures. Culture can be a notoriously difficult concept to pin down (González, 2005). Nevertheless, such a frame can enable certain kinds of understanding and practice critical for effective work with emergent bilinguals. Readers can find reference to teacher education courses bringing aspects of culture into focus in Chapters 6 and 11.

RECOMMENDATIONS

Boldly but Thoughtfully Commit to a Frame!

In this chapter, we have argued that conceptual frames afford specific kinds of learning and can do so differently for different groups of preservice teachers. We thus call for teacher educators to thoughtfully choose and commit to a frame that they think will promote learning and practice among their preservice teachers related to teaching emergent bilinguals while integrating new understandings with the core content of their courses.

In cases where teacher educators are unsure which frame may best serve them or suit their learners'—preservice teachers'—current knowledge and commitments, we encourage teacher educators to boldly choose one frame and discover its affordances and limitations. We did not know what would work as we began, and we are still revising our work. More important than getting it "right" the first time is simply to begin the ongoing learning and perspective-taking that comes with looking through frames. There may be some advantage to teacher educators trying more than one frame in different years for their own development.

We offer the following advice for instructors intentionally choosing a frame for their course:

1. Choose a frame that suits your preservice teachers. Be student-focused in choosing and developing a frame. We must start with where *our students*—our preservice teachers—are. The commitments, knowledge, and strengths they bring can be used as a bridge or source of motivation to strengthen the knowledge, pedagogical practices, and dispositions we seek to develop.
2. Choose a frame that allows for integration. Identify a frame that most powerfully lets you introduce and integrate learning about emergent bilinguals into the broader objectives and outcomes of your course. The frame should complement (reinforce, build on, or deepen) other course content and themes.
3. Embrace the reality of constraints. Each of the frames we identify—and more we haven't named—will likely afford certain learning

opportunities and constrain others. There is no one frame that can bring all into view that you may want. Constraints can even be viewed as a facilitator of growth by focusing preservice teachers on certain kinds of ideas and relationships. Constraints bound potential action and learning in ways that allow more focus and depth. In this view, constraint is not the opposite of an affordance, but a complement or further facilitator of the affordance (Brown, Stillman, & Herbert, 2004).

Work with Colleagues

One can choose a frame based on attention to one's preservice teachers and course content; a programmatic view might increase even more the effectiveness of a frame and the odds that preservice teachers synthesize what they are learning across courses. Working closely with colleagues will ensure linkages between the content and frame you choose and what others do related to emergent bilinguals. Thinking programmatically also avoids duplication and allows for extension. For example, an instructor can deepen what preservice teachers have already learned about culture and culturally relevant pedagogy in prior coursework, or she can decide that another frame suits her material and would be a more logical complement to what has gone before or will follow.

CONCLUSION

The work of infusing learning about emergent bilinguals should not be seen as just introducing a new topic into existing courses. Instructors, at minimum, must help preservice teachers link the new topic to their own course content. Instructors should also work together to help teachers develop more powerful conceptual frameworks for making sense of their work with emergent bilinguals across courses. Thoughtful and intentional use of conceptual frames can help teacher educators and their preservice teachers to do this important work.

While we have argued for choosing one frame, in courses that naturally focus on language—such as a foreign language or secondary English methods course—it may be easy to introduce a language-related frame and a second frame. For most courses, however, even if instructors later introduce a fully developed second frame, we think it makes sense to identify which frame would serve most powerfully to organize and influence whatever content—or frames—follow, and to lead with it. Presenting too many frames jeopardizes the focus and organizing affordances of a single well-developed frame. In summary, leading with a well-chosen, conceptual frame offers preservice teachers the opportunity to both pull together new learning in a coherent way and internalize the frame itself, increasing the odds that they can view their future teaching and students through multiple powerful frames.

REFERENCES

Banks, J. A. (1997). *Educating citizens in a multicultural society.* New York: Teachers College Press.
Boyle-Baise, M., & McIntyre, D. J. (2008). What kind of experience? Preparing teachers in PDS or community settings. In M. Cochran-Smith, S. Feiman-Nemser, D. J. McIntyre, & K. E. Demers (Eds.), *Handbook of research on teacher education: Enduring questions in changing context* (3rd ed., pp. 307–330). New York: Routledge.
Brown, J., Stillman, G., & Herbert, S. (2004). Can the notion of affordances be of use in the design of a technology enriched mathematics curriculum. In I. Putt, R. Faragher, & M. McLean (Eds.), *Proceedings of the 27th annual conference of the Mathematics Education Research Group of Australasia, Townsville* (Vol. 1, pp. 119–126). Sydney, AU: MERGA. Retrieved June 3, 2013, from http://www.merga.net.au/documents/RP122004.pdf
Cole, M. (1996). *Cultural psychology: A once and future discipline.* Cambridge, MA: Belknap Press of Harvard University.
Cummins, N. L., & Miramontes, O. B. (2006). Addressing linguistic diversity from the outset. *Journal of Teacher Education, 57,* 240–246.
de Jong, E. J., & Harper, C. A. (2005). Preparing mainstream teachers for English language learners. *Teacher Education Quarterly, 32*(2), 101–124.
Echevarría, J., Vogt, M., & Short, D. (2008). *Making content comprehensible for English learners: The SIOP® model* (3rd ed.). Boston: Allyn & Bacon.
Engeström, Y., & Miettinen, R. (1999). Introduction. In Y. Engeström, R. Miettinen, & R.-L. Punamäki (Eds.), *Perspectives on activity theory* (pp. 1–16). New York: Cambridge University Press.
Gay, G. (2010). *Culturally responsive teaching: Theory, research, and practice.* New York: Teachers College Press.
Gonzáles, N. (2005). Beyond culture: The hybridity of funds of knowledge. In N. González, L. C. Moll, & C. Amanti (Eds.), *Funds of knowledge: Theorizing practices in households, communities, and classrooms* (pp. 29–45). New York: Routledge.
Gonzáles, N., Moll, L. C., & Amanti, C. (2005). *Funds of knowledge: Theorizing practices in households, communities, and classrooms.* New York: Routledge.
Grosslight, L., Unger, C., Jay, E., & Smith, C. L. (1991). Understanding models and their use in science: Conceptions of middle and high school students and experts. *Journal of Research in Science Teaching, 28,* 799–822.
Halliday, M. A. K. (1975). Some aspects of sociolinguistics. In E. Jacobson (Ed.), *Interactions between linguistics and mathematics education: Final report of the symposium by UNESCO, CEDO and ICMI, Nairobi, Kenya, September 1–11, 1974* (UNESCO Report No. ED74/CONF.808) (pp. 64–73). Retrieved November 13, 2013, from http://unesdoc.unesco.org/images/0001/000149/014932eb.pdf
Johnson, D. W., & Johnson, R. T. (1994). Structuring academic controversy. In S. Sharan (Ed.), *Handbook of cooperative learning methods* (pp. 66–81). Westport, CT: Greenwood Press.

Ladson-Billings, G. (2009). *The Dreamkeepers: Successful teachers of African American children* (2nd ed.). San Francisco, CA: Jossey-Bass.
Lave, J., & Wenger, E. (1991). *Situated learning: Legitimate peripheral participation.* New York: Cambridge University Press.
Lee, C. D. (1995). A culturally based cognitive apprenticeship: Teaching African American high school students' skills in literary interpretation. *Reading Research Quarterly, 30*(4), 608–631.
Orkwis, R. (2003). *Universally designed instruction* (Report No. EDO-EC-03-02). Washington, DC: Special Education Programs. (ERIC Document Reproduction Service No. ED475386)
Pimm, D. (1987). *Speaking mathematically: Communication in mathematics classrooms.* New York: Routledge.
Scarcella, R. (2002). Some key factors affecting English learners' development of advanced literacy. In M. J. Schleppegrell & M. C. Colombi (Eds.), *Developing advanced literacy in first and second languages: Meaning with power* (pp. 209–226). Mahwah, NJ: Lawrence Erlbaum Associates.
Scarcella, R. (2003). *Academic language: A conceptual framework* (Tech. Rep. 2003-1). Santa Barbara, CA: University of California Linguistic Minority Research Institute. Retrieved March 18, 2014 from http://escholarship.org/uc/item/6pd082d4.
Schleppegrell, M. J. (2004). *The language of schooling: A functional linguistics perspective.* Mahwah, NJ: Lawrence Erlbaum Associates.
Schleppegrell, M. J., & Fang, Z. (2008). *Reading in secondary content areas: A language-based pedagogy.* Ann Arbor, MI: University of Michigan Press.
Serra, M. (2001). *Discovering geometry: An investigative approach* (2nd ed.). Emeryville, CA: Key Curriculum Press/Kendall Hunt.
Yankees: Molina Catching Burnett. (2009). *YouTube.* Retrieved March 18, 2014, from http://www.youtube.com/watch?v=XcnfgoXA-fQ&NR=1
Zwiers, J. (2008). *Building academic language: Essential practices for content classrooms.* San Francisco, CA: Jossey-Bass.

APPENDIX A: SAMPLE PROGRESSION USING A LANGUAGE FRAME IN A SECONDARY MATH METHODS COURSE

Table 4.2 outlines a general progression of topics, along with course activities and readings, that Megan Staples has used when working with her secondary math education group in a math methods course. From year to year, there is variation, and the amount of time allocated for different topics varies as well.

Table 4.2 Progression of Topics and Course Materials Related to Language in a Secondary Math Education Methods Course

Topic and Goals	Course Activities/Assignments	Resources and Corresponding Readings
1. Introduction to the math register Raising awareness	Viewing sports-talk video, with discussion	Bonnie Bernstein—Yankees: Molina catching Burnett http://www.youtube.com/watch?v=XcnfgoXA-fQ&NR=1

Continued

Table 4.2 Continued

Topic and Goals	Course Activities/Assignments	Resources and Corresponding Readings
2. Focus on the math register and the language demands of mathematics What is it? What's challenging for students? Why is it important for us to consider?	Activity: Language Demands—the Math Register (see below) PowerPoint-supported segment focused on how students express the following kinds of mathematical ideas: a) the language of proportional reasoning—focused on question of "which grew more?" and student work samples from Chapter 3 of Lamon (2006). b) the language of expressing a generalization while looking at a pattern task and student work samples from a partner high school. PowerPoint presentation also included examples from math texts.	Kotsopoulos, D. (2007). Mathematics discourse: it's like hearing a foreign language. *Mathematics Teacher*, 101(4), 301–305 Pimm, D. (1987). *Speaking mathematically: Communication in mathematics classrooms*. New York: Routledge and Kegan Paul. Selections from Chapter 4: *The Mathematics Register*, pp. 77–99.
3. Language objectives Clarifying different language skills and potential foci for language objectives. Considering the relationship between language objectives and content objectives.	Language Objective Sorting Activity: students are given a set of objectives and they sort them into content objectives and language objectives. Discussion follows. Students begin writing content and language objectives for next lesson plan. A volunteer shares his/her in advance with the instructor to be workshopped during class. Others workshopped in small groups.	Thompson, D., & Rubenstein, R. (2000). Learning mathematics vocabulary: Potential pitfalls and instructional strategies. *Mathematics Teacher*, 93, 568–574 Echeverria, J., Vogt, M., & Short, D. (2008). *Making content comprehensible for English learners: The SIOP model* (3rd ed.). Boston, MA: Pearson Education, Inc. Chapters 1 and 2. Optional: Staples, M., & Truxaw, M. (2011, Fall). Using language objectives to support linguistically diverse students in mathematics classes. *The Connecticut Mathematics Journal*, pp. 18–35.
4. Lesson design and strategies How do we design lessons to meet language objectives? How do we know they have been met?	Engage students with, *How Likely Is It?*, an introductory activity to bridge everyday to academic language. A version of that lesson can be found at http://www.crme.uconn.edu/lessons/lesson_detail.cfm?lessonid=37. Debrief.	Echeverria, J., Vogt, M., & Short, D. (2008). *Making content comprehensible for English learners: The SIOP model* (3rd ed.). Boston, MA: Pearson Education, Inc. Chapters 5 and 7.

Table 4.2 Continued

Topic and Goals	Course Activities/Assignments	Resources and Corresponding Readings
	Share/model additional strategies such as the Conga Line, using Language Frames (cloze sentences). Journal assignment: Structured portion of their weekly journal focuses on language-instruction and ELLs at their school sites– see below for specific prompts. (Also relevant for Topic and Goals #5.)	Enright, K. A. (2009). Mathematics instruction and academic English: Adapting problems for varying English proficiencies. In A. Flores (Ed.), *Mathematics for every student: Responding to diversity. Grades 9–12* (pp. 29–38). Reston, VA: National Council of Teachers of Mathematics.
5. English language learners Who are our ELLs in CT? What may be unique resources or issues?	Journal assignment: Structured portion of their weekly journal focuses on language-instruction and ELLs at their school sites– see below for specific prompts. (Also relevant for Topic and Goals #4.) Activity: Analyzing and re-writing word problem prompts from our State's high school exit exam to make them more accessible to ELLs.	Title II Project ALL & Office of Professional Practice ad Induction. (2004). *Supporting English Language Learners in Mainstream Classrooms*. Boston, MA: Boston College, Lynch School of Education. Retrieved from http://www.bc.edu/content/bc/schools/lsoe/title-iii/resources/manuals.html on 8 Nov 2013. Bielenberg, B., & Fillmore, L. W. (2005). The English they need for the test. *Educational Leadership*, 62, 45–49.

APPENDIX B: SAMPLES MATH METHODS ACTIVITIES FOCUSING ON LANGUAGE AND MATHEMATICS

The following two activities were designed to facilitate preservice teachers' understanding of the mathematics register and the role of language in teaching and learning mathematics. The assignment in Figure 4.1 prompts attention to a component of the mathematics register, specialized words. The second assignment is a journal prompt linked to the clinic experience.

Journal Prompt

Preservice teachers completed bi-weekly journals linked to their clinic placements. They always completed an unstructured section and a structured section. This journal prompt is the fourth one assigned for the structured section in the semester.

Language Demands—The Mathematics Register

Each Box A–C has a description of words we use in math class that are part of the mathematics register. Fill in each box with examples of words that fit the description. For Box D, try to come up with other language challenges you see.

A. Words **exclusive to mathematics register** (or math and other specialized registers). These words are not found in standard, everyday talk. e.g., 1. Coefficient 2. Polynomial *Students make meaning of these new words by drawing on everyday language and prior language developed in the mathematics register*	B. Words in the **mathematics register** that are **also** in the **everyday register** but which have a specialized meaning or different meaning in the mathematics register e.g., 1. "curve" – in mathematics, it refers to a graph, and can also be a straight line. In everyday use, it is usually something that bends, or something that curves (like a curve in the road) 2. "similar" -- In math, we have a very precise definition, all criteria must be met. In everyday use, it means "sharing some characteristics." The phrase, *She and Barbie are similar*, mean very different things in the 2 registers.
C. Pairs of words – **one from the everyday register** and **one from the mathematics register**—that have the **same or very similar meanings**. (The everyday term is likely to have a meaning that is slightly different or more precise in the mathematics register). e.g. 1. vertex (math term) is corner (everyday) 2. diamond (everyday) vs rhombus (math)	D. Other places where language and registers could play an important role. For example, possible points of confusion, places for extra attention because students will refer to their everyday discourse, etc. e.g. 1. *Intersect* and *intercept* (sound so similar, and even are similar in meaning, but inter*cepts* are where graphs inter*sect* the axis) 2. "No slope" in the everyday register would mean flat. In math, "no slope" is an attribute of vertical lines (they have no slope b/c slope is undefined) whereas something that is flat has slope of 0.

Use the back if you need more room. →

Figure 4.1 In-class activity focused on language and mathematics.

Structured Section: Focus on Language and Mathematics

1. As you observe lessons during these next two weeks, note how your cooperating teacher introduces and reinforces new vocabulary in class—paying particular attention to the technique(s) used to have students refine their understanding of the new terminology and ability to use it appropriately in context. The important point here is that language is not just about words; it's about ideas.
2. In addition, select one lesson to focus your observation on students' language use, which is an important feature of the SIOP model (Feature 6). (i) What opportunities do students have to PRODUCE language during a lesson? (ii) Identify two to three changes to that specific lesson that would increase these opportunities without significantly altering the lesson. (The not-so-subtle goal here is to have

you think about how small modifications to a lesson can significantly impact student language use—promoting their language development, potentially enhancing students' engagement and understandings, and increasing the richness of information available to you as a teacher for learning about students' thinking.)
3. Find out the percentage of students in your clinic school classified as ELLs, or receiving other supports for language, and a bit about who they are. (Are they newcomers to the country? U.S.-born, growing up in ethnic communities? Those leaving political or civil unrest? Those with parents in academia, perhaps who are fluent English speakers?) Identify *who* in the school (or district) a teacher, such as yourself, can go to with questions about how to support students who are English language learners in your own classroom.

5 Solving Problems of Space, Time, and Knowledge

How to Fit Learning about Linguistic and Cultural Diversity into Teacher Education Courses

Douglas Kaufman, Mary P. Truxaw, Alan S. Marcus, Sandra B. Billings, and Manuela Wagner

THE OVERARCHING CHALLENGE

As our work with Project PREPARE-ELLs commenced and we began our attempts to revise our courses to address the needs of culturally and linguistically diverse K-12 learners, we encountered an enormous challenge: how do we fit even more into teacher education courses that are already overflowing with content? Chapter 4, on conceptual framing, offers one invaluable approach for infusing new materials and assignments into any teacher education course. Adopting this approach, however, still leaves us grappling with a logistical conundrum. In this chapter, five teacher educators share their insights into how they addressed a number of complicated but related problems that any teacher educator might expect to face in the attempt to explore issues of linguistic and cultural diversity in content area courses. How do we fit these issues into our courses so that they enhance what we already do? How do we introduce such issues so that they re-contextualize what we already teach and provide a more holistic, inclusionary perspective of skills, methods, and content knowledge?

WHO WE ARE

The five authors of this chapter are all teacher educators who work within the teacher preparation programs at the University of Connecticut's Neag School of Education. Sandra Billings teaches several courses in our one-year Teacher Certification Program for College Graduates (TCPCG), for students who are returning to full-time graduate study to obtain certification in high-need secondary areas. Doug Kaufman teaches literacy and language arts courses to elementary education students in our five-year Integrated Bachelor's/Master's (IBM) program. Alan Marcus teaches secondary history and social studies education courses in the IBM program. Mary

Truxaw teaches elementary mathematics education courses in the IBM program. Manuela Wagner teaches foreign language education through the Department of Literatures, Cultures, and Languages.

We share many common goals, but because we teach within different content areas and can serve different populations of students, each of us also has unique interests, perspectives, and challenges. We systematically examined our syllabi and course activity and then used a memoing protocol (Corbin & Strauss, 2008) to uncover the relationships between them and the specific challenges and responses to challenges that we experienced when incorporating new material into our existing teacher preparation courses. In this chapter, we describe key challenges and suggest ways to address and overcome them.

THE CHALLENGE OF FITTING IT ALL IN

As you began to read this chapter, you might have immediately empathized, experiencing the classic anxiety of the overextended teacher educator and asking, "How can I fit any more *stuff* into my course?" Teacher educators never have enough time, and our own struggles to find space to introduce issues of language and culture competently into each of our courses factored into almost every other challenge that we experienced: the dual role of teaching both subject area material and a new knowledge set focused on language and culture was daunting. For some, like Mary, whose intensive math methods course was limited to a five-week block, the challenge was even more pronounced. Several related tensions seemed to work against us.

Competing with External Mandates

Many of us felt compelled to address state certification requirements and the looming specter of the Common Core State Standards to ensure that students were prepared for them. Addressing these new external mandates made it daunting to envision a comprehensive approach to also addressing other complex issues.

Competing with Multiple Content Requirements

Each subject area also faced its own unique time and space challenges. While state testing requirements directly influenced the curriculum in some methods courses, others also felt the pressure to prepare the preservice teachers to teach across multiple themes. For instance, Alan's social studies methods course, while not bogged down by state testing issues, covered a range of topics, including U.S. history, world history, geography, economics, government, and psychology. He struggled with matters of proportion and emphasis. As he put it, "My methods course focuses on the teaching methods of history/social studies. Therefore, I feel a tension between teaching about ELLs more broadly and keeping the focus on history/social studies." All instructors struggled to carve away content-specific material from what they were already teaching in order to replace it with content related to language and culture.

Selecting and Sequencing Course Materials

Relatedly, once we committed to a new focus on emergent bilingual education, we all had to decide what materials and lessons to include or exclude, how much time to spend on each topic, what resources to use, what readings to assign, and what activities in which to engage. While learning to address the needs of emergent bilinguals was imperative to us, we struggled over how to shape each of our courses. Each time we decided to include a new focus on emergent bilinguals, we realized that we needed to remove, truncate, or otherwise adapt material that we found extremely important to our students. It was an age-old breadth versus depth dilemma that complicated every move we made.

Similarly, we also struggled with issues of timing and sequence. As Alan commented, "I struggled to determine when during the semester was the most pedagogically effective time to introduce [diversity and language] topics, require in-depth engagement, connect to 'clinic placements,' etc." These challenges were ubiquitous. As Sandy summed up, "I needed to decide what to include in this course, what to leave out, and how to sequence the timing of assignments and activities."

Trying to Find Authentic Connections with the Preexisting Curriculum

To mitigate these difficulties, we increasingly tried to find the organic connections between current and new content. For Sandy and Mary, whose courses focused on general education and math topics, respectively, natural thematic connections appeared more difficult to uncover. Other courses seemed to lend themselves to integrating issues of language and culture more easily. Manuela's foreign language course already focused on issues of new language learning, Doug's literacy methods course explored linguistics and the processes of language acquisition, and Alan's social studies course embedded issues of cultural diversity, cultural education, and language into the syllabus. Some students brought backgrounds in foreign language and social studies to their respective teacher training, which may have helped them to value and acquire new understanding about language and culture.

Nevertheless, all of us were pushed to think deeply about the existing structures of our courses. Alan realized that preexisting foci on these issues might lead to complacency, explaining, "I worry the needs of emergent bilinguals could then be easily dismissed as 'basically what we already do' without realizing the significant knowledge and skills needed to effectively meet the needs of emergent bilingual students." Doug and Manuela concurred: their syllabi already dealt daily with language and culture issues. This somewhat eased their burden in terms of introducing "new material" but may have also initially given them the false impression that simply "introducing and discussing" issues of linguistic and cultural diversity without looking for deeper connections to the specific needs of emergent bilinguals could suffice in preparing their preservice teachers.

THE CHALLENGE OF PRESERVICE TEACHERS' LIMITED BACKGROUNDS AND EXPERIENCES

Another key dilemma was the preservice teachers' general lack of background regarding issues of language, culture, and diversity (see Chapter 8). In classes and during student teaching, many preservice teachers expressed concern about their lack of knowledge to support emergent bilinguals. In terms of its effect on the overarching problem of lack of time and curricular space, this problem meant that we had to provide our preservice teachers with more foundational information and intensive scaffolding before we could proceed.

In our teacher education programs, as in many programs across the U.S., our preservice teacher population tends to be relatively homogenous. Although we strive to create a population as diverse as possible, local socioeconomic demographics, historical trends regarding who enters the profession, and inadequate recruiting practices lead to this homogeneity. Many, although certainly not all, of our preservice teachers came into the program in positions of relative social and economic privilege and, as a group, were unrepresentative of the growing number of linguistically and culturally diverse students in our K-12 schools.

As a result, even the courses that traditionally dealt with issues of language and culture had students who struggled with the newly introduced concepts. Many of us noticed that the preservice teachers had difficulty transferring previously taught skills and knowledge into confronting diverse students' everyday realities. It was often difficult for them to put themselves in others' shoes: they often defined "reality" by a common acceptance of what *they* saw and knew. Manuela recognized the complexity of what she was asking her students to do in her world language course. She knew that even students who had spent time abroad had an understandably limited knowledge of inequality issues in language education. The goal in their minds often was to spread a love for language and culture in a general sense: more complex social and political issues related to language education were not necessarily part of their equation. Doug also recognized that students with backgrounds different from the majority had understandable reticence to share their personal experiences or state points of view that challenged commonly accepted ones.

Complicating the situation, we could not always expect our preservice teachers to be introduced to complex topics or diverse points of view in clinic placements, nor could we expect all of them to experience school models in which practicing teachers worked together on students' language education. The preservice teachers observed that the English teachers, world language teachers, and teachers of emergent bilinguals in their placements rarely considered the connections among their jobs and therefore collaborated infrequently.

Some of us were also challenged by the positions of our courses within the sequence of our programs. Sandy's general methods course, for instance, was held during the first semester summer session of her program before her preservice teachers could take any courses that explored issues of language, culture, and diversity. Her goal, therefore, was to give her preservice teachers "a baseline knowledge of the issues of emergent bilinguals, which would be reinforced and built upon in their subsequent courses." This was, of course, both admirable and essential, but the preservice teachers' initial lack of knowledge only exacerbated issues of time and space, complicating how we "fit it all in."

THE CHALLENGE OF TEACHER EDUCATORS' LIMITED BACKGROUNDS AND EXPERIENCES

Ultimately, our recognition of the preservice teachers' lack of experience and background knowledge also highlighted problems with our own histories. Alan's question, "What background knowledge and skills do preservice teachers need to maximize their learning about emergent bilingual issues?" underscored the fact that we as a group did not yet have a complete answer to the question. Until we answered it, we realized that it would be almost impossible to answer the pragmatic questions of what to include and how to include it.

We also knew that our own understandings of the complex issues of language, culture, and diversity were not strong enough. As teacher educators with diverse backgrounds in unique disciplines, we had varying degrees of expert knowledge when it came to issues of linguistic and cultural diversity. But even those of us who seemed to have a leg up because of our more complementary subject area expertise quickly realized we were underprepared to teach within this new context. Many of us simply did not know what particular knowledge sets, skills, and dispositions were most important to teach. (Our recognition of our own ignorance about these issues had, in fact, been what compelled us to develop Project PREPARE-ELLs in the first place.) We knew we had to continue learning if we were to move forward effectively.

However, in the midst of the myriad and often fragmented responsibilities of the university teacher educator, we again struggled to find the time to learn about new concepts and materials for ourselves. Sometimes feeling that we were barely treading water with our other obligations, it took a formal, concerted effort to grow and change.

HOW WE ADDRESSED OUR CHALLENGES

Step One: Simply Start and Start Simply

At the beginning of the process, some of us felt so overwhelmed with the apparent enormity of our task that we had difficulty even getting started. The initial solution for many of us was to give ourselves permission to start small, as Sandy did when she focused on offering "a baseline knowledge of emergent bilinguals" that could be extended in later courses. Mary wrote that the act of joining Project PREPARE-ELLs "motivated me to confront my excuses. *Deciding* to do something was a critical first step. I gave myself permission to start small with the recognition that even 'baby steps' move one forward." To begin, she set a series of initial goals that she used as a scaffold for her subsequent attempts. She said, "I set initial goals that I thought would be both doable and meaningful." One overarching goal was for her preservice teachers to recognize that language is an integral part of the teaching and learning of mathematics for all students, and especially for emergent bilinguals. Therefore, her related goals also included preservice teachers learning how to:

- increase their awareness of the need to support emergent bilinguals in mathematics education;
- use selected SIOP strategies in math lesson preparation and planning, including using language objectives, language frames, and key vocabulary (Echevarría, Vogt, & Short, 2008);
- increase their awareness of—and ability to apply strategies for—making mathematics content comprehensible (e.g., through active classroom discourse, modeling, visuals, hands-on experiences, etc.) (Echevarría, Vogt, & Short, 2008); and
- support interaction through group work, cooperative learning, partner talk, and scaffolded discussion (Chapin, O'Connor, & Anderson, 2009; Echevarría et al., 2008).

Reviewing this list, we quickly recognized the universality of their application to any of our own subject-area courses.

Because Alan's social studies methods course already focused on issues of culture and social dynamics, he did not feel the need to make drastic curricular changes. However, he did want to make connections to the needs of emergent bilinguals more explicit. Therefore, at the beginning of the course, he conducted a mini-presentation that discussed changing demographics and rising language diversity in schools. As a result, he articulated a clear rationale for the need to address issues of language and culture and provided a context for the later modeling of strategies that added depth and complexity to the typical social studies lesson.

How We Infused Issues of Language, Culture, and Diversity into Our Existing Course Structures

Our most important finding, after we had examined our work across our separate courses, was that our greatest successes occurred when we were able to infuse issues of language, culture, and diversity into preexisting topics, themes, and activities in ways that not only addressed the learning of emergent bilinguals but also enhanced our ability to meet the needs of the general population. We knew that we could not simply add more material and achieve success. Instead, we had to operate strategically, assuming roles as action researchers to uncover areas of our existing curricula to which we could connect issues of language and culture within the context of existing subject matter. Again, for some of us, these connections were more easily identifiable because of our course foci, but we all discovered that language and communication were ubiquitous features of all of our work, regardless of subject. As we experimented, each of us discovered different practices and assignments that lent themselves to a more organic inclusion of new issues. Some addressed challenges holistically, whereas others discovered that their preservice teachers needed to learn specific methods and strategies as well as theoretical perspectives.

Lessons and Presentations

As we began to revise our lessons, we found ourselves placing a greater emphasis on clear, well-crafted objectives. It was the most effective way to both orient and organize ourselves as we worked to incorporate multiple themes into the lessons. For some, an overarching objective pertaining to emergent bilinguals served as a reminder of our new emphasis. Alan, for instance, added an explicit objective for supporting the needs of emergent bilinguals in his secondary social studies course: "Students will cultivate an appreciation for the unique needs of English Language Learners (ELL) and explore strategies to promote ELL success in their classrooms." These types of objectives served as a foundation and influenced the way we introduced homework readings, specific class activities, connections to fieldwork, and explicit connections to class assignments.

Other objectives were more fine-grained and specific to individual sessions of our course. For instance, in revising lessons in our own courses, we were used to writing content objectives. Following the SIOP protocol, we now sought to define content and language objectives with preservice teachers and share these publicly. This served the dual purpose of ensuring that our students received regular instruction in issues of language and also saw us explicitly model the use of language objectives. When we made concerted efforts to focus on both content and language objectives, we visually and verbally shared examples of our own objectives at the beginning of each class and revisited them at the end of each class.

One Example Lesson: Sentence Frames

In one example of how instructors created lessons that supported language-content connections, Mary introduced, modeled the use of, and had preservice teachers practice using *sentence frames*. Sentence frames are printed structures for writing or speaking. They scaffold English sentence grammar structures and help language learners to think about appropriate vocabulary. They consist of grammatically correct sentences in which key words or terms have been left out so that students can practice completing the sentences with appropriate additions. They differ from cloze sentences in that there is often more than one appropriate word that can be used to fill in a blank. For example, sentence frames like "_____ is a correct answer because _____" and "I agree/disagree with _____ (idea) because _____" provide language learners with scaffolding grammar structures while compelling them to think carefully about vocabulary, terminology, sentence meaning, and content. Mary introduced sentence frames as her preservice teachers studied how to teach whole number subtraction with regrouping. While small groups used place value materials to create and make sense of sample problems, Mary asked them to develop sentence frames that their students might be able to use. They recorded these on sentence strips and shared them with the whole class. Some of the sentence frames they created included:

- "I regrouped _____ into _____ because _____."
- "I can make _____ (2-digit number) by using _____ tens and ones."
- "The number _____ can be regrouped as _____."

The use of sentence frames is one approach that can be adapted for any subject area course, helping students to learn and use content-specific language.

As preservice teachers across courses created and critically examined these types of scaffolding structures through our presentations and lessons, they began to accumulate a larger cache of potential activities to use during their own teaching. They also began to think of every aspect of their teaching as requiring differentiation.

We also found ourselves more readily adapting our instruction, either incorporating or revising practices that were relevant to teaching emergent bilinguals effectively. These included modeling scaffolding techniques, providing reading guides, introducing pacing instruction, creating more group work experiences, teaching students how to peer review effectively, and providing as many relevant scaffolding resources as possible, such as "brick and mortar" vocabulary lists (Dutro & Moran, 2003): lists that offer students both necessary content-specific words and connective language that help emergent bilinguals to articulate more complex concepts.

Assignments

Our focus on language objectives continued through the assignments that we gave to our preservice teachers. While remaining true to the original objectives of the assignments, we now often asked our students to think about the inherent connections to issues of language that may have previously been unrecognized.

Student-Created Lesson Plan and Teaching Assignments

A common assignment across many of the courses was for students to develop their own lesson plans. We recognized that the most obvious revision we could make to these assignments was that they include clear language objectives, as we had been providing explicit modeling of this practice on an ongoing basis. The instructors approached this revision in several ways. Given the existing connections among their courses, the elementary methods instructors (social studies, science, mathematics, and literacy) chose to work together to develop a common general lesson plan template that included attention to SIOP strategies. The template was then customized by the instructors for each curricular area, but all included both content and language objectives, key vocabulary, and a "checklist" of selected SIOP features (Echevarría, Vogt, & Short, 2008). In classes, the preservice teachers received these templates, which served as scaffolds as they thought about how to support emergent bilinguals during specific learning events (a sample template appears in the appendix).

Our lesson plan assignments had always required preservice teachers to include clear content objectives that focused on student learning and content standards. The addition of language objectives was the simplest, most straightforward way to attend to the needs of emergent bilinguals. In Mary's math methods course, for instance, her preservice teachers had always worked in teams to develop content objectives that aligned with the mathematics standards relevant to the grade of each of their field placement classes. Mary simply adjusted this activity to include both content *and* language objectives. Teams wrote their objectives on "sentence strips" and posted and shared these with the rest of the class. A Grade 2 content objective that the preservice teachers would create might be, "Students will be able to show the place value of each digit in numbers with 1s, 10s, and 100s places using place value blocks." Now they also developed a language objective that would help emergent bilinguals master new language skills, such as, "Students will be able to verbally articulate the place value related to the content objective." The lesson then had to include instruction on and practice with developing those verbal skills.

As Sandy added language objectives to her lesson plan assignments, she recognized their added benefit in meeting the Common Core State Standards (CCSS), which emphasize content area language skills. Focusing on the connection between the language objectives and the CCSS, she asked her preservice teachers to explain how they would use the language areas of reading, writing, speaking, and listening in each lesson. Her lesson plan assignment also required the preservice teachers to include a section on differentiation where they provided adaptations that would support emergent bilinguals, as well as students with special needs and talents. Ultimately, her preservice teachers had to teach the mini-lessons and enact the specific strategies.

Curriculum Unit Assignments

Assignments also included larger, more long-term projects than a single lesson plan. For instance, the culminating project that Alan used as a summative assessment for his methods course was a two-week curricular unit that provided all supporting teaching materials. Alan's preservice teachers were required to include specific language objectives within all of the unit lessons, explicit modifications for emergent bilinguals, and a narrative about how they met emergent bilingual needs through the lesson. Alan's unit assessment focused on their strategy use, particularly their attention to reading, writing, listening, and speaking activities.

Assignments That Critically Examine Materials and Practices

Important to all of us was that students began to adopt a critical lens that would allow them to analyze all the teaching approaches that they were learning in regard to their potential effectiveness in addressing the needs of emergent bilinguals. In one assignment, Manuela asked her preservice teachers to examine SIOP features and their applications in world language classrooms. They discovered that, as teachers of foreign language learners, they already used many of the strategies described in the SIOP and that they and other teachers could use its protocol as a tool to check their use of those strategies.

A major assignment in Mary's math methods course was a "video lesson project," in which each preservice teacher developed a mathematics lesson plan, taught the lesson in his or her field placement, video recorded it, and formally reflected on it. One preservice teacher, observing her video through a new critical lens, discovered how her students had been "conditioned to believe that math is about numbers, not language," which gave rise to opportunities to refine her teaching to address the phenomenon. Preservice teachers' critical examinations of their own work in light of language and culture issues became a key component of their development.

In-Class Activities and Discussions

In-class activities and discussions gave preservice teachers opportunities to apply and process the concepts, skills, and strategies that we had introduced through presentations. Every instructor found a specific class to work on and talk about issues important to emergent bilinguals' growth. Alan provided a series of activities that integrated whole-group discussion with small-group work, which focused on components of SIOP, developing language objectives, providing content-specific vocabulary, employing scaffolding techniques, and attending to the language arts skills of reading, writing, listening, and speaking.

Before our project began, Mary already utilized Chapin, O'Connor, and Anderson's (2009) concept of "talk tools," a series of five complementary talk moves developed in linguistically diverse Boston schools, which supported meaningful talk in math classrooms. The five moves included *revoicing* (reiterating what a student says), *reasoning* (asking students to apply their own reasoning to someone else's reasoning through; e.g., agreeing/disagreeing), *repeating* (asking students to restate someone else's reasoning in their own words), *adding on* (prompting students for further participation), and *waiting* (using wait time). During the semester, Mary and her preservice teachers modeled, practiced, and reflected on these moves, with each one of them taking on the role of "teacher" at least once. The talk moves provided both emergent bilinguals and others who were learning new content-specific language with a scaffold for improving talk skills and understandings during discussion.

Fieldwork

Every semester, our preservice teachers engage in fieldwork, observing and teaching in public school classrooms for at least six hours per week. Feeling the tight constraints of including new material in our classes, we recognized that the students' field placements offered perfect opportunities to strengthen connections to—and reflections on—teaching emergent bilinguals. Some of these placements offered preservice teachers opportunities to interact with culturally and linguistically diverse children in real classrooms.

Acting on our goal to not overwhelm ourselves with elaborate or complicated revisions, we adapted field experience assignments through a direct but simple change: instead of giving our preservice teachers the generic directive to observe, work with, and reflect on "students" in their placements, we now asked them to focus their attention on emergent bilinguals for at least part of the time. Alan now required his preservice teachers to interview a student who spoke English as a second language. The preservice teachers asked their interviewees about their attitudes toward history classes, how they felt that they best learned history, what class activities helped them learn, what class activities they enjoyed the most, how they learned about history outside of class (through watching films, visiting museums, and talking with family), and how they felt that their speaking, writing, reading, and listening impacted their learning in the history classroom. The preservice teachers then brought their interview notes to class and participated in an extensive discussion, which resulted in new understandings about the perspectives of emergent bilinguals. It also provided them with an "a-ha moment," in which they realized the importance of speaking with students as a means of developing rapport.

Many of Doug's and Manuela's assignments also asked students to work with both native English speakers and emergent bilinguals within clinic placements. Doug asked his students to interview students, perform running records (Clay, 2000, 2001), and create and give a reading lesson that specifically addressed the needs of emergent bilinguals (see Chapter 6).

These experiences often resulted in our preservice teachers thinking in new ways about how to enhance their own investigations of language and culture. For instance, Manuela's foreign language education students proposed teaching a lesson in a language other than English to other preservice teachers in their cohort in order to put them in the shoes of language learners.

Readings

An obvious component available for revision was the course reading list. We all experimented with readings, looking for new texts to incorporate without overwhelming students with a greater workload. Reviewing our syllabi, we discovered that some of our existing readings discussed issues already related to our new focus on emergent bilinguals, such as how to support reading and writing across proficiency levels, understanding students' backgrounds as a way to support them, the centrality of cultural knowledge to content learning, and the use of visual materials. Using these existing resources, we worked to engage in more explicit discussions about how their information might impact emergent bilinguals' instruction.

In various ways, we all used *Making Content Comprehensible for English Learners: The SIOP Model* (Echevarría, Vogt, & Short, 2008) as a foundational text because we accepted that its focus on language objectives as well as content objectives was beneficial in teaching new language skills to every student, regardless of first language. Some of us had students read specific sections at different points during the semester; others used it more as a reference that they would cite in class when issues of language diversity in teaching arose.

Additionally, each of us felt that our specific readings, in order to not be add-ons, also had to make clear connections between the subject area and the teaching of emergent bilinguals. Sandy, who taught general methods, used *Not for ESOL Teachers: What Every Classroom Teacher Needs to Know about the Linguistically, Culturally, and Ethnically Diverse Student* (Ariza, 2010) because of its case studies intended for an audience of teachers across subject areas and grade levels. After learning more about the implementation of strategies through Project PREPARE-ELLs, she also included *Working with English Language Learners: Answers to Teachers' Top Ten Questions* (Cary, 2007), which dealt directly with strategies that addressed general, pragmatic classroom problems.

Alan and Doug also found readings that were relevant to their specific content areas. Alan added readings from the book *Teaching Social Studies to English Language Learners* (Cruz & Thornton, 2008) as well as an article, "Social Studies for English Language Learners: Teaching Social Studies That Matters" (Cruz & Thornton, 2009). Doug added literacy articles for practitioners, such as "Using Writing to Understand Bilingual Children's Literacy Development" (Rubin & Carlan, 2005) and "What Does Research Tell Us about Teaching Reading to English Language Learners?" (Irujo, 2007). For each instructor, these types of readings directly connected issues of the learning and teaching of emergent bilinguals to the existing course content. (A short list of selected readings from each instructor can be found at the end of this chapter.)

Despite our best efforts, we still sometimes found it difficult to incorporate new readings because of curricular time and space restrictions. Each of us addressed this challenge in different ways. In one case, Sandy exploited the fact that her preservice teachers went through their classes together as a cohort and that she worked with them from the beginning of their program to the end. As a result, during an orientation meeting that occurred a month prior to their first class in the program, she distributed a packet of articles with readings that focused on emergent bilingual issues, thus offering some necessary prior knowledge before they even started the program. She also divided the preservice teachers' reading of *Working with English Language Learners* between her general methods course and their subsequent student teaching experience, minimizing the amount of material they read in one course while still giving them the full experience of the book over time.

We expect that, for any teacher educator, the limited amount of time available for even traditional curriculum will pose a challenge when exploring the teaching of emergent bilinguals. Nonetheless, while tensions always remained, we were able to mitigate problems by carefully considering all aspects of our planning, organizations, and teaching, and focusing on creating clear curricular connections between new and existing content. Communication was key, and Project PREPARE-ELLs meetings served as a forum for mulling over problems and sharing solutions.

How We Addressed Preservice Teachers' Limited Backgrounds and Experiences

As noted in Chapter 4, when we conceptually framed new material about emergent bilinguals, we could more easily weave it into the existing themes and ideas of a course, thus reducing the amount of other important content that we have to eliminate. Nevertheless, helping our students understand the complexity of issues surrounding language and diversity in classrooms did require reducing some of the time that was previously spent on subject-area matters.

But we also learned that if we spent time up front helping our students to develop stronger tools for inquiry and reflection, we made up time in the long run. The field experiences that we described earlier certainly provided key opportunities, as every preservice teacher worked in different, diverse districts across semesters. Now we made a more conscious and systematic effort to identify the already available language and cultural opportunities, tweak our syllabi and teaching approaches to take more advantage of them, and have students reflect more deeply on their experiences with emergent bilingual students. Any stress on our existing time and resource load was reduced once we completed this initial planning.

Individually and as a group, we also utilized a couple of other focused approaches.

Asking Questions to Challenge Existing Assumptions

Manuela and Doug concluded that it was essential for their preservice teachers to reflect on critical issues of language advocacy and for them to become aware of the deficit models under which some language teaching operated (and which teachers, parents, administrators, and even emergent bilinguals commonly accepted). They strongly believed that teacher education courses should provide students with the tools to advocate for all language learners. This entailed making sure that their preservice teachers reflected deeply on how their emerging subject area skills, knowledge, and attitudes related directly to emergent bilingual students' learning. Their most helpful strategy was to provide preservice teachers with specific reflection questions and the opportunities and incentives to discuss them, with the expectation that the preservice teachers would begin to ask these questions to themselves and to others. They repeatedly pushed their students to explore language learners' experiences from a variety of perspectives through class discussions, reflections, and presentations. One question that they posed was, "What are my own notions, biases, and prejudices about languages and cultures?"

- Doug asked another question every time he introduced a new concept, method, or skill: "So, if we have been looking at this case as being for a *general* population of students, what might it mean for

emergent bilinguals?" He wanted to challenge native English speakers to contemplate perspectives currently invisible to them. He had been greatly influenced by the book, *Why Are All the Black Kids Sitting Together in the Cafeteria?* (Tatum, 2003), which highlights the difficulty of putting yourself in someone else's shoes when you come from a position of relative privilege. His question pushed preservice teachers to contemplate and complicate the issues at hand from a new perspective.
- Manuela assigned her preservice teachers case studies that introduced them to bilingual education situations. She asked them to critically examine language education policies and ponder how these policies affect various students, teachers, and schools.
- To help their preservice teachers to see the many opportunities for collaboration, they both asked questions such as, How can we create an atmosphere in which diversity is valued? With whom can I collaborate in the school to promote the understanding of emergent bilingualism, including "foreign" language and English teachers? How can I recognize the power of other language systems such as American Sign Language and African American Vernacular? How can I become a resource for others and share what I know? How can I learn from others?
- In general, Manuela and Doug worked to create a culture of continuous inquiry, asking their preservice teachers to reflect on, question, and challenge every aspect of the material and concepts with which they were presented. This was good general practice, but, in response to the goals at hand, they shaped the focus of their inquiry more specifically to the knowledge, needs, and situations of emergent bilinguals.

Helping Preservice Teachers to Discover Their Own Backgrounds in Relation to Issues of Language and Culture

On the first day of his course, Doug engaged in several activities in which the preservice teachers revealed the languages they spoke and the cultures and countries from which they came. In subsequent classes, he highlighted the value of multilingualism and invited students to share personal understandings and experiences regarding emergent bilingual issues. Because he invited rather than forced individuals to speak, his students said that they felt more comfortable sharing their knowledge on their own terms. Two spoke about coming to the U.S. with no prior exposure to the English language and their experiences in working toward English proficiency. The differences in their stories helped native English speakers to see that there was no universal formula for acquiring a new language. As bilingual students spoke directly about the teachers, environments, and personal initiative that helped them to learn language, their stories become part of the course's subject matter.

How We Addressed Our Own Ignorance

It is inevitably more comfortable to acknowledge others' lack of knowledge than it is our own, but as a group, we committed ourselves to challenging our own ignorance and working to overcome it. We operated on the assumption that if we started early and sustained our efforts in a regular way, we would save time and frustration in the long run. So the first step we took was an attitude check: a personal mandate on each of our parts to accept roles as perpetual learners. If we could do this publicly, in front of our preservice teachers, we would have the added benefit of authentically modeling behaviors that we expected from them.

Forming Project PREPARE-ELLs

The simple act of recognizing the gaps in our knowledge and teaching and resolving to do something about it was the most important thing we did. The result was the formation of Project PREPARE-ELLs, which served as our forum for tackling our ignorance, discussing our attempts to learn, and sharing our successes. If there is any advice that we can give in terms of beginning an endeavor similar to ours, it is to create and formalize a group that will meet on an uncompromisingly regular basis with a clear agenda of learning to teach emergent bilinguals better than you already know how to do.

Adopting Mentors

When we began Project PREPARE-ELLs, each one of us received a mentor, a teacher educator who was an expert in the field of bilingual education. Some of our mentors were in-house, from the University of Connecticut, while others worked in universities across the country.

Each of our mentors became an essential guide: someone who could answer our questions, address our fears, and gently disabuse us of ill-conceived ideas, preconceptions, or prejudices. Our mentors also pointed us to a rich array of resources. Many of the readings that we introduced into our courses came through their suggestions. In these ways, mentors were tremendous time savers, flattening our learning curves, providing support, and guiding us toward materials and approaches in efficient ways.

Communicating across Courses

One weakness that we knew we had was communicating across courses. In the midst of our busy days, it was quite easy to become myopic and bore in on only our personal concerns. However, this approach led to inefficiency and more difficult integration when we gave redundant assignments, conveyed conflicting messages, or exploited time that could be more valuably used in other courses. By discussing together the key issues of language, culture, and diversity from both theoretical and practical/instructional standpoints, we more effectively coordinated our class curricula and agenda. We also learned how these issues influence and are influenced by the larger, more holistic context of the full program. Finding the time to solve the logistical challenges of this coordination has remained a challenge, but our regular Project PREPARE-ELLs meetings have helped enormously. During each meeting, one instructor conducts a formal presentation, outlining the work that he or she has been doing. Again, the practice of learning from others takes center stage as colleagues ask questions about how they might incorporate or complement others' work into their own.

As we move foreword, we are working to set up a formal system in which every course focuses on specific issues and materials, integrates complementary teaching across courses, eliminates even more redundancy and inefficiency, and formulates a clear transdisciplinary agenda. In each case, we look to create systems with which we can confront our own ignorance and create new understandings that will help us move forward.

RECOMMENDATIONS

As we engage in this continuous process of learning, we know that we don't yet have all the answers. However, we hope the following insights will help other teacher educators trying to fit important new information and activities into tight schedules. Reflecting on our work, we have developed a list of some of the actions that have helped us, and we offer them in the spirit of suggestions that are adaptable to your own unique situations:

- Accept that challenges exist, but move ahead anyway, and don't be afraid to start small. Even "baby steps" will get you started. Once you make a commitment, the momentum can help you to continue to move forward.
- Set clear goals from the outset. Determine what is unique within your discipline that may impact how emergent bilinguals learn. Consider how you might infuse issues of language and culture into your course through content, core discipline ideas, curricular standards, and assessment.
- Don't throw out your entire curriculum; instead, look across all of its elements for places where you can make natural connections with what you already do. Modify lessons, assignments, activities, and discussions to include issues important to emergent bilingual education. You will discover that much of the work that you already do will have indirect connections that you can make more explicit.
- Recognize that you may need to make a few hard choices, eliminating old material that you hold dear or compromising on some new goals because they are logistically impossible. However, when we

have made thoughtful revisions with a clear goal of understanding the needs of emergent bilinguals, it has enhanced and given new vitality to our teaching and has transformed our preservice teachers' own attitudes and approaches.

- Our greatest successes occurred when we were able to infuse issues of language, culture, and diversity into preexisting topics, themes, and activities in ways that not only addressed the learning of emergent bilinguals but also enhanced our ability to meet the needs of the general population.
- Recognize students' lack of experience with issues of language and culture as a curricular issue: something that needs to be addressed in class in the same ways that their lack of instructional skills or content knowledge is. While counterintuitive, taking the extra time to build their prior knowledge saves time in the long run.
- Recognize your own lack of knowledge and then create a formal system for learning more. Our system was Project PREPARE-ELLs, and any committed group of teacher educators can create a project that essentially compels you to examine issues of language and culture on a regular schedule. Committing to the schedule in the long term is key; once it becomes a ubiquitous aspect of your professional commitments, it, too, leads to more focused, efficient, and effective teaching and learning.

CONCLUSION

Reflecting on the work that we have done to date, we note that our modifications to our previous approaches have served not only the needs of emergent bilinguals but also other classroom populations. Our revisions have given us new insight on how to individualize our approaches and meet the disparate needs of very different students. When we began to focus on issues of language and culture from larger perspectives, we saw how each student could benefit from clearer objectives, more explicit instruction on how language is used to make meaning, and a clearer understanding of how to navigate within a classroom culture of multiple perspectives, understanding, talents, and needs. As a result, our initial fears about how to fit more in were largely mitigated: the changes we made were not mere add-ons. They became organic components of a larger agenda committed to embracing diversity to the greatest extent possible.

REFERENCES

Ariza, E. N. (2010). *Not for ESOL teachers: What every classroom teacher needs to know about the linguistically, culturally and ethnically diverse student* (2nd ed.). Boston: Allyn & Bacon.

Cary, S. (2007). *Working with English language learners: Answers to teachers' top ten questions* (2nd ed.). Portsmouth, NH: Heinemann.
Chapin, S. H., O'Connor, C., & Anderson, N. C. (2009). *Classroom discussions using math talk to help students learn, grades 1–6* (2nd ed.). Sausalito, CA: Math Solutions Publications.
Clay, M. M. (2000). *Running records for classroom teachers.* Portsmouth, NH: Heinemann.
Clay, M. M. (2001). *Change over time in children's literacy development.* Portsmouth, NH: Heinemann.
Corbin, J., & Strauss, A. (2008). *Basics of qualitative research* (3rd ed.). Thousand Oaks, CA: Sage.
Cruz, B., & Thornton, S. (2008). *Teaching social studies to English language learners.* New York: Routledge.
Cruz, B., & Thornton, S. (2009). Social studies for English language learners: Teaching social studies that matters. *Social Education, 73*(6), 270–273.
Dutro, S., & Moran, C. (2003). Rethinking English language instruction: An architectural approach. In G. Garcia (Ed.), *English learners reaching the highest level of literacy* (pp. 227–258). Newark, DE: International Reading Association.
Echevarría, J., Vogt, M. E., & Short, D. (2008). *Making content comprehensible for English learners: The SIOP model* (3rd ed.). Boston, MA: Pearson Education.
Irujo, S. (2007). *What does research tell us about teaching reading to English Language Learners?* Retrieved March 14, 2004 from <http://www.usc.edu/dept/education/CMMR/543/543IrujoResearchReadingsELLS.pdf.
Rubin, R., & Carlan, V.G. (2005). Using writing to understand bilingual children's literacy development. *The Reading Teacher, 58*(8), 728–739.
Tatum, B. (2003). *Why are all the Black kids sitting together in the cafeteria? And other conversations about race.* New York: Basic.

Selected Books and Articles Used by Authors in Courses

Ariza, E. N. (2010). *Not for ESOL teachers: What every classroom teacher needs to know about the linguistically, culturally and ethnically diverse student* (2nd ed.). Boston: Allyn & Bacon.
Cary, S. (2007). *Working with English language learners, Answers to teachers top ten questions* (2nd ed.). Portsmouth, NH: Heinemann.
Chapin, S. H., O'Connor, C., & Anderson, N. C. (2009). *Classroom discussions using math talk to help students learn, grades 1–6* (2nd ed.). Sausalito CA: Math Solutions Publications. (A resource for learning how to incorporate "talk moves.")
Cruz, B., & Thornton, S. (2009). Social studies for English language learners: Teaching social studies that matters. *Social Education, 73*(6), 270–273.
Echevarría, J., Vogt, M. E., & Short, D. (2008). *Making content comprehensible for English learners: The SIOP model* (3rd ed.). Boston, MA: Pearson Education.
Garcia, O. (2009). Emergent bilinguals and TESOL: What's in a name? *TESOL Quarterly, 43*(2), 322–326.
Garland, S. (2012). Education nation: Finding classroom success in noisy mix of Spanish, English. *The Hechinger Report.* Retrieved March 14, 2004 from http://hechingerreport.org/content/education-nation-finding-classroom-success-in-noisy-mix-of-spanish-english_9637/.
Irujo, S. (2007). *What does research tell us about teaching reading to English Language Learners?* Retrieved March 14, 2004 from <http://www.usc.edu/dept/education/CMMR/543/543IrujoResearchReadingsELLS.pdf.

Kumaravadivelu, B. (2006). TESOL methods: Changing tracks, challenging trends. *Tesol Quarterly, 40*(1), 59–81.

Marinova-Todd, S., Marshall, D. B., & Snow, C. E. (2000). Three misconceptions about age and second-language learning. *TESOL Quarterly, 34*(1), 9–34.

Rubin, R., & Carlan, V.G. (2005). Using writing to understand bilingual children's literacy development. *The Reading Teacher, 58* (8), 728–739.

APPENDIX

Elementary Math Methods Course Lesson Plan Template

Elementary methods courses use variations of the following lesson plan template. In elementary math and science, they produce a fuller unit plan, whereas in math, they proceed to enact, video, and reflect on this specific lesson. Asterisks precede elements that focus our preservice teachers on planning for instruction that is more effective for emergent bilinguals.

Title/Topic:
Background of School & Students:
Standards/Frameworks (Common Core State Standards [CCSS]):
Initiation:
Lesson Development:
Closure:
Opportunity to engage in higher-order thinking (H.O.T.):
Differentiation:
*Assessment (Please identify the objectives being assessed by each assessment, e.g., CO1, LO2)

*Selected SIOP Features Checklist (you may add others)

Preparation:

___ Content objectives
___ Language objectives

Comprehensible Input:

___ Clear explanation of academic tasks
___ Variety of techniques

Building Background:

___ Links to background experience
___ Links to past learning
___ Key vocabulary

Strategies:

___ Questions & tasks to promote H.O.T.

6 Teaching Preservice Teachers How to Learn from—and about—Their Emergent Bilingual Students
The Foundation for Everything Else

Douglas Kaufman

THE OVERARCHING CHALLENGE

Due to a variety of factors, largely political in nature, we exist in an environment in which classroom teaching and teacher education focus strongly on the learning of isolated skills, strategies, and content matter (Pease-Alvarez, Samway, & Cifka-Herrera, 2010; Sleeter & Stillman, 2005). While attention to these components is arguably necessary, we also know that it is insufficient (Darling-Hammond, 2006a, 2006b). By narrowing the curriculum to a few of the more easily "testable" features—often in pursuit of higher standardized scores and federal funding that is tied to tightly circumscribed assessment mandates—we fail to attend to a condition that is less quantifiable but just as essential: teacher listening and learning. In this context, listening to learn is a process of deep engrossment (Noddings, 1992) in what students do and say. This is accompanied by a process of reflection that allows the teacher to act toward students in new and more effective ways according to what he or she discovers (Kaufman, 2000). Treated as an ingrained, systematic classroom practice, listening to learn from children about their multifaceted lives helps teachers to target their responses to each student's current knowledge base, proclivities, and needs (Haroutunian-Gordon & Laverty, 2011; Kaufman, 2000; Lucas, Villegas, & Freedson-Gonzales, 2008; National Council of Teachers of English, 2006; Newkirk & Kittle, 2013). In the specific case of working with emergent bilinguals, who often have significantly different sociocultural and linguistic backgrounds than those who teach them (Barron & Menken, 2002; Kindler, 2002), teacher listening and learning is all the more important: any lack of background knowledge that *we* have regarding emergent bilinguals makes it as difficult for us to teach them as their own lack of background knowledge may make it difficult for them to learn in English-dominant classrooms. In this chapter, I argue for our need to listen and learn as a conscious, continuous practice—and as a disposition that helps us to challenge ineffective existing practices—in order to best serve emergent bilinguals. I also present some of the teaching practices with which I have recently experimented (often in a trial-and-error fashion) in order to illustrate possibilities for reshaping curricula and instruction so that they promote a culture of sustained listening and learning.

Current Approaches to Supporting Emergent Bilinguals in K-12 Classrooms, and the Problems with Them

Although we have recently paid greater attention to the teaching of emergent bilinguals than we have in the past, much of the material used for instruction in teacher preparation courses focuses on a fairly narrow set of features. Reading through several commercially available materials designed to address English language learner (ELL) instruction (e.g., Cooper, Pikulski, & McPhail, 2003; Herrell & Jordan, 2011; Hill & Flynn, 2006; Peregoy & Boyle, 2012; Stanford Graduate School of Education, 2012), you will find some clear general patterns, one of which is the limited or tokenized use of the students' native languages during instruction. Others include:

- a focus on specific skills and strategies for English language instruction;
- models of teaching that occur in described instructional stages, which provides sequential, boundaried instruction;
- a heavy emphasis on teaching cognates;
- a focus on explicit instruction;
- a focus on teaching academic language;
- a focus on building students' background knowledge in order to help them learn English and academic concepts in English; and
- the use of language objectives to teach content language and vocabulary in English.

The inattention to the emergent bilingual's native language may be indefensible, but the other foci, when introduced within a proper context, can clearly support a more overarching approach to teaching emergent bilinguals. However, most, if presented in an isolated, decontextualized, or homogenized fashion, can also limit the menu of possibilities for teaching a broader number of emergent bilinguals more effectively (Ford, Cabell, Konold, Invernizzi, & Gartland, 2012; Fu, 2009; Hernandez, 1991). Less prevalent in the commercial materials is mention of other conditions and practices essential to a comprehensive approach to teaching emergent bilinguals. These include:

- attending to learners' attitudes, dispositions, and learning styles;
- using flexible teaching approaches in response to identified student needs;
- using students' native languages as powerful scaffolds to support English learning;

- introducing contextualized learning experiences and students' independent exploration into the new language;
- using and teaching language specific to different social and cultural groups; and
- most important to this chapter, enacting teacher learning practices that reveal students' individual and group strengths, understandings, and needs.

Beyond materials, we can find similar limitations in even the most well-known and respected larger approaches, including the Sheltered Instruction Observational Protocol (SIOP) (Echevarria, Short, & Powers, 2006). The SIOP is perhaps the most widely known and successful approach in the nation for teaching emergent bilinguals in schools. I appreciate the SIOP for its strong research base and thoroughness in integrating targeted emergent bilingual instruction across the curriculum. Nevertheless, I find one distressingly underemphasized component. The research-based protocol that drives sheltered instruction includes 30 features of instruction, and the SIOP identifies itself as a complete approach for helping emergent bilinguals to learn subject area content while also gaining language skills. Although the SIOP clearly attends to the important task of *building* the background knowledge of students so that they can connect more effectively to new language learning, much less prevalent in the program is the component of teacher learning that would allow us to discover and take advantage of students' preexisting background knowledge and values. It is implied and suggested in places, but missing is an explicit, clearly articulated, consistent, systematic approach to discovering students' own "funds of knowledge" (González, Moll, & Amanti, 2004).

Working with colleagues to "develop innovations in teaching that draw upon the knowledge and skills in local households" in underserved Latino communities in Arizona (Moll, Amanti, Neff, & Gonzalez, 1992, p. 132), Moll defined funds of knowledge as "those historically accumulated and culturally developed bodies of knowledge and skills essential for household and individual functioning and well-being" (Moll & González, 1994, p. 443). In relation to their identities as classroom students, emergent bilinguals can bring in funds of knowledge that are bankrolled by their prior language experiences in both their primary and secondary languages; their previous experiences with both language learning and content learning; their individual talents and skill sets; their individual tastes; their previous experiences with classrooms, school dynamics, and school structural and organizational features; their previous experiences with curriculum distribution; their previous social and political interactions; their previous roles in the community, society, and educational institutions (Rojas & Ortiz, 2010); their motivations; their family and community support systems; their cultural understandings; and the accumulated cultural capital gained from all of these experiences. These funds can serve both emergent bilinguals and their teachers if the teachers can set up conditions whereby students' attributes are recognized and welcomed into the curriculum and then examined to determine their power to scaffold new learning. But, as of now, in the commercial materials and the larger integrative approaches to emergent bilingual instruction, there is not enough intentionality—no clear approach for the teacher to learn about his or her students. Importantly, for teachers who do not share their emergent bilingual students' linguistic and cultural knowledge, emergent bilinguals' funds of knowledge are that much harder to discover and understand.

The results can be destructive. Without learning from and about their students, teachers enter the field and engage with emergent bilingual students in extremely inefficient and ineffective ways (Colombo, 2007). Their lack of knowledge leads to both a lack of confidence and an inability to address student need appropriately (Dunn, Kirova, Coolie, & Ogilvie, 2009; Wenger & Dinsmore, 2005). As a result, teachers experience a reduced sense of personal agency, which can lead them to rely even more on prepackaged curricula as a crutch, often to such an extent that their interaction with students devolves into formulaic instruction that is disconnected from the students' actual needs. Every year as a teacher educator, I have listened to trepidatious preservice teachers ask for materials that "tell me what to do." But their attainment of those materials can result in a continuous loop of instruction that focuses disproportionately on the teaching of isolated, predetermined skills and strategies (Paris & McNaughton, 2010). As formula reduces the need to respond to new learning and immediate situations, it can also promote a myopic and discriminatory mode of thinking that emphasizes the "rightness" of the teacher's point of view and discourages collaboration and social learning. By not regarding the language knowledge and cultural capital that students already possess as essential information to shape our teaching, skill and strategy instruction becomes further decontextualized from the larger purposes of learning English and contributing to a multilinguistic, multicultural society. It denies students the opportunity to develop a broad commitment to becoming responsible, responsive citizens of a social democracy existing within a continuously changing and challenging world.

The purpose of this chapter, then, is to offer possibilities arising out of my own struggles with learning to teach at the same time I teach about emergent bilinguals. I come from a background that heavily influences my ability to teach preservice teachers about emergent bilinguals: I am a native English speaker with only the most rudimentary skills in a second language (Spanish), although I am trying to learn more. In short, I am a teacher who is ignorant of language in much the same way that many teachers and teacher educators in the U.S. are. I am privileged in being able to speak the dominant language in a society where my monolingualism rarely harms me and allows me to remain ignorant of and less empathic toward those learning English, if I so choose. McIntosh's (1988) and Tatum's (1997) seminal works on the numbing effects of privilege on our ability to recognize the damage that lack of privilege and opportunity has on others speaks to the danger of not making a conscious effort to learn about our students.

Therefore, I try to live through a philosophy which emphasizes that good teaching arises out of good learning. In this chapter, I share my attempts to teach my preservice teachers how to learn from their own students in order to teach them more powerfully. Much of my work focuses on modeling the learning actions and behaviors that I expect my students to adopt—to such an extent that the traditional definition of modeling as a primarily academic endeavor is superseded by one more aptly characterized as living publicly the life of a learner (Kaufman, 2002, 2009). As I position myself as a proactive learner, I work to create corresponding instructional and pedagogical approaches that are more intensive, systematic, and comprehensive than those found in the current literature or in my own past practice.

Teaching teachers how to learn about—and from—their students provides an essential context for their success in addressing key issues that impact not only learning the English language itself but also learning subject matter *in* English. When teachers listen to their students, the students' backgrounds immediately become the foundation off of which they successfully build new content and language learning. Here are some examples of how I worked to develop a classroom culture of learning in one methods course where teacher learning became a ubiquitous part of both the curriculum and the classroom activity.

Creating a Listening and Learning Classroom

The premise that modeling was the best approach to introduce and nurture classroom listening and learning drove my activity. How we listen to others is a cultural characteristic, and I felt that in order to develop and sustain a learning culture, I had to promote it by living a life of deep attention to my students. If I wanted these preservice teachers to learn the strengths and needs of young students, I had to learn *their* strengths and needs first. My conscious, explicit examination of how I listen and learn effectively, along with regular practice in learning about other communities, was essential.

My Approach

My work took place in a methods course titled *Teaching Reading and Writing in the Elementary School*. I taught this course on-site at a local public elementary school (Pre-K-4) with a population of about 200 students. Although the majority of these students were first language English speakers, some (18%) came from households where the primary language was not English, due to the presence of a nearby university with many international faculty and graduate students. Among these households, 14 different languages were represented (Connecticut State Department of Education, 2013). Being on-site, the preservice teachers were able to observe and work with elementary students on a weekly basis.

In my course, I try to complicate my approach to methods instruction. While articulating the value of knowing specific teaching skills, strategies, approaches, and methods to preservice teachers, I also place extraordinary emphasis on learning *how* to learn these things, helping students to develop ways of exploring and processing that will help them to make meaning of, use, and articulate newly discovered information. Then, when they inevitably leave my course not knowing everything they need to know, they can use these exploration and process skills for the rest of their careers. Many teacher educators address learning and process approaches, but for me, they are at the core—they drive everything else. The subject matter becomes the landscape within which we learn how to learn (Kaufman, 2003). The payoff is that students learn the subject matter even more deeply than if we focused on it as material to be memorized.

Syllabus Changes

I began my journey by analyzing my existing language arts-focused syllabus and trying to figure out where I could infuse issues related to emergent bilinguals into the curriculum seamlessly. I recognized that I had written nothing in the syllabus that spoke to my goals—nothing that would help either me or my students create a starting point for ourselves. Therefore, my first change to the course was a simple announcement within the syllabus, which I read aloud and discussed with students on the first day of class. It described this particular revision of the course from previous years' courses (Please note that since this time, I have come to prefer the term "emergent bilingual" to "English language learner" as it recognizes students' native language proficiencies as having equal value to new ones):

> *A New Focus: English Language Learners (ELLs)*: This year we will also begin to incorporate learning about a growing segment of our school populations: ELLs. Incorporated within our different activities will be inquiry and discussion about learning from—and teaching—students who are learning a new language. You should be committed to looking out for issues pertaining to ELLs during your field experiences. We will discuss this as the semester continues.

My wording was intentional: learning about people was paramount to the mission. I wanted my students to focus immediately on learning about emergent bilinguals even more than they focused on how to teach them. My commitment to promoting preservice teachers' identities as agents of inquiry was important to me, so I articulated this commitment in writing. In discussing the syllabus with them on the first day, I highlighted my wording choices and my belief in their need to be learners first. This was the first of many occasions on different days when I would highlight this theme.

A Regular Emphasis in the Classroom on the Teacher as a Learner

From the beginning, I tried to regularly articulate my educational philosophy and research that has centered on the concept of the teacher as learner (Kaufman, 2000, 2002, 2003, 2009). From the first class to the final, I tried to model publicly my own learning and orient my preservice students toward adopting a similar identity. As I taught, conferred, and listened during discussions, I always kept a notebook at my side, and I would take notes as I learned information that I thought might be important. On several occasions, I would stop during my own presentations when a student asked a thought-provoking question or made a comment that I hadn't expected. Portable technologies helped as well. As students conferred or worked together on projects, I could also audio or video record them with a smart phone. (Consult your own university's policies regarding obtaining permission to record in your classroom.)

The result was that I had a body of observation data to which I could turn after class, searching for patterns in preservice teachers' thoughts, confusions, and epiphanies. I could use this information to revise my preestablished plans. I could also read back to them the things I had recorded to get further feedback about what was happening in class.

I also continually exhorted preservice teachers to ask themselves what they didn't know about classroom students, and then I challenged them to find effective ways of learning more about them. In an early class I said, "We can't teach them well unless we know what they can do, know what their preferences are, and know what they need." My preservice teachers, who had been accepted into our highly competitive program, had generally been very successful throughout their 15-plus years of formal schooling. While their acumen had its obvious benefits, I discovered that it could also blind them to the more complex and multidimensional aspects of education. As successful performers in their high school and college classes, they usually spent most of their time associating with a crowd similar to themselves. During the second class, I told them:

> If you "got" how school worked—if you knew how it operated, and you felt comfortable navigating within its system—then you probably know only *that* part of school. If you were "top ten percent" and you try to teach your future students with the approaches that were successful to you, your teaching will not work for ninety percent of your students. We all need to learn how the system doesn't work for so many other students, simply because they don't fit a inside very small box of items that we use to evaluate them for "success." Assume that you are ignorant, and then spend your entire career as a learner, happy that you can get a little less ignorant every day.

The Repeated Introduction of the Question, "What Might This Mean for Emergent Bilinguals?"

I tried to ask this question during every class as a follow-up to discussions that approached a given topic more generically (see Chapter 5). For instance, in one early class, my students and I discussed the various conditions that might influence literacy learning. The students talked about physical classroom structures and setups, the teachers' teaching styles, the students' background knowledge, the socioeconomic conditions of the neighborhood, and many other influences. I then narrowed the focus of the discussion and asked, "Okay, so what conditions might make it more challenging for emergent bilinguals in U.S. schools?" I asked the students to quickly write down a list of conditions, not censoring anything that came into their heads. Then we held a discussion, during which I wrote down and consolidated the students' different answers. The most prevalent responses were these:

- Prior schooling experiences
- Out-of-school experiences
- Family literacies
- Family culture
- Cultural references
- Different languages
- Behavioral norms

This list was not treated as comprehensive, nor did I treat any particular item as "right" or "wrong" (although these initial answers clearly reflect a deficit perspective regarding emergent bilinguals), but I wanted my preservice teachers to consciously identify and articulate, from their current perspectives, potential points of dissonance that emergent bilinguals might face when entering a situation where their own funds of knowledge might not be recognized or even sanctioned by the members of the dominant culture and language. As we spoke, I asked them to view the list as a starting point from which they could begin to envision how our ignorance of different life experiences might get in the way of helping students take advantage of new experiences.

At the same time, I challenged my preservice teachers to consider what funds of knowledge emerging bilinguals might bring into the classroom—what unique experiences, understandings, and language skills they possessed that the typical native English speaker might not possess. As they discussed, my preservice teachers began to recognize that their list of "deficits" could also be viewed from a diametric perspective—as *benefits* that would enrich a more meager classroom culture. The experiences, cultural backgrounds, and language backgrounds of emergent bilinguals only appeared as deficits in their minds because they were *different*—different from what they had traditionally accepted as standard in their particular social system. However, as they began to recognize diversity as an opportunity to expand their own experiences and understandings, their perspective shifted.

By recognizing students' sociocultural and linguistic capital, teachers enrich their own backgrounds, contextualizing their own understandings through newly available worldview comparisons. They suddenly see the value in what the emergent bilingual brings to the classroom. And when they value something, they attend to it more deeply, and they begin to learn more actively about it. I pushed my preservice teachers to see every facet of the emergent bilingual's life as valuable knowledge and information that their classrooms never would have had if those "different" children had not stepped into them.

Asking the preservice teachers to utilize their own background knowledge, no matter how limited it might be, forced them to imagine the potential consequences—both positive and negative—of creating certain classroom conditions when emergent bilinguals were present. Asking them to discover and reimagine what counted and didn't count as legitimate linguistic and cultural capital was the next step in their progress.

A Focus on Discovering the Logic Behind Emergent Bilinguals' Language Use

Despite my own limited knowledge in dealing with issues of English language learning in the classroom, I had noticed through the years that my students often operated from a deficit model when discussing linguistically and culturally diverse students. At times they talked about having to teach students how to speak "the right way," and because of their own limited backgrounds, they sometimes misunderstood particular behaviors that they saw in emergent bilinguals. For instance, some preservice teachers worried about emergent bilingual students' spelling, which appeared to be illogical to them as they learned how to recognize the patterns in native English-speaking students' invented spellings. The patterns in the Spanish-speaking and Chinese-speaking students with whom they were working didn't seem to fit. Listening to their concerns, I revised my teaching plans to approach the matter.

The next week I suggested to them that the emergent bilinguals were employing sophisticated strategies as they learned how to use English. To illustrate, I displayed examples of invented spelling by emergent bilinguals and compared them to examples written by native English speakers. I said,

> Let us assume that there is *always* some sort of logic behind any behavior exhibited by any person. What is it that these students have and are using that native English speakers don't usually have? What logic are they using to come up with the word approximations that they do?

The answer was, of course, that the emergent bilinguals had an ingrained knowledge of different language systems—ones that included different pronunciations of, and accents on, words and letters. Through discussion and inductive inquiry, the preservice teachers quickly recognized how the young students' phonemic awareness and phonics knowledge in relation to their first languages helped them to make plausible, sophisticated approximations of English words. My repeated emphasis on discovering the logic behind young students' decision making and activity, heavily influenced by their specific linguistic and cultural understanding, helped the preservice teachers to see that it was almost always our own ignorance of their pupils' backgrounds that interfered with learning rather than their pupils' alleged lack of knowledge or intelligence. If they learned to search for—*listen* for—the logic behind any behavior, then they could more readily recognize its value and exploit it as a learning scaffold.

Revised Assignments That Focus on Learning from Emergent Bilinguals

In my methods course, I already had several general assignments designed to help preservice teachers learn the backgrounds, tastes, and strengths of their students. During the summer before the school year began, I fretted about how to incorporate this new focus on emergent bilinguals into my course in authentic, organic, and symbiotic ways. I always attempt to look at each component of my class holistically, and I wanted my students to see the natural connections among all learners in ways that also allowed them to discover their diversity. Therefore, I worked on the assumption that if my assignments already focused on teachers learning about students in general, I could also use them to focus on particular populations. I realized that these new iterations of my assignments might also offer points of comparison that would shatter some old stereotypes and myths.

Literacy Interviews with Emergent Bilinguals

One of the earliest general assignments that I had my students complete was to interview K-6 pupils in order to learn about their reading and writing understandings, beliefs, and practices. In the past, I had simply asked the preservice teachers to choose any willing students from their clinic placements or the school where we held our methods course, but I revised the assignment so that each preservice teacher would interview at least one native English speaker and at least one emergent bilingual. (We discussed how they might revise the wording of questions to support emergent bilinguals, although most whom they ultimately interviewed had fairly strong oral language skills in English.) I told them,

> The mission will be to find out as much as you can about each student, not so that you can "fix" any one of them, but so that you can discover

their sometimes hidden talents and interesting perspectives. These are the elements that will help you to teach to both their strengths and their needs, and you will also give them opportunities to teach you and others about themselves.

The preservice teachers worked in small groups to develop questions that they felt would help them to learn about young students' reading and writing understandings and practices. After they had conducted and transcribed interviews, they combined their data to compare different students' answers, looking for both patterns of commonality and patterns of difference. Aggregating these data in multiple ways allowed them to look at the responses of the emergent bilingual students from both individual and group perspectives.

Running Records with Emergent Bilinguals

In terms of learning a child's reading habits and strategies, a running record is one of the most powerful modes of formative assessment (Clay, 1985; Ross, 2004). Created specifically to document what students do well as they read, a running record requires a teacher to watch, listen to, and record the reading strategies and behaviors of a child reading out loud. Counterintuitively, a teacher learns about the reader's strengths by analyzing his or her *mistakes*, which reveal the strategies that the reader might use predominantly over other complementary strategies. For instance, a running record can reveal, through the way a first grader speaks and the mistakes that she makes as she reads, that sounding out is her primary mode of decoding. (If she read completely fluently, the teacher would not know which strategies she relied on the most.) The teacher now recognizes sounding out is a relative strength that can ground and support the student's subsequent reading while the teacher reinforces complementary strategies, such as looking for context clues in the text to figure out the correct words and intended meanings. A running record is also usually accompanied by the student's "retelling" of the text, in which she provides a brief synopsis of the story and answers questions from the teacher designed to reveal her comprehension. Through a retelling, a teacher again looks for the strengths in comprehension and expression that the child brings to the conversation.

When teaching my preservice teachers about running records, I again introduced the procedure to them as another way to learn from their students rather than to "fix" them. I told them, "I want you to focus on finding out what your readers *know* so that you can build off of their strengths when you respond to them through teaching. Strengths are harder to isolate than weaknesses, but they are the foundation off of which you build everything else."

In the past, as was the case with the interview assignment, I had simply asked the preservice teachers to find age-appropriate students with whom to conduct running records. Now, I specifically asked them to conduct at least one running record and accompanying retelling with a native English speaker and one with an emergent bilingual. The preservice teachers would then analyze their data and subsequently compare and contrast the reading behaviors of the children. (I also repeatedly admonished them not to generalize to larger populations from the limited data that they had collected.) The preservice teachers, in small groups, then wrote up reports focusing on what they had learned from the students. Finally, they discussed their analyses in class in order to determine what learning patterns appeared across multiple students and what unique behaviors and strategies individual students possessed.

Read-Aloud Sessions That Teach the Teacher

My preservice teachers' access to working classrooms through their clinic placements gave me the opportunity to have them develop original reading activities and then document how children responded to them. Once again, my emphasis was as much on teacher learning as it was on teaching. I asked each preservice teacher to document how students responded to the activity, what appeared to work for them, what appeared to distract them, and so on. Now, however, I asked them to create more formal lesson plans than I had asked in the past, following the SIOP format (Echevarria, Short, & Powers, 2006), which ensured that they included specific content and language objectives that would provide background and focused practice in language learning to emergent bilinguals. This emphasis would help orient the preservice teachers to what emergent bilinguals were doing and how they were reacting. For every action I expected my students to take, I also expected them to create an accompanying opportunity for reflection that would help them determine its value. Commensurately, for every action the preservice teachers expected their own pupils to take, I expected them to engage in some form of formative assessment to learn who their students were and how they operated within a literacy lesson. Their final assignments had to include a write-up of what they had learned.

Initial Discoveries

Recently, my graduate assistant Jennifer Dolan and I conducted research on the potential effect of these curricular changes on my students (Kaufman & Dolan, 2012). We analyzed our observational notes on class activities and discussions as well as the preservice teachers' written reflections, running records, interviews with students, lesson plans, and final project assignments for the course. Our findings indicated that the preservice teachers: (a) depicted emergent bilinguals in more nuanced and holistic ways in their writing and discussions than they had in the past, actively looking for social and academic strengths; (b) attempted multiple strategies for differentiating instruction for linguistically diverse students; (c) searched more for linguistically and culturally relevant texts to use in teaching; and (d) recognized and expressed surprise that in many instances the emergent bilinguals exhibited more sophisticated reading behaviors and better comprehension than their native English-speaking classmates. They also began to recognize patterns in emergent bilinguals' reading that had been supported by their native language proficiencies. My preservice teachers could now more easily regard language differences as strengths rather than deficits, and therefore determine how to use them to scaffold the young readers' subsequent reading in English. They began to conceive of lessons that compared and contrasted the pronunciations of different vowel sounds, highlighted cognates, and provided new cultural contexts that would help readers to see writers' intended meaning.

To be sure, their new perspectives were sometimes superficial, difficult for them to transfer into effective teaching, and fraught with dissonance, but the recognizable shift in their understandings and active attempts to change their approaches appeared to be a powerful change from previous years.

Implications for Learners

Together, the changes to the course caused a dynamic shift in its tone and focus. While always cognizant of the general need of the teacher to listen and learn, my work with the members of Project PREPARE-ELLs has taught me that we can identify *particular* aspects of our students and our instruction that require more attention, and we can tailor our listening approaches to address their specifics head on. As I listened to my preservice teachers and tried to help them listen to their own students, we talked together regularly about what the most important actions were that we could take to become better listeners. Several general pieces of advice arose as they shared their various experiences. Contemplating them, I realized that they hold just as true for teacher educators as they do for classroom teachers:

- Whether you teach in a teacher education program or in a K-12 classroom, learn first what the emergent bilingual's strengths are. Remember that each has a wealth of experiences that he or she brings to the classroom. These experiences may not seem immediately relevant to our traditionally prescribed definitions of academic learning, but they may nonetheless work as powerful bridges into new learning if we discover them. Find daily, systematic ways to learn what your students know and can do. Find ways to record, document, and review what you have learned in order to transform your teaching based on evidence.
- Learn where your inevitable ignorance lies. Again, assume that there is logic behind your students' actions and behaviors. Learn what social, cultural, linguistic, and experiential backgrounds they bring

to the classroom, which we may be initially blind to but may account for the things they do that surprise or confuse us.
- Learn to read your students in the present, taking special effort to recognize moments of frustration and moments of epiphany. As you do with any form of good responsive teaching, look for the teachable moment and be willing to adapt instruction according to immediate need, even if it requires a shift from the original agenda.
- Learn what you can about the individual languages of your emergent bilingual learners. You won't become an expert in all, but a child will appreciate your honest effort to learn basic words and phrases. This will also make the corresponding English words and phrases easier to teach.
- Learn a second language yourself. It is time to revisit a common suggestion that every teacher should have vastly more training in another language. Some teacher education programs have language requirements, but many of them are superficial. Given the changing demographics of our schools and the modeling value of learning something that we expect our own students to learn, our own efforts to become bilingual as a larger community become necessary.

As I write this conclusion, I am in Chile, working for five weeks at a university here. The experience has helped me to become even more acutely aware of the struggles that many emergent bilinguals face when they enter our schools. I usually travel to other countries as a tourist, and in that role, I have access to the support systems of hotel employees and tour guides who cater to people who don't know the language. Here, I am much more on my own, navigating in the professional world of Spanish-speaking experts in my field. Many speak flawless English, but many don't speak English at all. My lack of Spanish language skills, when combined with a Chileno accent that often significantly alters the pronunciations that I learned during my rudimentary language education, have put me in a position of understanding much less than even I thought I would. As I told a group of faculty members the other day, "To me, right now, your language sounds like a beautiful symphony of rising and falling notes with no words." The people with whom I interact are wonderful, but the confusion that I feel on a daily basis as I try to navigate the Metro, buy groceries, carry on a simple conversation with new acquaintances, or convince a Spanish-speaking academic of my professional competence often turns to fear and embarrassment. As I try to learn the language, there are days where I honestly feel that my Spanish is becoming progressively worse: whereas I could initially use basic phrases to get to my apartment from the airport or find a public bathroom, I now find myself tongue-tied as I try to conjugate a verb or remember a more sophisticated word that I looked up in the dictionary yesterday but did not memorize. On a daily basis I feel stupid, and on some days I have to willfully force myself not to retreat into a shell of public silence because of my difficulties. As I contemplate my experience, I realize how grateful I am for the people who stop and listen for what I might need. I am grateful when they are willing to slow down their conversation (a difficult thing for any Chileno to do!), try to use simpler words to express complex ideas, include what few words of English they might speak, use hand gestures, smile with encouragement and pat my back when they see my frustration, take the time to try to learn about me, or tell me about themselves even when the communication is muddy. These people are good listeners and good learners: they not only hear my superficial words but also read my more complex expressions and body language, and they share of themselves. They search continually for a connection between the meaning that I can currently make and my larger intentions. They assume that there is an intelligent man behind that inarticulate babble or that embarrassed silence, and they spend good time trying to find him.

I have learned and done so many edifying things while here, but the trip would be worth it if only for the experience of being able to put myself into the shoes of the struggling language learner for more than the few days that the usual vacation trip offers. My commitment to creating a space where new language learners can be heard for who they are and what they can do—rather than for who they aren't and what they can't—is greatly strengthened. My attempts to make a listening, learning classroom for my preservice teachers—so that they can make a listening, learning classroom for their future students—are just a beginning, and I see this project as a continually evolving endeavor. If I am doing my job well, I will continue to learn and change; the equivalent of this chapter five years from now will look significantly different as the cycle of learning and growth renews itself.

REFERENCES

Barron, V., & Menken, K. (2002). *What are the characteristics of the bilingual education and ESL teacher shortage?* Washington, DC: National Clearinghouse for English Language Acquisition and Language Instruction Educational Programs.

Clay, M. (1985). *The early detection of reading difficulties* (3rd ed.). Portsmouth, NH: Heinemann.

Colombo, M. (2007). Developing cultural competence: Mainstream teachers and professional development. *Multicultural Perspectives, 9*(2), 10–16.

Connecticut State Department of Education. (2013). *Strategic school profile, 2011–2012.* Retrieved March 14, 2014 from http://sdeportal.ct.gov/Cedar/WEB/ResearchandReports/SSPReports.aspx?type=SSP.

Cooper, D. J., Pikulski, J. J., & McPhail, D. (2003). *Handbook for English language learners.* Boston: Houghton Mifflin.

Darling-Hammond, L. (2006a). *Powerful teacher education: Lessons from exemplary programs.* San Francisco: Jossey-Bass.

Darling-Hammond, L. (2006b). Constructing 21st-century teacher education. *Journal of Teacher Education, 57*(3), 300–314.

Dunn, W., Kirova, A., Cooley, M., & Ogilvie, G. (2009). Fostering intercultural inquiry in subject-area curriculum courses. *Canadian Journal of Education, 32*(3), 533–557.

Echevarria, J., Short, D., & Powers, K. (2006). School reform and standards-based education: A model for English-Language Learners. *Journal of Educational Research, 99*(4), 195–210.

Ford, K. L., Cabell, S. Q., Konold, T. L., Invernizzi, M., & Gartland, L. B. (2012). Diversity among Spanish-speaking English language learners: Profiles of early literacy skills in kindergarten. *Reading and Writing: An Interdisciplinary Journal, 26*(6), 889–912.

Fu, D. (2009). *Writing between languages: How English Language Learners make the transition to fluency, grades 4–12.* Portsmouth, NH: Heinemann.

González, G., Moll, L. C., & Amanti, C. (Eds.). (2004). *Funds of knowledge: Theorizing practices in households, communities, and classrooms.* Mahwah, NJ: Lawrence Erlbaum Associates.

Haroutunian-Gordon, S., & Laverty, M. J. (2011). Listening: An exploration of philosophical traditions. *Educational Theory, 61*(2), 117–124.

Hernandez, J. S. (1991). Assisted performance in reading comprehension strategies with non-English proficient students. *Journal of Educational Issues of Language Minority Students, 8,* 91–112.

Herrell, A. L., & Jordan, M. (2011). *50 strategies for teaching English Language Learners* (4th ed.). New York: Pearson.

Hill, J. D., & Flynn, K. M. (2006). *Classroom instruction that works with English Language Learners.* Alexandria, VA: Association for Supervision & Curriculum Development.

Kaufman, D. (2000). *Conference & conversations: Listening to the literate classroom.* Portsmouth, NH: Heinemann.

Kaufman, D. (2002). Living a literate life, revisited. *English Journal, 91*(6), 51–57.

Kaufman, D. (2003). Reading the world and writing to learn: Lessons from writers about creating transdisciplinary inquiry. In D. Kaufman, D. M. Moss, & T. A. Osborn (Eds.), *Beyond the boundaries: A transdisciplinary approach to learning and teaching* (pp. 155–166). Westport, CT: Praeger.

Kaufman, D. (2009). A teacher educator writes and shares: Student perceptions of a publicly literate life. *Journal of Teacher Education, 60*(3), 338–350.

Kaufman, D., & Dolan, J. (2012, December). *A non-expert's first attempts to incorporate ELL issues into a general literacy methods course: Implications for course development and teacher educator growth.* Paper presented at the annual conference of the Literacy Research Association, San Diego, CA.

Kindler, A. L. (2002). *Survey of the states' limited English proficient students and available educational programs and services 1999–2000 summary report.* Washington, DC: National Clearinghouse for English Language Acquisition and Language Instruction Education Programs (NCELA). Retrieved December 26, 2003, from http://www.ncela.gwu.edu

Lucas, T., Villegas, A. M., & Freedson-Gonzales, M. (2008). Linguistically responsive teacher education: Preparing classroom teachers to teach English Language Learners. *Journal of Teacher education, 59*(4), 361–373.

McIntosh, P. (1988). *White privilege and male privilege: A personal account of coming to see correspondence through working in women's studies.* Working paper #189. Wellesley, MA: Wellesley College Center for Research on Women.

Moll, L. C., Amanti, C., Neff, D., & González, N. (1992). Funds of knowledge for teaching: Using a qualitative approach to connect homes and classrooms. *Theory into Practice, 31*(2), 132–141.

Moll, L. C., & González, N. (1994). Lesson from research with language minority children. *Journal of Literacy Research, 26*(4), 439–456.

National Council of Teachers of English. (2006). *NCTE position paper on the role of English teachers in Educating English Language Learners (ELLs).* Retrieved

March 14, 2004 from http://www.ncte.org/positions/statements/teachersedu-catingell on March 14.

Newkirk, T., & Kittle, P. (Eds.). (2013). *Children want to write: Donald Graves and the revolution in children's writing.* Portsmouth, NH: Heinemann.

Noddings, N. (1992). *The challenge to care in schools: An alternative approach to education.* New York: Teachers College Press.

Paris, S. G., & McNaughton, S. (2010). Social and cultural influences on children's motivation for reading. In D. Wyse, R. Andrews, & J. Hoffman (Eds.), *The Routledge international handbook of English, language and literacy teaching* (pp. 11–21). London: Routledge.

Pease-Alvarez, L., Samway, K. D., & Cifka-Herrera, C. (2010). Working within the system: Teachers of English learners negotiating a literacy instruction mandate. *Language Policy, 9,* 313–334.

Peregoy, S. F., & Boyle, O. F. (2012). *Reading, writing, and learning in ESL: A resource book for teaching K-12 English learners* (6th ed.). New York: Pearson.

Rojas, E. D., & Ortiz, J. (2010). A research based analysis on students' individual achievement and standardized testing: Linguistical, cultural and social complexities, and its impact on students' failure. *Boletín de Investigación Educacional, 25*(2), 151–168.

Ross, J. A. (2004). Effects of running records assessment on early literacy achievement: Results of a controlled experiment. *Journal of Educational Research, 94*(4), 186–194.

Sleeter, C., & Stillman, J. (2005). Standardizing knowledge in a multicultural society. *Curriculum Inquiry, 35*(1), 27–46.

Stanford Graduate School of Education. (2012). *Understanding language: Language, literacy, and learning in the content areas.* Retrieved March 14, 2014 from http://ell.stanford.edu.

Tatum, B. (1997). *Why are all the Black kids sitting together in the cafeteria, and other conversations about race.* New York: Basic Books.

Wenger, K. J., & Dinsmore, J. (2005). Preparing rural preservice teachers for diversity. *Journal of Research in Rural Education, 20*(10), 1–15.

7 Leveraging Clinical Experiences to Prepare Teachers for Culturally and Linguistically Diverse Students

Rebecca D. Eckert, Susan L. Payne, Robin E. Hands, and René Roselle

Clinical experiences may be the ideal vehicle to develop and practice the skills and dispositions needed to work effectively with culturally and linguistically diverse students (Darling-Hammond, 2012; Valdés, Bunch, Snow, Lee, & Matos, 2005). According to the National Research Council, a "key element for successful learning is the opportunity to apply what is being learned and [to] refine it" within the context of a variety of clinical experiences (Hammerness, Darling-Hammond, Grossman, Rust, & Shulman, 2005, p. 401). Additionally, Darling-Hammond (2012) suggests that strong teacher preparation programs have "a common clear vision of good teaching that permeates all course work and clinical experiences, creating a coherent set of learning experiences," and they have "extended clinical experiences ... that are carefully chosen to support the ideas presented in simultaneous, closely interwoven course work" (p. 93). These scholarly recommendations are reflected regularly in the data collected from exit surveys of graduating preservice teachers in the Integrated Bachelor's/Master's (IBM) program at the University of Connecticut (UConn). As one respondent commented:

> The best aspect of my preparation at UConn was my clinical experience. This was a time to see methods put to practice and learn exactly how schools function. My teachers were able to provide me with thorough feedback on my strategies and work with me to improve my teaching methods. It also gave me a time to see the challenges in the field of education and work through some of those challenges.

Learning to teach is a developmental process, and these guided clinical experiences within varied classroom settings over time offer preservice teachers opportunities to confront and explore their beliefs about effectively teaching all learners.

THE OVERARCHING CHALLENGE

In many cases, preservice teachers continue to come from predominately white, suburban, high-achieving high schools and have had little, if any, life experiences to prepare them for working effectively with the growing numbers of students in K-12 classrooms who are emergent bilinguals (e.g., see demographics in Chapter 8). However, research suggests an urgent need for highly qualified teachers who can demonstrate both culturally responsive classroom practices along with the content area expertise needed to support academic language growth in all K-12 students (Darling-Hammond, 2012; Valdés et al., 2005). According to the Connecticut State Department of Education, Bureau of Data Collection, Research, and Evaluation (2012):

> While effective bilingual and ESL programs are essential, an important approach to narrowing the achievement gap should focus on the general education classroom, where ELL students receive most of their instruction. ELLs in general education classrooms need to receive differentiated instruction and ongoing support so they may simultaneously acquire academic vocabulary and content, as well as English language skills. (p. 9)

As such, from the beginning of our work with Project PREPARE-ELLs, clinical faculty recognized the importance of helping preservice teachers make sense of the cognitive dissonance that often accompanies fieldwork in classrooms and communities that are starkly different from many preservice teachers' prior experiences and understandings. Moreover, we knew that we had to be intentional and reflective in our own practice and planning as we worked toward ensuring supportive, practical "experiences for candidates to acquire and demonstrate the knowledge, skills, and professional dispositions necessary to help all students learn" (National Council for Accreditation of Teacher Education, 2008, p. 34). Finally, as we considered the array of clinic experiences available in partner schools, we recognized that university faculty are far from the only professional role models and guides aiding preservice teachers on their journey. School partners, lead teachers, cooperating teachers, and university supervisors also play a significant role in supporting cognitive and affective development in that they provide observational data and feedback to preservice teachers in clinical contexts.

This chapter addresses the question of how clinic placements can help prepare preservice teachers to work effectively with culturally and linguistically diverse students. Within the IBM program, we strive to use the powerful lever of purposeful clinical experiences with attention to where the students are developmentally. Seminars that correspond to junior, senior, and master's year provide time and space for preservice teachers to uncover misconceptions or stereotypes about diverse students and communities. Simultaneously, preservice teachers also expand their understanding of the purposes of public schooling as well as issues of equity and access in modern classrooms. This process is facilitated by the clinical structure provided in the program. Within the Neag School of Education IBM program, preservice teachers enter the program at the beginning of their junior year and complete the program after they finish their fifth-year post-graduate master's degree studies. During each semester in the program, preservice teachers participate in guided clinical experiences in a partner school. Each clinical experience is paired with a seminar class, which is used to provide structured learning tasks and opportunities for preservice teachers to reflect on experiences and begin to develop expertise in a range of clinic settings.

DEVELOPMENTAL CONSIDERATIONS: A JOURNEY RATHER THAN A DESTINATION

There are many different theories to describe the journey of growth and learning that accompany preservice teacher preparation (Hammerness et al., 2005). Several decades ago, Fuller (1969) recognized that changing preservice teachers' perspectives and classroom activities requires time, effort, and support; moreover, he noted that these eventual changes follow predictable developmental stages. This scholarly work led to the development of the *Stages of Concern* model by Hall and Hord (2011b), who have, over the past 40 years, studied change in schools and other settings. The *Stages of Concern* model provides a research-based framework for understanding an individual's feelings and perceptions as she progresses from novice to expert in any new situation requiring personal change or innovation. Hall and Hord view *change*—or the implementation of new practices or ideas in the profession of teaching—as linked to professional learning that will ultimately lead to improved levels of student learning and achievement. However, "introducing new practices alone seldom results in new practices being incorporated into ongoing classroom practices" (Hall & Hord, 2011a, p. 52). Educators need to spend time planning for and evaluating implementation of new ideas, practices, and beliefs. Essentially, we must attend to the journey of preservice teacher preparation as well as the desired destination.

Hall and Hord's (2011a, 2011b) model includes four developmental stages: Unrelated Concerns, Self-Concerns, Task Concerns, and Impact Concerns. Similar to many other models used by psychologists to describe and understand cognitive and affective development, these four stages represent a continuum of responses to an innovation that varies in duration and intensity depending on the individual. This process of the integration of new practices—and a recalibration of focus from self, to task, to impact—will happen countless times over the course of educators' career as they hone and expand their professional practice (Hall & Hord, 2011a).

Because of its focus on the implementation of new practices or ideas, the *Stages of Concern* model provides a basic, four-part frame for describing and understanding the journey of preservice teacher development within clinical experiences (Hall & Hord, 2011a, 2011b). Although all preservice teachers travel a unique path of growth and development as they integrate new professional skills and knowledge, the four developmental stages are used as a guide for designing and organizing developmentally appropriate clinical experiences for preservice teachers in the IBM program. Recognition of the various stages of concern and the differing needs, styles, and growth rates of preservice teachers as they progress toward expertise in working with emergent bilinguals can help faculty decide how to strategically establish structures and supports—also known as "implementation bridges"—within clinic experiences that will encourage the development of effective skills and dispositions needed for success in schools (Hall & Hord, 2011a). Because professional change is a developmental process rather than a single, one-day event, concerns should be monitored, both formally and informally, throughout clinical experiences to ensure that the proper support is being provided to fully prepare preservice teachers to work with culturally and linguistically diverse students (Hammerness et al., 2005; Hall & Hord, 2011b).

Each of the four *Stages of Concern* is described next through the lens of preservice teacher response to clinical experiences and working with culturally and linguistically diverse students. Because these are not the only factors influencing the journey of preservice teacher development, progress through these stages may not always be linear or clear-cut, nor does the cycle of innovation and implementation represented in this model end when preservice teachers graduate from our program.

1. Unrelated concerns. In many cases, preservice teachers at this early stage of development may have only briefly considered that the contexts of their clinic placements will differ somewhat from their own personal experiences as students in K-12 classrooms, and they are minimally aware of the growing diversity in today's public schools, especially with regard to emergent bilinguals. Depending on background, prior experiences, educational opportunities, and program entrance requirements, this stage may not be evident or particularly lengthy for most preservice teachers engaging in clinical experiences. Nevertheless, attention to these concerns is an essential aspect of beginning the journey toward the development of the knowledge, skills, and dispositions needed to support the learning of culturally and linguistically diverse students. To address these concerns, faculty should be prepared to provide general background information about the diversity of learners students will encounter in clinic experiences (as noted in the second case in Chapter 4), as well as specific instructions about professional expectations for conduct and interactions with adults and students for preservice teachers in school settings.

2. Self-concerns. The focus in this stage remains on the preservice teacher and his or her understanding and experiences rather than on students or acts of learning. At this stage, there is a growing awareness of the cultural and linguistic diversity of K-12 students and how it interacts with the role and responsibilities of educators. Observations and reflections from clinic placements are viewed and interpreted through the lens of prior experiences and existing belief systems about good teachers and learning communities, which affords multiple opportunities to explore, examine, and expand preservice teachers' perspectives. In instances where clinic experiences vary greatly from the student's own or are not supported with opportunities for reflection and feedback, preservice teachers working through this stage may view the presence of emergent bilinguals and culturally diverse students as a barrier to effective teaching and learning that must be overcome, rather than an opportunity to better understand and celebrate how education can support democratic principles. Similar to the previous stage, more information and background knowledge is needed to further the growth and development of preservice teachers. Seminar classes within the IBM program provide information about cultural and linguistic diversity and issues of democracy and social justice in schools. Faculty are also sensitive to the need to reassure preservice teachers that they are on a journey of self-discovery, and that all teachers require practice and a range of experiences to develop both the comfort and expertise needed to lead an inclusive learning community effectively.

3. Task concerns. Preservice teacher attention is focused on the skills and strategies needed to plan and implement effective instruction, with an emphasis on organization and efficiency. In this stage, marked by growing awareness and problem-solving skills, the focus is on the practicalities and realities of the classroom, and clinic experiences are often viewed as laboratories in which to test out and practice a variety of instructional strategies, methods, and resources taught as theoretical constructs in university coursework. Preservice teachers focused on task concerns have recognized and internalized their responsibility as educators to teach *all* of their students, and in many cases, they are eager to identify tools and strategies that will help them meet the needs of emergent bilinguals. Additionally, preservice teachers can feel overwhelmed at times by their perceived lack of experience in or resources for supporting the individual needs of culturally and linguistically diverse students. However, in many cases, they are also responsive to constructive feedback and practical suggestions from trusted colleagues in clinical settings, helping preservice teachers to build the skills and self-efficacy needed to continue their professional growth and development. For many preservice teachers, a focus on task concerns represents the longest stage of their developmental journey because of the vast amount of knowledge and skill in a variety of domains that must be mastered to successfully manage the demands of the inclusive classroom. Given the number of new responsibilities and procedures frequently juggled by preservice teachers in this lengthy stage, faculty should be providing practical "how-to supports" in a variety of flexible, accessible formats (e.g., reflective journals can be completed on paper or electronically). Moreover, attention should be given to the fact that university faculty are not the only educators coaching preservice teachers, and care should be taken that research-based information about working with culturally and linguistically diverse students is readily available for all professionals in clinic settings.

4. **Impact concerns.** As self- and task concerns decrease, the improvement of K-12 student outcomes moves to the center of preservice teacher concerns in this final stage of the developmental journey. In many ways, this stage represents the envisioned destination of a well-trained teacher who recognizes his or her students as unique individuals whose strengths and talents enrich the classroom learning community. This recognition has a positive and visible impact on the learning of K-12 students in all classrooms, but especially in those that are culturally and linguistically diverse. When focused on impact concerns in clinic placements, preservice teachers have the confidence, skills, and knowledge to select and use a variety of instructional strategies and resources to expand student academic language skills and vocabulary, and these choices are informed by formative and summative evaluation data. Although this stage is often marked by independence and confidence, it should not be viewed as a purely *solo performance* clinic experience. Many preservice teachers begin to demonstrate behaviors suggesting a shift of focus to impact concerns in the senior year during their full-time student teaching experience, where they continue to benefit from collaboration and reflection with other professionals in the clinic setting as the focus of the work together has shifted to positively impacting students who are emergent bilinguals rather than on teacher practice or classroom procedures. Moreover, to support continued growth of both preservice teachers and their students, there is room for experimentation, practice, mistakes, and reflective feedback in a supportive clinic environment. To address impact concerns, faculty provide support for recognizing successes and the positive impact on K-12 student performance of instructional choices tailored specifically to the needs of diverse groups of learners within the clinic setting.

CLINICAL EXPERIENCES DESIGNED TO SUPPORT THE CONTINUED JOURNEY OF PRESERVICE TEACHER PREPARATION FOR WORK WITH CULTURALLY AND LINGUISTICALLY DIVERSE STUDENTS

As clinical faculty began the work of supporting preservice teachers to better meet the needs of emergent bilinguals, we recognized that existing clinical experiences and assignments tied to clinical seminars could be adapted to provide powerful opportunities for supporting preservice teachers on their developmental journey. To that end, we used the *Stages of Concern* model to frame our decisions about how and when to incorporate certain tasks and supports (Hall & Hord, 2011b). As we discuss in this section, we were sensitive to the need for intentionality, creation of both intellectual and applied tasks, and reflection throughout all stages of development.

Attending to a Diversity of Experiences with Support and Intentionality

Because of their location in public schools, learning that occurs in clinic settings is shaped by context and opportunity. The disparities between schools in Connecticut are striking, and even within our network of partner schools, a short 10-minute drive can mean the difference between finding oneself in a highly resourced, high-achieving school district or a grossly underfunded, struggling educational community. Making sense of these differences and recognizing the needs of emergent bilinguals within various settings can challenge preservice teachers at various points in their journey.

Throughout the program, we work to ensure that all preservice teachers are provided with a concrete set of expectations and common vocabulary to explore and reflect on how to work effectively with culturally and linguistically diverse K-12 students. With preservice teachers at the beginning of their journey who are demonstrating behaviors of unrelated and self-concerns, seminar leaders identify and define specific common terms, vocabulary, and acronyms used in school settings. The goal is to foster a common language and understanding so that preservice teachers can discuss and "unpack" their clinic experiences with honesty and thought. These expectations and common vocabulary terms are then incorporated and expanded in subsequent clinic experiences and seminars.

Another way in which we intentionally encourage a common set of expectations and foundational skills is with the cooperation and support of education professionals in clinic settings. As preservice teachers progress toward the stage of task and impact concerns, we require that they are observed and receive prescriptive feedback. The cooperating teacher serves this function during the spring semester of the senior year when preservice teachers are doing their full-time student teaching. Also, the university supervisor, an experienced educator hired by the university, provides explicit and formal feedback to preservice teachers using a structured observation tool that includes descriptions of targeted professional teaching practices and prompts for reflection. Because university supervisors provide such a foundational role in the formation and implementation of teaching practices within the clinical context, it is important for them to have information regarding instructional strategies to support the needs of emergent bilinguals. To this end, a group of clinical and tenure-line faculty created an ad hoc group we titled Creating Learning among Supervisors and Schoolteachers about ELLs (CLASSE). We designed and then provided professional development for university supervisors focused on the purpose and use of sheltered instructional strategies. We have identified online resources that we will make accessible for supervisors and cooperating teachers; we plan to create a webpage that highlights practical resources and strategies that may prove particularly useful during student teaching. The goal is to make the information readily accessible and easy to incorporate amid the many task concerns that tend to dominate student teaching.

Creating Intellectual Space for the Journey through the Selection of Seminar Content

Whether you are learning to read or learning to teach algebra, automaticity of new skills and required knowledge takes time and intellectual space. As explained previously, each clinic experience within the UConn program is paired with a seminar course to help bridge the gap between theory and practice. Therefore, we reviewed the content selection for the seminars to ensure that it was developmentally appropriate and reflective of the concerns of students as they progress through the program.

Because new arrivals to the teacher preparation program often show evidence of self- and unrelated concerns, we recognized the primary need for raising awareness of and providing a framework for understanding the cultural and linguistic diversity found in schools. To that end, the junior seminar was recently redesigned. This work was significantly influenced by Adichie's (2009) TED talk, in which she spoke about how personal stories shape our conceptions, and that each person is the sum of what another perceives or assumes to be true about that person. Within the reflective activities of seminar, we explore Adichie's (2009) statement that, "[t]he single story creates stereotypes, and the problem with stereotypes is not that they are untrue, but that they are incomplete. They make one story become the only story." Using the "single story" theme, preservice teachers explore and expand their own stories as well as understandings and misunderstandings they hold of others (Roselle, Hands & Payne, 2013). In seminar, preservice teachers use art, poetry, and multi-media to reflect on their prior and current experiences in school and to deepen their understandings about emergent bilinguals. One example of a powerful assignment central to this learning objective included asking preservice teachers to write an "I'm From" poem based on the template by Lyon's (1999) poem, *Where I'm From*. In this poem, preservice teachers reflect on their own upbringing and schooling and the impact these experiences have had on forming their ideas about teaching and learning. The poems become a book that is used as a way to make explicit the importance of not reducing each other to a single story.

Assigned readings provide another example of how course content can be organized and selected to reflect the expected developmental journey of preservice teachers. During their first clinic experience, we assign the article *His Name Is Michael* written by Marriott (2002), a veteran teacher. This true story recounts the arrival in a busy classroom of a new student named Michael who did not speak English and the ways in which the teacher tried to help him assimilate into the classroom community.

When the student left the school a few months later, Marriott received paperwork that indicated that his name was actually "David." She questioned the fact that this was a brown child who did not even possess the power to explain to his teacher that his name was not Michael, but David. By reading and discussing the author's honest reflections, preservice teachers often overwhelmed with the many self-concerns of navigating their first clinic experiences are pushed to consider how simple actions like introductions can define power relationships and shape the lives of students in positive ways. As preservice teachers progress to senior year and the focus on task concerns increases, Cowhey's (2006) *Black Ants and Buddhists* is assigned. Cowhey's thoughtful, detailed descriptions of discussions and activities inside her first-grade classroom offer preservice teachers with an alternative model for addressing the many task concerns that emerge as they prepare for student teaching. In addition, Cowhey's narrative explains the instructional decisions she makes to challenge and engage her class of diverse learners (including emergent bilinguals) in culturally responsive and innovative ways. In this way, the reading provides a model of a teacher focused on impact concerns that can be capitalized on in seminar and clinic experiences. Some preservice teachers—having completed their student teaching—elect to research a topic related to emergent bilinguals and/or take a full course on sheltered instruction in the final year of the program. In many cases, this decision is spurred by impact concerns or the realization that developing more expertise for effectively teaching emergent bilinguals will allow them to better meet the needs of students in the internship setting or future classrooms. At this point, reading assignments are more self-directed and in-depth. See the appendix for a list of additional reading selections that may support growth and exploration of the *Stages of Concern* model.

Creating Applied Space for the Journey through Opportunities for Practice in Clinic Settings

To develop the habits and dispositions necessary to meet the needs of emergent bilinguals, preservice teachers must be afforded opportunities to repeat and refine their practice in authentic settings, facing authentic instructional challenges. When structuring these opportunities for application, clinical faculty use the *Stages of Concern* model to help them gauge what type of feedback and challenges are most likely to prove constructive for a preservice teacher and her students.

The ability to plan and execute instruction is a bedrock skill for every teacher and a complex process that is investigated in every clinic placement throughout the program. At each stage of the preservice teacher's developmental journey, opportunities to practice and apply a variety of teaching skills and dispositions can further student growth and continue to move them toward a focus on impact concerns. Moreover, small adjustments to clinic expectations can enhance recognition and understanding of the needs of learners who are culturally and linguistically diverse.

One example is an introduction to lesson planning that offers preservice teachers an opportunity to create a developmentally appropriate lesson plan for the classroom in which they are placed (Figure 7.1). They do this in a group format to start and then they individualize a lesson plan. This plan is iterative in the sense that they continue throughout the semester to make changes to it based on instructional strategies they are learning in both seminar class and their clinic placements, and in response to the various linguistic and academic needs they are observing in their students. They eventually have an opportunity to teach this lesson, receive feedback from their clinic teacher, and reflect on their practices. This cycle of teaching, learning, and reflecting continues in each new clinic setting. The instructional tasks and expectations become increasingly complex as preservice teachers master the skills and knowledge needed to promote student learning. To further their development and enhance their abilities for working with emergent bilinguals, preservice teachers should have opportunities to:

— create measurable learning and language objectives;
— establish and communicate high expectations for all students;
— plan and implement instruction;
— select, adapt, and develop instructional resources that reflect students' academic language skills and promote continued growth;
— evaluate student growth and progress toward objectives, standards, and other benchmarks;
— foster authentic, culturally responsive relationships with students and colleagues;
— apply appropriate flexible grouping strategies when warranted;
— implement culturally responsive classroom management strategies that promote positive interactions and efficient use of instructional time;
— reflect on practices; and
— communicate effectively with families and other community stakeholders (including strategies and resources for working with emergent bilinguals).

Another way in which clinical experiences are structured to help preservice teachers develop the skills and dispositions needed to work effectively with emergent bilinguals is through the use of the "Professional Practices" Observation Tool (UConn IBM Program, 2010). This observation protocol includes 24 teaching practices that preservice teachers must demonstrate at a level of acceptable proficiency during the student teaching experience. The purpose of the tool is twofold: to provide a formative and ongoing assessment of the student teacher's progress; and to preclude observers

OBSERVATION #5   LITERACY AND LANGUAGE TASKS

Student Observer _____ School _____

Class/Teacher _____ Grade(s) _____ Date _____

A. CLASSROOM OBSERVATION

BICS. *Describe at least one instance of a student demonstrating Basic Interpersonal Communication Skills. In what* **context** *was this experience embedded? Explain how the speaker and listener interacted and the result of the exchange.*

CONTENT LITERACY. *Describe at least one example of how the students are using reading and writing to further their understanding of a lesson's content or expand their academic language proficiency (CALP). Identify any abstract concepts or specialized vocabulary that is needed to complete the task.*

VOCABULARY. *Describe how new words are incorporated into classroom tasks and activities. Are all students responsible for learning/developing the same vocabulary or is there some differentiation occurring?*

HELPFUL CUES. *How does the teacher support student understanding of language based (CALP) tasks? Describe any body language, use of multiple media, practice with new vocabulary, or other classroom structures or procedures that may enhance student understanding in this realm.*

B. QUESTIONS I'D LIKE TO ASK MY CLINIC PLACEMENT TEACHER:

C. REFLECTION (Please respond to any of the following in your writing):

- *How does what I have observed compare to what I have learned in education classes, seminar readings, or prior experiences?*
- *What aspects of this lesson might challenge an English Language Learner with emergent CALP skills? How might (or was) the lesson be adapted to address these concerns?*
- *Did you see any examples of students who you believed were struggling with academic language tasks? What was the teacher's response or awareness to this perceived confusion?*
- *In what way might you incorporate some of the skills and strategies you have observed into your own teaching? What will you try?*

Figure 7.1 Structured observation and reflection task regarding literacy and language.

from dwelling on a pervasive issue or challenge that is presenting for the student teacher, affording a more holistic view of the application of practices. For each lesson observation conducted by either a cooperating teacher or university supervisor, student teachers select three practices on which to be observed. The observer then focuses on the three practices selected and documents what he sees and hears. A conference is held between the observer and the student teacher to debrief and discuss the comments he recorded. The student teacher then writes a corresponding reflection, and the entire completed document is maintained as part of the preservice teacher's electronic portfolio.

Many of the promising practices support and promote preservice teachers' work with culturally and linguistically diverse students and also highlight teacher behaviors that shift the focus toward impact concerns For example:

— #5 - Builds on students' prior knowledge and experience.
— #10 - Uses questioning to stimulate thinking and encourages all students to respond.
— #12 - Employs appropriate sheltered English or subject matter strategies for English learners.
— #15 - Provides many and varied opportunities for students to achieve competence.
— #16 - Accurately measures student achievement of, and progress toward, the learning objectives with a variety of formal and informal assessments, and uses results to plan further instruction.
— #22 - Encourages all students to believe that effort is a key to achievement.
— #23 - Works to promote achievement by all students without exception.

Infusing Opportunities for Reflection with an Attention to Practices That Support Emergent Bilingual

Becoming a reflective practitioner is imperative if preservice teachers are to fully develop the capacity necessary to understand the impact of their instructional choices on the learning of emergent bilinguals. Through observation and reflection, preservice teachers take field notes and become familiar with data collection and analysis. The goal for these reflection tasks is to use feedback and repeated practice to hone the essential teaching skills of observation and reflection, which are essential elements in shifting the focus of concerns from self to impact. Additionally, observations and thoughts can serve as a springboard for seminar discussions and may also broaden the understanding of the teacher's roles and responsibilities related to student learning.

The following example of a structured reflective task is used in the first clinic placement with preservice teachers who are likely focused on self- and task concerns. The goal of this assignment is to expand recognition of the use of language and literacy tasks in all K-12 classrooms, and to help preservice teachers connect those tasks to basic background knowledge they are gaining about the needs of culturally and linguistically diverse students. Ideally, this protocol is used while observing or participating in a class with emergent bilinguals; however, the observation form is generalizable and has enough utility to be used in settings without emergent bilinguals.

Another example of a reflection opportunity offered to preservice teachers is a culminating assignment in which they video themselves teaching and are asked to reflect on the impact of instruction on student learning. Clinical faculty revised this student teaching video project to convey the importance of effective instruction for emergent bilinguals and support preservice teacher exploration of impact concerns. The assignment requires all student teachers to videotape themselves in their clinic placements, teaching a formally designed lesson, to edit the video, and to write a reflection paper focusing on their instructional practices and student performance. (See the appendix for the complete assignment directions.)

As part of the assignment, student teachers are directed to identify segments of video that highlight various aspects of their teaching (e.g., something in the lesson that went well, something that they would do differently in the future, etc.). Preservice teachers are also asked to select and highlight a video segment to demonstrate one of four "Professional Practices" employed in the lesson:

— #12 - Employs appropriate sheltered English or subject matter strategies for English language learners.
— #14 - Provides regular and frequent feedback to students on their progress.
— #15 - Differentiates instruction by providing many and varied opportunities for students to achieve competence.
— #16 - Accurately measures student achievement of, and progress toward, the learning objectives with a variety of formal and informal assessments, and uses results to plan further instruction.

All of the selected professional practices focus on interactions with K-12 students in ways that will promote learning. Practice #12, which highlights sheltered instruction and work with emergent bilinguals, was included in the assignment after Project Prepare-ELLs training. Because the video project is a required culminating assignment maintained in students' electronic portfolios, this simple addition acknowledges and encourages students in their integration of and reflection about responsive instructional practices while allowing clinical faculty to evaluate the integration of these practices throughout the program.

CONCLUSION

The importance of the clinic experience in teacher preparation cannot be overestimated; preservice teachers will not develop knowledge, skills, and dispositions of culturally and linguistically responsive teachers from only engaging in theoretical coursework in a teacher preparation program. Diverse clinical experiences coupled with a theoretical framework such as the *Stages of Concern* model can be used to support preservice teachers in their work with K-12 students and professional colleagues. When planning clinical experiences that attend to the developmental journey of preservice teachers, it is important to consider diverse experiences, intellectual and applied space, and opportunities for reflection. Attending to this journey allows preservice teachers to reach their fullest potential to impact the learning of emergent bilinguals.

REFERENCES

Adichie, C. (2009). *Chimamanda Adichie: The danger of a single story* [TED video]. Retrieved March 14, 2014 from http://www.ted.com/talks/chimamanda adichie the danger of a single story.html..

Connecticut State Department of Education, Bureau of Data Collection, Research and Evaluation. (June 2012*).* *Data Bulletin: English Language Learners, School Year 2011–2012.* Retrieved March 14, 2014 from http://sdeportal.ct.gov/Cedar/Files/Pdf/Reports/ELL_Data_Bulletin_2012.pdf.

Cowhey, M. (2006). *Black ants and Buddhists.* Portland, ME: Stenhouse Publishers.

Darling-Hammond, L. (2012). Building a profession of teaching: Teacher educators as change agents. In M. Ben-Peretz, S. Kleeman, R. Reichenberg, & S. Shimoni (Eds.), *Teacher educators as members of an evolving profession* (pp. 87–102). New York: Rowman & Littlefield.

Fuller, F. F. (1969). Concerns of teachers: A developmental conceptualization. *American Educational Research Journal, 6*(2), 207–226.

Hall, G. E., & Hord, S. M. (2011a). Implementation: Learning builds the bridge between research and practice. *The Journal of Staff Development, 32*(4), 52–57.

Hall, G. E., & Hord, S. M. (2011b). *Implementing change: Patterns, principles, and potholes* (3rd ed.). Upper Saddle River, NJ: Pearson.

Hammerness, K., Darling-Hammond, L., Bransford, J., Berliner, D., Cochran-Smith, M., McDonald, M., & Zeichner, K. (2005). How teachers learn and develop. In L. Darling-Hammond & J. Bransford (Eds.), *Preparing teachers for a changing world: What teachers should learn and be able to do* (pp. 358–389). San Francisco, CA: Jossey-Bass.

Hammerness, K., Darling-Hammond, L., Grossman, P., Rust, F., & Shulman, L. (2005). The design of teacher education programs. In L. Darling-Hammond & J. Bransford (Eds.), *Preparing teachers for a changing world: What teachers should learn and be able to do* (pp. 390–441). San Francisco, CA: Jossey-Bass.

Lyon, G. E. (1999). *Where I'm from, where poems come from.* Spring, Texas: Absey & Co.

Marriott, D. (2002, October 9). "His name is Michael": A lesson on the voices we unknowingly silence. *Education Week,* p. 35.

National Council for Accreditation of Teacher Education. (2008). *Professional standards for the accreditation of teacher preparation institutions.* Washington, DC: Author.

Roselle, R., Hands, R. E., & Payne, S. (2013). The danger of a single story: Preparing preservice teachers to teach for social justice. In K. Zenkov, D. Corrigan, & R. Beebe (Eds.), *Professional development schools and social justice: Schools and universities partnering to make a difference,* pp 91–110. Lanham, MD: Lexington Books.

UConn IBM Program. (2010). *"Professional practices" observation tool.* Retrieved March 14, 2014 from http://assessment.education.uconn.edu/assessment/assets/File/Professional%20Practices%20Observation%20Tool%2C%202014.pdf.

Valdés, G., Bunch, G., Snow, C., Lee, C., & Matos, L. (2005). Enhancing the development of students' language(s). In L. Darling-Hammond & J. Bransford (Eds.), *Preparing teachers for a changing world: What teachers should learn and be able to do* (pp. 128–135). San Francisco, CA: Jossey-Bass.

APPENDIX

Suggested Readings to Guide the Journey

This list provides examples of readings used in seminar courses in the Neag School's IBM program to support and promote preservice teacher growth and progression within the *Stages of Concern* model.

Unrelated Concerns

Choi, Y. (2003). *The name jar*. New York: Dragonfly Books.
Smith, D. J., & Armstrong, S. (2011). *If the world were a village: A book about the world's people* (2nd ed.). Tonawanda, NY: Kids Can Press.
State of Connecticut. (2012). *Connecticut code of professional responsibility for educators: Regulations of Connecticut State Agencies, section 10–145d-400a*. Retrieved May 29, 2013, from http://www.sde.ct.gov/sde/cwp/view.asp?a=2613&q=321332
Handbooks, websites, and reports issued from partner schools

Self-Concerns

Bronson, P., & Merryman A. (2009). Why white parents don't talk about race. In *Nurture shock: New thinking about children* (pp. 45–70). Boston, MA: Twelve.
Bunting, E., & Lewin, T. (2006). *One green apple*. New York: Clarion Books.
Davis, C., & Yang, A. (2006, April). Welcoming families of different cultures. *Responsive Classroom Newsletter*, pp. 6–7.
Kilman, C. (2009). Lonely language learners? *Teaching Tolerance, 75*(2), 16–20.
Marriott, D. (2002, October 9). "His name is Michael": A lesson on the voices we unknowingly silence. *Education Week*, p. 35.
Nobisso, J., & Ziborova, D. (2003). *In English, of course*. New York: Gingerbread House.
Weinbaum, L. M. (2007). Culture clash: Why some otherwise concerned parents stay away from school. *Teacher Magazine, 18*(4), 50–52.

Task Concerns

Author. (2009). Supporting the needs of English Language Learners—theme issue. *Educational Leadership, 66*(7).
Bronson, P., & Merryman A. (2009). Why Hannah talks and Alyssa doesn't. In *Nurture shock: New thinking about children* (pp. 197–224). Boston, MA: Twelve.
Delpit, L. (2003). Teaching teenagers who are still learning English. In *Fires in the bathroom: Advice for teachers from high school students* (pp. 145–161). New York: The New Press.
Ford, K. (2011). *Differentiated instruction for English language learners*. Retrieved May 29, 2013, from http://www.colorincolorado.org/article/41025/
Jules, J. (2007). *No English*. Ann Arbor, MI: Mitten Press.
Vogt, M. E., & Echevarria, J. (2007). *99 ideas and activities for teaching English learners with the SIOP model*. Boston, MA: Pearson Education.

Impact Concerns

Cowhey, M. (2006). *Black ants and Buddhists: Thinking critically and teaching differently in the primary grades*. Portland, ME: Stenhouse Publishers.
Echevarria, J., Vogt, M. E., & Short, D. J. (2012). *Making content comprehensible for English learners: The SIOP model* (4th ed.). Boston, MA: Pearson Education.

Part III
Assessing Outcomes and Learning Along the Way

8 Assessing Progress Within and Across Cohorts

Elizabeth R. Howard, Megan E. Welsh, Thomas H. Levine, and David M. Moss

THE OVERARCHING CHALLENGE

How can a faculty learning community gauge impact on its preservice teachers at a programmatic level? Over time, what changes can be noted among preservice teachers within and across cohorts? As our efforts at the University of Connecticut (UConn) have progressed, these questions have come to the forefront, and there has been a corresponding shift in our focus to document program-level changes and establish the extent to which these changes permeate entire cohorts of teacher candidates. Our emphasis on program-level data has been motivated by two key factors. First, as noted in Chapter 2, this project developed out of a larger effort to use assessment results to focus our continuous improvement effort. Exit surveys administered to graduates of the teacher education program revealed that graduates did not feel adequately prepared to work effectively with emergent bilingual students. As a result, we initiated the faculty learning community with the intent of bringing about program-wide change that would have a long-term impact on the practice of the teachers we graduate. Such data-driven, programmatic-level work is consistent with our ongoing accreditation activity.

Second, UConn is a research university/very high research activity (RU/VH university) as indicated by the Carnegie classifications, and carrying out research is a clear priority for individual faculty members and the institution as a whole. Incorporating systematic and ongoing data collection into the project increased faculty buy-in and institutional support. Some of these efforts are addressed in other chapters. For example, Chapter 5 describes individual faculty efforts to document changes in teaching and learning in content-specific methods courses, and Chapter 9 describes project-level efforts to document change in the instructional practices of preservice teachers through observation and interviews with a subset of students.

This chapter conveys the story of a further effort, our approach to documenting program-wide shifts in the self-efficacy of preservice teachers with regard to their ability to teach this group. Self-Efficacy Theory (Bandura, 1977) maintains that the way people perceive themselves influences their effort and persistence in pursuing a goal, which in turn influence actual performance. Self-efficacy is also affected by personal experiences of success or failure and by observation of others' success. That is, building self-efficacy improves performance, which begets future success. In the teacher education context, this would mean that preservice teachers who feel confident about their ability to work effectively with emergent bilinguals would put forth more effort and show greater persistence in their work with these students, resulting in improved teaching practices.

In addition, because tracking teaching performance after graduating from the teacher education program was untenable, we decided that measuring change in an important precursor to teaching success was an acceptable proxy for the long-term impact we hoped to create. We also knew that we wanted to collect data at multiple time points on a large number of people across a variety of concentrations and teacher education programs. A survey instrument seemed to be the most appropriate data-collection instrument in that it is relatively easy to administer.

Finally, because we expected to improve our own teaching as the faculty learning community matured, we decided to examine growth within and across cohorts of preservice teachers. We also examined the extent to which differing patterns emerged across our two teacher preparation programs, one geared toward undergraduate students (Integrated Bachelor's/Master's [IBM]) and one for mid-career professionals (Teacher Certification Program for College Graduates [TCPCG]).

We begin with an overview of the measure and the process that we went through to develop it. We then describe the preservice teachers we serve in terms of their familiarity with the challenges emergent bilinguals face, discuss our data-collection efforts within each program, and share descriptive findings. We conclude with recommendations for other projects that may wish to collect systemic data to inform program improvement and research. Specifically, this chapter responds to the following two questions: (a) In what ways does preservice teachers' self-efficacy with regard to teaching emergent bilinguals change over time? (b) How, if at all, has self-efficacy at program exit changed throughout the time of implementation of the project?

METHODS

Development of the Teaching English Language Learners Self-Efficacy Scale (TELLSES)

The first step in developing any effective measure is to conduct a review of the literature, both to learn about different aspects of the construct you intend to measure to ensure that the measure addresses the full range of beliefs (content representativeness) and the most important aspects (content relevance) of the construct you intend to measure (Allen & Yen, 2001). The literature review also alerts instrument developers to any existing measures that address the construct of interest. In the event that a high-quality measure already exists, it makes sense to administer it. In our case, Liz Howard (lead author of this chapter) had already created a questionnaire for her work with dual language educators as part of the Center for Research on Education, Diversity & Excellence (CREDE) (http://www.cal.org/crede/). This instrument served as a point of departure, which Tom Levine revised into a provisional version of the Teaching English Language Learners Self-Efficacy Scale (TELLSES).

The provisional version of the questionnaire was introduced with the following directions: "Please rate how confident you are about your ability to do the things described in each statement below, using a scale of 0 (*completely disagree*) to 10 (*completely agree*) as follows." Participants were then asked to respond to the stem, "When it comes to English language learners (ELLs), I am confident that I can . . . ," followed by a series of 28 statements designed to tap into self-efficacy in relation to four abilities: (a) identifying challenges and needs of ELLs; (b) drawing on—or helping students draw on—the prior knowledge, experiences, family and community resources, and cultural and linguistic capital that ELLs have; (c) identifying pedagogical strategies and knowledge to support ELLs; and (d) implementing strategies to support ELLs in actual teaching.

Three content experts in the field of bilingual/ELL education reviewed the statements. These experts indicated which of the domains, if any, each statement related to; their certainty in assigning a domain to each statement (1 = *not very sure*, 2 = *pretty sure*, or 3 = *very sure*); and their assessment of how relevant each item was for its category (L = *low/no relevance*, M = *mostly relevant*, or H = *highly relevant*). We only kept items when at least two of three raters indicated that they were both very sure of their assignment of the item to one of our intended domains and felt the item was "highly relevant" to this domain. Experts were also asked to provide feedback on a few open-ended questions designed to tap into specific strategies and approaches preservice teachers might enact when working with emergent bilinguals. Experts helped us revise our definition of ELL, agreed that the domains were appropriate, and provided ratings and qualitative input. Based on the feedback from the content experts, the TELLSES was shortened to 20 items designed to tap into three domains:

1. five items target "challenges faced by emergent bilinguals" (e.g., "When it comes to ELLs, I am confident that I can describe challenges many ELLs face as they learn concepts and skills in the specific subject(s) I teach");
2. six items target "resources that emergent bilinguals bring with them" (e.g., "When it comes to ELLs, I am confident that I can draw on ELLs' native language abilities, life experiences, and knowledge to promote their ability to read and write in English"); and

3. nine items target "effective pedagogical strategies to support emergent bilinguals" (e.g., "When it comes to ELLs, I am confident that I can effectively implement strategies that help ELLs learn concepts and skills for the subject(s) I teach").

The operational version of the instrument also includes open-ended questions that address pedagogical tasks specific to each content area and grade level (e.g., teaching slope in a secondary mathematics class) due to feedback from reviewers that the original open-ended items were too vague. These tasks require preservice teachers to indicate specific strategies they would use to support emergent bilinguals to be successful for that lesson, and why they would use each one.

Finally, because self-efficacy builds from prior experiences, and because we felt it was important to get a more in-depth profile of our students to help tailor instruction as we move forward with our learning community and other changes in our teacher education program, the operational version of the TELLSES also includes a series of demographic questions designed to tap into students' background experiences, as well as a series of questions that specifically inquire about the extent to which prior courses and other experiences within the Neag School of Education (e.g., student teaching and internships) have increased their confidence about working with emergent bilinguals. The responses to these questions have been used to create a rich profile of our students, as described in the Participants section.

The next step in instrument development typically involves administering the questionnaire to a group of participants and using exploratory factor analysis to evaluate whether the items cluster within the intended constructs, revising the instrument as needed, and administering the revised version to a new sample to confirm that the proposed factor structure holds (McCoach, Gable, & Madura, 2013). However, each of these steps requires a sample of at least 200 students for a "fair" sample size (Comrey & Lee, 1992), although more recent work has shown that the number of variables, the number of factors, and the correlation between factors all affect the sample size required to obtain a stable solution (MacCallum, Widaman, Zhang, & Hong, 1999). Because our teacher education program is small by design, this approach would have required the participation of approximately four cohorts of students. Instead, we proceeded with the content validated instrument with plans to conduct factor analyses as the requisite sample sizes were met. Those validation efforts are ongoing and will not be addressed here, as this chapter focuses solely on global self-efficacy as determined by a composite score across all 20 items. As will be discussed later in the Findings section, reliability for the measure as a whole was found to be quite high.

Participants

The instrument was administered to teacher candidates in both the TCPCG and IBM programs over a four-year period between 2009 and 2013.

During each of those years, between 109 and 133 students entered the IBM program, and approximately 88% of those students went on to program completion at the end of three years. The TCPCG program is somewhat smaller, with cohort sizes at the West Hartford campus ranging from 47 to 58 students over the same four-year period. TCPCG graduation rates for those cohorts were consistently high, ranging from 92% to 98%. New TCPCG programs also serve preservice teachers at the Waterbury, CT, and Avery Point, CT, branch campuses, but only West Hartford, CT, data are reported here.

Drawing on the demographic information provided in the TELLSES responses, a profile of the various cohorts within the IBM and TCPCG programs is provided in the following paragraphs. Only responses from the final wave of data collection were used to generate these profiles in order to avoid counting responses from the same student on more than one occasion. Because the second research question focuses specifically on this final time point, this was the logical wave of data to use to create the profiles.

To gauge how many preservice teachers were emergent bilinguals, we asked them to indicate their native language. Over the cohorts, between 93% and 96% of IBM students indicated that English is their native language depending on cohort studied. The TCPCG cohorts varied more widely, from a low of 86% to a high of 100% of students who reported that English is their native language. That is, most of the teacher candidates we train do not have direct personal experience of what it is like to be an emergent bilingual in U.S. schools. Interestingly, relatively few of the teacher candidates with a non-English native language are native Spanish speakers or native Spanish-English bilinguals, indicating that few represent the most common demographic of emergent bilinguals in the U.S. today (Batalova & McHugh, 2010).

To further explore preservice teachers' personal experiences as second language learners, we also asked respondents to indicate the second language in which they have the highest level of proficiency. As shown in Table 8.1, most

Table 8.1 Preservice Teachers' Second Language

Program	Cohort	None	English	Spanish	Others
IB/M	2009	25.3%	1.2%	50.6%	22.9%
	2010	13.7%	1.1%	60.0%	25.3%
	2011	34.7%	5.6%	43.1%	16.7%
	2012	24.8%	4.0%	56.4%	14.9%
TCPCG	2009	9.1%	13.6%	45.5%	31.8%
	2010	0.0%	0.0%	75.0%	25.0%
	2011	35.5%	3.2%	35.5%	25.8%
	2012	32.7%	11.5%	32.7%	23.1%

teacher candidates (64%–100%) indicated that they have gained at least some proficiency in a language other than English, most likely through mandated foreign language courses in high school and/or college. We deem this proficiency valuable, in that the teacher candidates have some awareness of the challenges learners face and the resources they bring to bear in developing proficiency in a second language, albeit in a different context. Moreover, the most common reported second language is Spanish, providing teacher candidates a base on which to build when working with emergent bilinguals in the U.S., the majority of whom are native Spanish speakers.

To better gauge the extent to which these second language skills might be brought to bear on instruction, we also asked preservice teachers to self-report their level of proficiency in their second language on a 5-point scale ranging from 1 (*basic*) to 5 (*fluent*) (see Table 8.2). Brief descriptions were provided for these labels, i.e., "beginner—I could purchase food or get directions in this language, but real conversation is hard." The second highest rating, "advanced," was defined as being able to communicate facts and talk about current events and personal interests with some grammar errors and groping for words.

Across all cohorts in both programs, approximately 50% or more of preservice teachers identified themselves as having low levels of second language proficiency (basic or beginner). Much smaller percentages of preservice teachers (2%–28%) rated themselves as having high levels of proficiency (advanced or fluent), and this was particularly the case among those in the IBM program. These results indicate that a minority of preservice teachers have experienced the kinds of conditions that lead to advanced second language proficiency and are therefore unlikely to be able to draw on such experiences when providing instruction to emergent bilinguals. In other words, without opportunities to further develop their second language proficiency, most preservice teachers do not possess sufficient fluency to provide instruction in their second language. Rather, they have rudimentary skills that would need to be built on to be useful in instruction and/or communication with parents. Moreover, it indicates that a possible area of future expansion for the teacher education programs at UConn may be to more actively promote advanced second language proficiency among preservice teachers, such as through content courses taught in Spanish or other high-frequency languages and/or study-abroad experiences in countries where other languages are spoken.

Another potential indicator of familiarity with the experiences of emergent bilinguals is the amount of time spent in non-English-speaking countries. These cross-cultural travel experiences frequently require individuals to negotiate daily life tasks in another language and culture, thereby enabling them to directly experience some of challenges and frustrations that emergent bilinguals in the U.S. may encounter on a regular basis. In response to this question, there is a difference across programs, with higher percentages of preservice teachers in the TCPCG program reporting more time spent in non-English-speaking countries. Across all cohorts, approximately 25% of IBM students reported having spent more

Table 8.2 Preservice Teachers' Second Language Oral Proficiency

Program	Cohort	Basic	Beginner	Intermediate	Advanced	Fluent
IB/M	2009	35.9%	21.9%	29.7%	6.3%	6.3%
	2010	31.0%	29.8%	26.2%	8.3%	4.8%
	2011	30.0%	28.0%	40.0%	0.0%	2.0%
	2012	36.0%	32.6%	20.9%	3.5%	7.0%
TCPCG	2009	40.0%	25.0%	10.0%	10.0%	15.0%
	2010	42.9%	14.3%	28.6%	14.3%	0.0%
	2011	23.8%	33.3%	19.0%	19.0%	4.8%
	2012	39.5%	20.9%	11.6%	9.3%	18.6%

than one month in a non-English-speaking country, whereas nearly 40% of TCPCG did so. Additionally, 25% of IBM students reported having spent no time whatsoever in a non-English-speaking country, whereas only about 10% of TCPCG students did so. This may be a function of age, as TCPCG students have already completed college and sometimes have considerable life experience prior to enrolling in the program, whereas IBM students begin the program as undergraduates. As mentioned earlier, expanding the program offerings to include more teacher education study abroad experiences in non-English-speaking countries could have the double advantage of increasing preservice teachers' experiences abroad as a cultural and linguistic "other" as well as promoting greater second language proficiency.

Finally, we asked preservice teachers to indicate their exposure to emergent bilinguals in a classroom setting through their clinic or internship placements. As shown in Table 8.3, reported exposure is variable, but a sizeable

Table 8.3 Quantity of ELLs in Classrooms Where Preservice Teachers Taught or Interned

Program	Cohort	None	1 or 2	A Few	20% or More
IB/M	2009	25.3%	33.7%	20.5%	20.5%
	2010	23.2%	34.7%	20.0%	22.1%
	2011	17.8%	31.5%	26.0%	24.7%
	2012	19.0%	35.0%	23.0%	23.0%
TCPCG	2009	45.5%	31.8%	22.7%	0.0%
	2010	28.6%	57.1%	0.0%	14.3%
	2011	30.0%	63.3%	3.3%	3.3%
	2012	31.4%	35.3%	19.6%	13.7%

minority reported no exposure at all, particularly in the TCPCG program. It is important to remember that these are self-reported data, and the low incidence of reported exposure to emergent bilinguals may be at least in part a function of preservice teachers' inability to identify emergent bilinguals. Still, it is likely that these general trends still hold, and they point to the need for continued efforts on the part of the teacher education programs to recruit a more diverse student population and provide more experiences where preservice teachers can interact with emergent bilinguals on a regular basis.

Overall, this profile of preservice teachers in the IBM and TCPCG programs indicates that teacher candidates enroll in the program with relatively little exposure to emergent bilinguals, and the challenges they face provides compelling evidence for the need to address emergent bilinguals in our teacher education program. This, combined with the steady increase in ELLs in Connecticut schools (from 4% in 2002–2003 to 5.6% in 2010–2011; National Center for Education Statistics, 2012) indicates that an explicit emphasis on this population should be infused throughout the program.

Data Collection

Because we wanted to capture the effects of our efforts on individual cohorts of preservice teachers as they progressed through the program, as well as the effects brought about by the faculty learning community across different cohorts of preservice teachers, we repeatedly administered the TELLSES questionnaire to successive cohorts of preservice teachers in both the IBM and TCPCG programs from 2009 through 2013. Within the IBM program, preservice teachers were assessed at five points: (a) fall of junior year (baseline—entry point of program), (b) fall of senior year (prior to methods course), (c) winter of senior year (following methods course but prior to student teaching), (d) spring of senior year (following student teaching), and (e) spring of master's year (program completion). Within the TCPCG program, which is a 12-month program, the TELLSES was administered at three points: (a) summer (baseline—program entry), (b) late fall or early spring (program midpoint), and (c) late spring (program completion). This schedule has allowed us to monitor change within and across cohorts and to note differences at seminal points in the IBM program. It should be noted that the earliest cohorts were not administered the first wave(s) of the TELLSES because they were already partially through their respective programs at the onset of data collection. Likewise, data collection/data entry for the more recent cohorts has not yet been completed, and so the later waves of TELLSES results are not yet available for those cohorts.

To ensure the confidentiality of participants and to protect their rights as human subjects, the TELLSES was administered in targeted classes by a member of the Project PREPARE-ELLs research team and not by the course instructor, so as to assure preservice teachers that there would be no connection between survey completion and course grade. Participants were reminded of their right to opt out of taking the survey at any time. Moreover, respondent anonymity was ensured because we did not collect any identifying information on the surveys. This seemed particularly important in this project, given that the preservice teachers enter into long-term and high-stakes relationships with many of the faculty participating in Project PREPARE-ELLs, as they take courses that lead to degree completion and teacher certification from a number of different faculty members throughout their course of study.

This approach does have its drawbacks, however, chief among them the fact that it is impossible to identify non-respondents (e.g., preservice teachers who happened to be absent from class during a period of data collection) and follow up with them. As such, it is important to note that our sample sizes for each cohort fluctuate across time points, meaning that it is not always the exact same sample from point to point. In the IBM program, response rates for 13 of 16 data-collection points (five cohorts, each over one to five time points) are above 80%, with the remaining three between 60% and 80%. Among respondents in the TCPCG program, the response rate at one data-collection point (four cohorts, each over one to three time points) was lower than 20%; for three data-collection points, it ranged from 35% to 50%, and for five data-collection points, it was above 60%. Thus, for the IBM data, we have assurance that the sample mean for any cohort at any point represented that overall cohort reasonably well; unfortunately, our confidence in the representativeness of our TCPCG data is less strong, and this underscores the preferability of being able to follow up with individual students to promote higher response rates.

Another considerable drawback to not having student-level identification on the surveys is that it is impossible to track the growth in self-efficacy of individuals over time. As a result, our analyses are limited to examining group-level trends, but this was deemed an appropriate trade-off given the ongoing relationships among teacher educators and preservice teachers that were being mentored throughout the duration of this project.

Data were entered into an ACCESS database by trained research assistants who were supervised by Graduate Assistants Cory Maley and Eileen Gonzalez, with oversight from project leaders. Before analyzing data, an accuracy check across time points, programs, and data entry personnel was conducted on 5% of the surveys entered, checking all 55 individual items entered for each survey. The check revealed a 99.8% accuracy rate. Perhaps most important, the accuracy check helped the researchers identify and correct systematic sources of error for the 95% of entries that were not checked, further increasing the trustworthiness of data in the database.

Data Analysis

To respond to our two research questions, we created a mean score across all 20 self-efficacy items for each individual at each time point, so as to

148   Elizabeth R. Howard, et al.

have a global indicator of self-efficacy. A scale reliability analysis found strong evidence for all 20 items to be reported as a single factor (α=.964), with all items contributing to the reliability of the measure. We then generated descriptive statistics for each cohort at each time point and conducted analyses of variance (ANOVAs) cohort by cohort to determine whether the level of self-efficacy in teaching ELLs improved over the course of the teacher training programs. Finally, we conducted a second set of ANOVAs to determine whether there were significant mean differences across cohorts at the time of program completion.

FINDINGS

Improvements in Preservice Teacher Self-Efficacy within Cohorts over Time

The first research question focuses on potential changes in mean self-efficacy within cohorts of preservice teachers over time. Mean self-efficacy ratings, by cohort and time point, are presented in Figures 8.1 (IBM) and 8.2 (TCPCG). As the figures show, each cohort showed gains in self-efficacy over the course of their program. Substantively, the gains seem to move teacher candidates from a neutral stance in terms of their self-efficacy to teach ELLs to "agreeing" with statements that they feel confident that they can address the various challenges associated with educating emergent bilinguals, with 2011 and 2012 TCPCG students recording the largest self-efficacy gains.

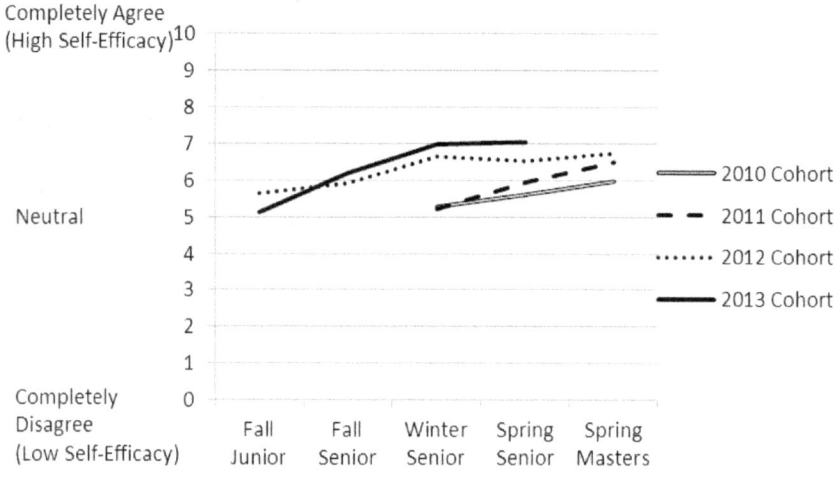

Figure 8.1   Change in IBM preservice teacher self-efficacy over time for each cohort.

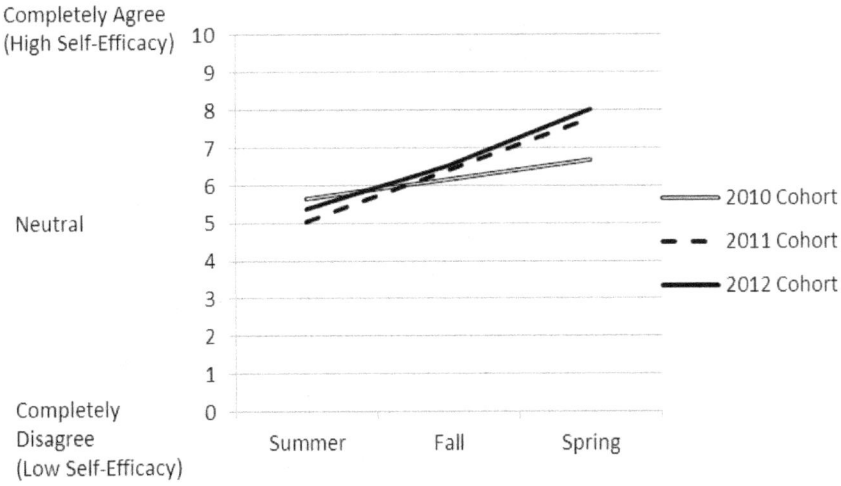

Figure 8.2 Change in TCPCG self-efficacy over time for each cohort.

Table 8.4 TELLSES ANOVA Results by Cohort within Program

Program	Cohort	F	df Between	df Within	p	η^2
IB/M	2010	5.003	2	222	0.007	0.043
	2011	20.956	2	236	<0.001	0.151
	2012	12.105	4	577	<0.001	0.077
	2013	62.325	3	490	<0.001	0.276
TCPCG	2010	2.447	1	33	0.127	0.690
	2011	32.872	2	95	<0.001	0.409
	2012	53.369	2	117	<0.001	0.477

ANOVAs yielded statistically significant differences, except for the TCPCG 2010 cohort, with a medium-to-large effect observed for all but two cohorts (Table 8.4). It is important to recall the sometimes suppressed response rates of TCPCG cohorts and interpret these findings with caution. However, the fact that similar trends were noted among IBM cohorts, who typically had higher response rates, lends support to the findings. As noted in the Participants section, the preservice teachers typically entered the teacher preparation program with limited experience or knowledge about second language learners, and this likely resulted in lower baseline self-perceptions and enhanced our ability to see gains over time. Future analyses will explore this possibility further, using multiple regression analyses to investigate the effects of prior experiences on self-efficacy.

Improvements in Preservice Teacher Self-Efficacy across Cohorts over Time

The second research question asks whether mean scores at time of program completion have changed over time. Ideally, we would examine differences in self-efficacy at program completion after controlling for initial self-efficacy levels so that we could examine whether participation in the faculty learning group improved over time after adjusting for differences between cohorts of teacher candidates. Looking back to Figures 8.1 and 8.2, we see that most cohorts started their programs with a neutral level of self-efficacy, with the 2012 IBM cohort and the 2010 TCPCG cohort having slightly higher initial levels of self-efficacy. In comparing self-efficacy at program completion, we would like to be able to control for these fluctuations in initial self-efficacy, but we are unable to do so because we don't know that the same students completed the surveys at the beginning and end of their respective program.

That said, we did detect between-year differences at program completion in preservice teacher self-efficacy to teach emergent bilinguals, with higher mean self-efficacy in cohorts graduating once the faculty learning community had matured (Figures 8.3 and 8.4). Omnibus F tests calculated using one-way ANOVA revealed differences among IBM cohorts [$F(3, 354) = 10.20, p < 0.01, \eta^2 = 0.080$] and TCPCG cohorts [$F(3, 112) = 11.43, p < 0.01, \eta^2 = 0.234$] at program completion. Bonferroni posthoc analyses revealed that mean self-efficacy scores between IBM cohorts at least two years apart are statistically different. That is, the mean self-efficacy of the 2011($M = 6.51, SD = 1.33$) and 2012 ($M = 6.73, SD = 1.61$) cohorts are significantly different from the 2009 cohort ($M = 5.66, SD = 1.44; p < 0.01$ and $p < 0.001$, respectively), and the mean self-efficacy score of the 2012 cohort is also significantly different from the 2010 cohort ($M = 5.98, SD = 1.41; p < 0.01$). Among TCPCG graduates, the program exit self-efficacy mean score of the 2011 cohort ($M = 7.78, SD = 0.97$) is significantly higher than those of both the 2009 cohort ($M = 6.68, SD = 1.26; p < 0.01$) and the 2010 cohort ($M = 6.67, SD = 1.26; p < 0.05$), as is the program exit self-efficacy mean score of the 2012 cohort ($M = 7.59, SD = 1.19; p < 0.001$ and $p < 0.01$, respectively). Again, because of the suppressed response rates among TCPCG cohorts, it is important to exercise caution when interpreting these findings, but the comparability of results for the IBM cohorts lends support.

Overall, the findings for both research questions are encouraging, as they seem to indicate that Project PREPARE-ELLs is having the intended effect on preservice teachers, at least in the realm of self-efficacy. That is, preservice teachers' level of self-efficacy seems to improve during their time in the teacher education programs, and the teacher education programs seem to have heightened impact as the faculty gain experience in focusing on the needs of emergent bilinguals. As discussed in Chapter 9, continued work is required to help preservice teachers make firmer connections to practice.

Assessing Progress Within and Across Cohorts 151

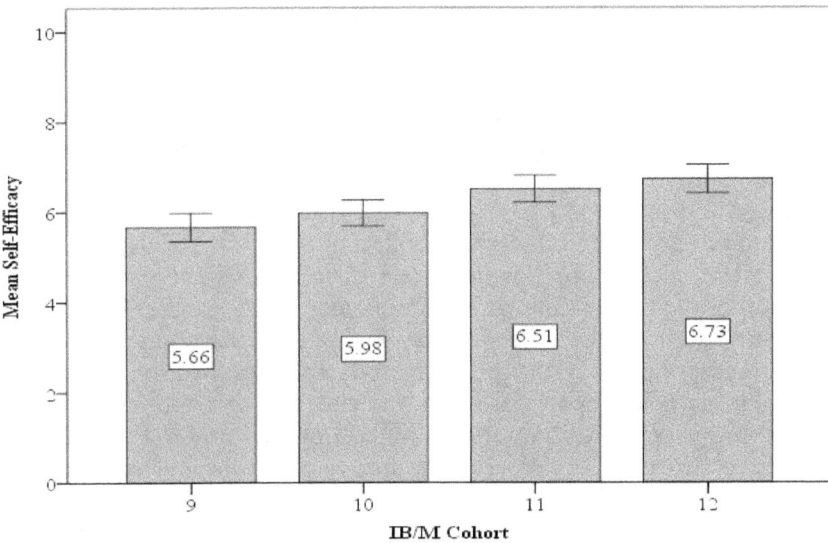

Figure 8.3 Mean self-efficacy at program completion by IBM cohort.

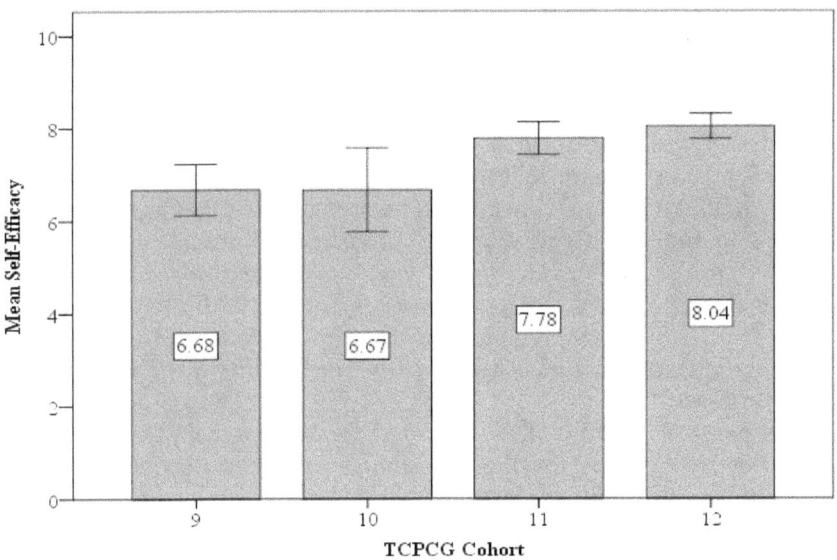

Figure 8.4 Mean self-efficacy at program completion by TCPCG cohort.

Recommendations

Based on what has worked well for us as well as the challenges and limitations we have faced, we offer the following recommendations to other programs that may wish to collect similar project-level outcome data:

1. Start with a needs assessment to determine what skills and experiences teacher candidates typically bring with them into the program. Use this information to guide decisions about where to focus programmatic efforts and to support requests for resources. Ideally, your measure would also gain baseline data about some variables you seek to impact in preservice teachers.
2. Decide what your goals are at the outset, including what forms of project-level data you want to collect at what points in the program and why. For example, in our case, we decided that self-efficacy was an important and feasible project-level outcome, so we decided to focus our project-level data collection on that issue across the continuum of our programs. Other programs may prefer to focus on other areas of teacher development, such as knowledge or dispositions at various strategic points within the development of their preservice teachers.
3. Capitalize on existing data-collection mechanisms and existing measures (such as those essential for accreditation) to initiate and sustain project-level data-collection efforts. In our case, we were able to work from an existing measure, which facilitated our work in creating the TELLSES. In our institution, we are fortunate to have a Director of Assessment who administers some surveys to current students and alumnae and provides findings to faculty on a regular basis. This infrastructure was largely responsible for the motivation for our project, as exit surveys from graduates revealed a lack of preparation to work effectively with emergent bilinguals. Whatever routines and personnel with relevant expertise or responsibilities an institution has might assist in data collection.
4. Develop or select the measure(s) before initiating the faculty learning community so that you can assess baseline performance. In our case, we created the measure in the first year of the project and so were unable to completely capture baseline data. In addition, because our project built from previous work from individuals and small groups within the teacher education faculty, the baseline was not as clear in our case.
5. If possible, gain permission to identify students (e.g., through a student ID number) to allow for enhanced data-collection and data-analysis possibilities. Specifically, by linking surveys to individual students, it will be possible to follow up with any students who may not have completed a survey at a given time point. It will also allow for additional analytic possibilities such as individual growth modeling and the ability to control for prior status in determining program impact.
6. Administer the measure(s) repeatedly—at least pre/post for each cohort, and across multiple cohorts, to be able to gauge long-term effects. As we've demonstrated in this chapter, the ability to track cohort changes over time and changes across cohorts at the same time

point is extremely important because it provides compelling information about the potential effects of the project.

Taken together, following these recommendations will increase the likelihood of being able to capture project-level outcomes in a systematic way. This information is useful from a practical standpoint because it provides insight and guidance for further work. It also has relevance from a scholarly perspective because it provides useful data for publication, accreditation, and seeking extramural funding to support the work of teacher education reform.

REFERENCES

Allen, M. J., & Yen, W. M. (2001). *Introduction to measurement theory.* Long Grove, IL: Waveland Press.
Bandura, A. (1977). Self-efficacy: Toward a unifying theory of behaviorial change. *Psychological Review, 84*(2), 191–215.
Batalova, J., & McHugh, M. (2010). *Top languages spoken by English language learners nationally and by state.* Washington, DC: Migration Policy Institute.
Comrey, A. L., & Lee, H. B. (1992). *A first course in factor analysis* (2nd ed.). Hillsdale, NJ: Lawrence Erlbaum Associates.
MacCallum, R. C., Widaman, K. F., Zhang, S., & Hong, S. (1999). Sample size in factor analysis. *Psychological Methods, 4*(1), 84–99.
McCoach, D. B., Gable, R. K., & Madura, J. P. (2013). *Instrument development in the affective domain: School and corporate applications.* New York: Springer.
National Center for Education Statistics. (2012). *Digest of education statistics.* Washington, DC: Institute of Education Sciences, U.S. Department of Education. Retrieved March 14, 2014 from https://nces.ed.gov/programs/digest/d12/tables/dt12_047.asp.

9 Instruction in Progress
In Search of Effective Practices for Emergent Bilinguals

Cory Wright-Maley, Thomas H. Levine, and Eileen M. González

THE OVERARCHING CHALLENGE

Does what we do in our teacher education coursework result in preservice teachers enacting effective practices for emergent bilinguals when they are with K-12 students? How can we collect data that tell us whether preservice teachers are able to implement effective practices for emergent bilinguals? Further, how can we learn more about preservice teachers' self-perceptions of their progress and challenges working with emergent bilinguals?

While these questions cut to the core of our work in Project PREPARE-ELLs, they also comprise a larger challenge for teacher education in general. Teacher training programs often frontload preservice teachers with access to learning theory, discussions about pedagogies, readings about classroom management, and similar content, hoping that preservice teachers will later be able to apply what they learned in clinical settings (Grossman et al., 2009). Some people believe that "teacher education is a weak intervention" (Feiman-Nemser, 1990, p. 229) whose effects get "washed out by school experience" (Zeichner & Tabachnik, 1981, p. 7), thus preventing many new teachers from implementing the research-based approaches championed in the academy (see also Ballantyne, 2007; Levine, 2011; Wideen, Mayer-Smith, & Moon, 1998).

Reform-oriented pedagogies and approaches to teaching may create additional classroom organization and management hurdles (Kaufman & Moss, 2010) and thus may present extra obstacles—or disincentives—to enactment by new teachers. This doesn't mean that teacher education should prepare teachers for simpler methods of conveying content and controlling classrooms. It does suggest to us that teacher education programs that are serious about empowering ambitious practice must identify methods of determining whether their more ambitious aims translate into enacted practice; they should also explore the facilitators of and obstacles to enactment. In this chapter, we address this need. We describe methods that we used in one of our programs—the three-year Integrated Bachelor's/Master's (IBM) teacher education program—to go beyond self-reported data to see how preparation for work with emergent bilinguals was translating into observable practice in clinical settings. We describe the methods we used to learn what preservice teachers were doing and experiencing while teaching emergent bilinguals, what struggles they were having, and what suggestions they had for us. We proceed to illustrate the kind of things such methods revealed about our work, organizing our findings under the following question: What practices do preservice teachers currently use with emergent bilinguals? What did preservice teachers find challenging? What do preservice teachers recommend we do differently to help future preservice teachers?

In the case of our IBM program, our data showed us that most of our teachers were able to implement some features of instruction that help emergent bilinguals; data also helped us see where we need to do more, including in the area of the linguistic demands of classroom tasks and the kind of linguistic supports most likely to help emergent bilinguals. There appeared to be overall improvement from the first to second year, particularly with using language objectives. Our preservice teachers' suggestions about improving our program would likely benefit others as well. In summary, the kinds of data collection we propose—and other methods we note in our closing recommendations—can inform the ongoing work of teacher education, providing a feedback loop to guide instructors' ongoing efforts. Our closing recommendations include ideas for programs with limited resources for data collection.

METHODS OF COLLECTING DATA REGARDING PRESERVICE TEACHERS' WORK WITH EMERGENT BILINGUALS

As we set out to improve teacher preparation for emergent bilinguals, we wanted to know what our preservice teachers were and were not actually doing with their emergent bilingual students. We have repeatedly administered TELLSES surveys, as described in Chapter 8, to explore whether our cohorts of future teachers attain self-efficacy for teaching emergent bilinguals during their time in the program, and whether the patterns of mean change for each cohort vary across years as we have made ongoing programmatic changes. Conceptions and intentions that preservice teachers have about their practices, however, do not always translate into actual practice (Bryan, 2003; van Hover & Yeager, 2003). Thus, as we were constructing our project, we designed methods to capture actual practice through observations paired with debriefing interviews to gain insight into the lived experiences of our student teachers. We hoped that through this design, we would be better able to capture what our preservice teachers knew and were able to do, as well as why they engaged with their students as they did. We also sought their feedback about what they found challenging, and what more they wished we would do before student teaching to prepare them for work with emergent bilinguals.

THE CHALLENGE OF RECRUITING VULNERABLE PRESERVICE TEACHERS

To initiate recruitment, as preservice teachers completed TELLSES surveys before student teaching, we sought volunteers to participate in one interview and one observation of their student teaching. We knew that we would be asking permission to view student teachers at a time when they lack confidence (i.e., their first full-time and sustained teaching in schools). Thus, we emphasized that we would be asking preservice teachers to assess our efforts to prepare them rather than judging their teaching, appealed to participants' idealism by explaining how their help would improve our program for future preservice teachers, and offered participants' a modest $20 Amazon gift card. We did not find it easy to reach our goal of two volunteers in each of the secondary subject areas and three in elementary education.

When there were not enough initial volunteers, we sent out an email invitation to the preservice teachers who were in placements with high numbers of emergent bilinguals. To avoid undue influence on preservice teachers whom we would observe and interview, faculty members who served as advisors and/or methods instructors did not directly recruit preservice teachers or know who had agreed to participate. In each of the first two years of data collection, we were able to recruit 11 preservice teachers from across multiple disciplines, including special education, elementary education, secondary English, math, science, and social studies (see Table 9.1).

We faced two challenges that are likely to affect other programs doing similar work. First, we wanted to observe preservice teachers who actually had emergent bilinguals in their classes to get a more accurate picture of what our preservice teachers now could do when working with these students. Three of our six partner school districts for the IBM program lacked substantial emergent bilingual populations. Thus, a number of our preservice teachers who were willing to participate turned out to be ineligible. Second, preservice teachers often lack the confidence to have a person they

Table 9.1 Preservice Teachers' Disciplinary Backgrounds by Cohort

Discipline	2011	2012
Special Education	1	1
Elementary Education	3	3
English	1	1
Math	2	2
Science	2	2
Social Studies	2	2
Total	11	11

do not know come into their classrooms to evaluate their teaching practices. Student teachers are already observed and evaluated by a university-based supervisor six times during the semester, and some also get a visit from their faculty advisor or a coordinator linking the partner district and our university. Asking self-conscious and vulnerable novices being judged by others to endure one more observation could be a barrier to participation. We re-visit recommendations for others interested in collecting data from potentially self-conscious novice teachers at the end of this chapter.

Seeking Evidence of Observable Practice in Student Teaching

Clinical Observations

We observed each of the student teachers during one class period (or lesson in the case of the elementary teachers). These preservice teachers knew the day when we would watch them and interview them. Thus, teachers knew in advance that we would be observing their teaching of emergent bilinguals and that they should provide a lesson plan in advance of the observation. Because preservice teachers knew the focus, it is possible that they made some extra effort to use what they had learned regarding emergent bilinguals. We understood that these observations might not capture everyday practice, but we do believe this approach lets us talk about what our preservice teachers are capable of doing for emergent bilinguals. Each of the teachers had at least one emergent bilingual in the class we observed. Most worked in the urban districts that partner with our program.

Instrument for Observations

To guide our observations, we used the Sheltered Instruction Observational Protocol (SIOP), a research-based instrument comprising 30 instructional features that have been shown to help emergent bilinguals learn academic content and develop language and literacy skills (Echevarria, Vogt, & Short, 2012). The observer took extensive field notes on SIOP checklists denoting the presence or absence of the 30 SIOP features of instruction. He also took notes describing practices, activities, or materials relevant to any of the features. We chose to use the SIOP to guide our classroom observations for three reasons. First, as already noted, it is a research-based instrument that was developed through a rigorous research process (Short & Echevarria, 1999) and has been used for more than a decade in a variety of small- and large-scale research studies with emergent bilinguals and other students (e.g., Echevarria, 2012; Echevarria & Short, 2004; Echevarria, Short, & Powers, 2006). Second, the SIOP is an instrument and instructional approach that Project PREPARE-ELLs members were all familiar with. As described in Chapter 3, we initiated our faculty learning community with a five-day summer in-service, four days of which consisted of intensive SIOP training with Deborah Short. Moreover, Project PREPARE-ELLs Co-Director Liz Howard is well versed in the measure and associated instructional approach, having worked with Deborah Short at the Center for Applied Linguistics at the time of its development and having developed an associated measure for dual language programs, the Two-Way Immersion Observation Protocol (TWIOP) (Howard, Sugarman, & Coburn, 2006). Finally, it is widely used in schools, including the urban PDCs in which our preservice teachers are placed, and therefore had the potential to be reinforced by mentor teachers.

Analysis of Observation Data

To enhance the trustworthiness of our data, we conducted three initial observations for the purpose of ensuring inter-rater reliability. Project personnel rated the observations independently of one another and then met with Liz Howard to discuss their observations and ratings and come to consensus about how to interpret various observed behaviors using the SIOP framework. Initially, we planned for a binary assessment to judge whether preservice teachers were incorporating each of the 30 SIOP features in a single instance of observed instruction. After discussions based on the three initial observations, we decided to create a third, or "emergent," category to capture preservice teachers who were partially meeting the SIOP criteria for a feature but clearly missing other elements. In this way we depart from the SIOP; whereas its creators developed a much more fine-tuned scale for evaluating the degree to which various features of instruction are present and well implemented (Echevarria, Vogt, & Short, 2012), we simplified our ratings to this three-point system.

Seeking Preservice Teachers' Explanations and Insights

We also wanted to understand how our student teachers viewed their experiences of working with emergent bilinguals and hear their feedback about what more teacher educators could be doing to support them. We also knew that limiting our observations to the SIOP and observing each teacher only once might lead us to overlook important strategies that teachers use. To augment what we could see preservice teachers doing during a single visit, we conducted follow-up interviews with preservice teachers on the same day as an observation; when possible, interviews took place immediately following the class period or lesson observed.

Interview Protocol

We used an interview protocol to debrief our teachers (see the appendix). The interview was broken into three sections. First, we asked questions related to teachers' general practices and perspectives related to emergent bilinguals.

Second, we asked questions related to the lesson we observed. Third, we asked preservice teachers to reflect on their experiences working with emergent bilinguals. Each interview took approximately 30 minutes and was audio recorded with the permission of the preservice teachers. At the end of the interview, the recording device was turned off, and participants were asked whether teachers had any questions or concerns. If preservice teachers asked for feedback, constructive feedback was provided. Part of our recruitment strategy was to minimize our preservice teachers' feelings that they were being judged; thus, feedback was not provided unless requested.

Data Analysis

We conducted deductive and inductive analyses of the data. To do so we utilized a structural approach to coding, using the interview questions as primary categories with which to organize data (MacQueen, McLellan-Lemal, Bartholow, & Milstein, 2008, cited in Saldaña, 2009). Within these question-based categories, we utilized open coding in order to identify the salient features of our preservice teachers' experiences (Merriam, 2009). After we had completed our deductive analysis, we returned to the transcripts using open coding to allow for the emergence of items that may not have directly addressed the interview questions.

FINDINGS

What Practices Do Student Teachers Currently Use with Emergent Bilinguals?

The nature of information we have collected is from a small number of preservice teachers in one specific program. We recognize that findings from our specific program may or may not generalize to any other cases (Yin, 1994); we offer findings to illustrate the value of collecting these kinds of data while seeking to improve teacher preparation for linguistic diversity and invite readers to consider whether the insights we uncovered might apply in their contexts. To get as robust a view of patterns as our small numbers permit, we aggregate observations across two years and all program areas, although we'll later pull out several findings that resulted from looking at sub-groups within the sample. We believe that this approach to data collection is most useful for illuminating a snapshot of practice, and we have relied on our surveys (see Chapter 8) for a more comprehensive view of project impact.

Findings from Clinical Observations

Our observations using the SIOP protocol give evidence that our teachers are able to implement some features of instruction that help emergent bilinguals and show us that there is more to be done. While some individual methods instructors had been incorporating changes related to emergent bilinguals into their courses for many years (see Chapter 3), the 2011 cohort was the first group of preservice teachers to receive systematically infused methods and clinical instruction that was influenced by large-scale faculty participation in the Project PREPARE-ELLs faculty learning community. This cohort of preservice teachers did not experience the newly infused material in junior-year courses that were starting up as these preservice teachers were seniors. Tables 9.2 and 9.3 show the frequency of enactment for the most and least frequently enacted SIOP features. These kinds of data are particularly helpful for identifying practices that we may seek to emphasize within courses or feedback on students' written work and clinical practice.

Features of Instruction That Many Teachers Use

Our preservice teachers demonstrated an ability to use some practices that support emergent bilinguals (Table 9.2). At least 17 of 22 preservice teachers—more than three quarters—fully implemented the following SIOP features, which we note in terms of their name and their order in the protocol itself: age appropriate concepts (SIOP 3, or the third of the 30 features), a variety of techniques (SIOP 12); scaffolding (SIOP 14); applying knowledge and language in the classroom (SIOP 21); conducting assessments (SIOP 30). As shown in the table, there were three more features where 16 of 22

Table 9.2 Most Frequently Enacted SIOP Features

STOP Number	STOP Feature	Full Enactment	Partial Enactment
3	Content concepts appropriate for age and educational background level of students	22	0
30	Conducts assessment of student comprehension and learning of all lesson objectives	19	5
12	Uses a variety of techniques to make content concepts clear	17	5
14	Consistent use of scaffolding techniques throughout the lesson, assisting and supporting student understanding	17	4
21	Provides activities for students to apply content and language knowledge in the classroom	17	4

Note: SIOP feature descriptors are taken from the Sheltered Observational Protocol (see Echevarria, Vogt, & Short [2004], pp. 187–195).

preservice teachers fully implemented the feature: opportunities for interaction (SIOP 16); integrated language activities (SIOP 22); and feedback to students (SIOP 29). (We use labels based upon SIOP categories, but to get the exact names and fuller definitions of these SIOP features, refer to Echevarria, Vogt, & Short, 2004.)

Less often implemented features of instruction. Our observation of preservice teachers also revealed that there are SIOP features of instruction that they don't often use to support emergent bilinguals (Table 9.3). Five of the seven least frequent practices relate to supporting language development and comprehension: encouraging students to clarify concepts in their first language (SIOP 19); encouraging the use of language objectives not only in lesson plans, but as things to be visually displayed *and* orally reviewed during the lesson itself (SIOP 2); designing lessons that support the language objectives (SIOP 24); incorporating comprehensive review of vocabulary (SIOP 27) and content concepts (SIOP 28) at the end of lessons.

These data suggest that we need to do even more to help our preservice teachers understand the linguistic demands of learning content and building academic English. It is also possible that secondary teachers do not see themselves as teachers of language; all but one of the elementary participants were in the top third of participating student teachers in terms of their implementation of SIOP features.

Of the seven least frequent areas, the other two are reviewing already-introduced content concepts (SIOP 28) and in-class use of content objectives (SIOP 1). Our teachers specify content objectives in lesson plans, and 15 actually had written language objectives (SIOP 2) into lesson plans; however, we didn't count the mere appearance of objectives in lesson plans as

Table 9.3 Least Frequently Enacted SIOP Features

SIOP Number	SIOP Feature	Full Enactment	Partial Enactment
1	Clearly defined content objectives for students	4	10
19	Ample opportunities for students to clarify key concepts in L1 as needed with aide, peer, or L1 text	5	3
2	Clearly defined language objectives for students	2	7
27	Comprehensive review of key vocabulary	3	1
28	Comprehensive review of key content concepts	2	3

Note: SIOP feature descriptors are taken from the Sheltered Observational Protocol(see Echevarria, Vogt, & Short [2004], pp. 187–195).

even partial enactment. SIOP expects content objectives to also show up in instruction when teachers both visually display and orally review them.

The use of language objectives was the only SIOP feature that was not fully enacted by any participant in the first year of the study. The first year, language objectives were only partially enacted by two participants. Language objectives—which require teachers to target and develop language while teaching academic content—are a hallmark of the SIOP. Our 40 hour summer institute prior to our first year of implementation helped all teacher educators learn about this important practice for supporting language development and scaffolding learning of rigorous academic content. In our first year of systematically teaching about language objectives in methods courses—which was also our first year of observing student teachers—we found that five of eleven student teachers put language objectives into written lesson plans. This suggests that we were having some impact; nevertheless, we were discouraged that none of the eleven student teachers shared these objectives aloud, and only two posted them on the board with the content objectives. Again, full implementation of this SIOP standard requires sharing language objectives visually and orally calling students attention to them. As a result of this data collection, instructors redoubled their efforts to emphasize the use of language objectives. We then saw the biggest gain in implementation of a single SIOP feature that we observed in our participants from one year to the next. The number of students fully or partially implementing language objectives more than tripled from the first cohort. Of eleven preservice teachers observed during the second year, two fully implemented language objectives and five partially implemented them.

Student Teachers' Perceptions of their Practices with Emergent Bilinguals

When we invited our preservice teachers to describe their general practices to support emergent bilinguals in the classroom, our preservice teachers described using strategies that align with many of the areas where we observed the greatest levels of acceptable proficiency in SIOP features, suggesting to us that our use of the SIOP protocol to collect data about preservice teacher practice did not miss some approach used by many teachers that did not appear on the SIOP.

Student teachers' self-reported patterns of practice. Our preservice teachers see themselves employing a variety of techniques in their practice in order to help emergent bilinguals. There is, however, a wide variation among teachers. Collectively, the 22 preservice teachers identified the use of 29 different strategies, but only five of these strategies were highlighted by half or more of the interviewees as strategies they employed regularly (see Table 9.4. Note that we intentionally sought out candidates' self-descriptions of strategies—rather than use the SIOP in particular—so that we might capture how our future teachers see their own work and so that we could see if there were important approaches we had missed with our explicit focus on the SIOP.

Table 9.4 Student Teachers' Self-Described Strategies for Working with Emergent Bilinguals, 2011 and 2012

Strategies Reported by a Majority of Preservice Teachers	Number of Preservice Teachers Who Stated That They Use This Strategy (n = 22)
Use of visuals	18
Scaffolding	16
Vocabulary-based strategies and supports	14
Checking in with emergent bilinguals during or after class to ensure they understood the instructions and content	13
Encouraging students to use multiple forms of language (reading, writing, speaking, and listening)	12

First among these five strategies was the use of visuals, which was cited most frequently (40% more often than the next most common strategy) and by the greatest number of teachers (18 individuals). The salience of using visuals suggests a jumping-off point for further development of our teachers. We find it helpful to consider whether and how preservice teachers' self-identified approaches map onto the SIOP, the framework we had been trained in and introduced to preservice teachers. Visuals could correspond with—or be part of—three SIOP categories, but it is not clear that teachers yet see its import as a necessary part of developing supplementary materials (SIOP 4), as employing a variety of techniques during instruction (SIOP 13), and as scaffolding (SIOP 15). These data invite us to understand what visuals mean to preservice teachers and whether our preservice teachers' use of them deepens over time. In other words, we now must aim to have preservice teachers introduce visuals and build on them in ways deeply supportive of learning content and language learning rather than just throwing one more picture or diagram somewhere into a lesson. The salience of visuals—and the underlying student understanding of visual modes of learning—could also be a bridge to help students think about hands-on activities (SIOP 20), which only half of the student teachers implemented fully.

Scaffolding (related to SIOP 14) appeared in a number of forms, including the use of graphic organizers and similar supports such as Venn diagrams, guided notes, and sentence stems. Scaffolding was identified in interviews by 16 student teachers. In contrast to more limited attention to vocabulary that we observed, 14 student teachers explained that they used vocabulary-based activities or supports in their effort to support their emergent bilinguals (related to SIOP 9). Thirteen reported providing individual help to students by checking in with them during or after class to ensure they understood the instructions and content (related to SIOP 30); our in-class observations can not provide corroborating evidence of such efforts. Finally, 12 teachers described their use of activities that encouraged students to use multiple forms of language, such as reading, writing, speaking, and listening (related to SIOP 21 and SIOP 24; see Table 9.4). With the exception of preservice teachers' strategy of providing extra social attention to individual students, their self-reported strategies did not differ greatly from SIOP's features of instruction, giving us more faith that our observations were capturing patterns of instruction.

Perspectives on Students' Use of Their L1

Interview data can allow programs to ask about specific features they are promoting or struggling with in a given year. We chose to explore further our preservice teachers' experience of emergent bilinguals using their first language, or L1, in class, which turns out to be a feature that the majority of our preservice teachers don't yet promote in their own instruction.

Of our student teachers, 18 of 22 reported that they noticed students' use of their L1 in the classroom, and of those, 14 reported that they were comfortable with students' use of their first language. Four noted some ambivalence or confusion, and one stated that she did not feel comfortable when students spoke in their L1. In addition to noticing the use of other languages in their classrooms, 11 of the teachers reported using emergent bilinguals' L1s in some way as a means to help support their understanding of the content (SIOP 19). Four student teachers told us that they incorporated Spanish to make comparisons or clarify student understanding, but even this number seems low given what we know of the desirability of using students' L1 to help students learn content (August & Shanahan, 2006; Echevarria, Vogt, & Short, 2004; Goldenberg & Coleman, 2010). This finding may speak to the need to expand preservice teachers' access to other languages, including a Spanish-for-Educators course, extending student abroad/teaching internships in countries where high-frequency languages are spoken, or providing opportunities for summer language retreats (see Chapter 8 for more data and discussion of having preservice teachers learn a second language). This finding suggests the need to value students' first language and develop means to help students use that language regardless of whether teachers themselves speak the first language(s) of their students.

What Did Teachers Find Challenging?

Communication with Emergent Bilinguals

Our student teachers described a number of challenges in their efforts to better serve emergent bilinguals. Perhaps not surprisingly given the low incidence of observed native language support, communication with emergent bilinguals and their families was rated as the top concern. Ten of our student teachers expressed that they have difficulty at times communicating with students because of a language barrier that exists between them. Teachers perceived such a barrier when they discussed their inability to understand what the student is saying, to discern whether the student understands the content, or to clarify their instructions in a different way if students do not initially understand. Given that a plurality of preservice teachers felt this way, emphasizing the SIOP features that address this—and making the link to communication—could help preservice teachers, including multiple methods for clarifying tasks, building background, and providing comprehensible input.

Preservice teachers may also need encouragement to make additional efforts to communicate with their students during or after class, perhaps using additional supports or methods. To the extent that our preservice teachers—and others in similar programs—experience communication with emergent bilinguals as challenging, we suspect there is a larger opportunity. Preservice teachers' brief experiences of discomfort communicating with emergent bilinguals could be framed to help them consider emergent bilinguals' experience of communication with teachers. Emergent bilinguals are negotiating almost all of their interactions with peers and students in their second language; thus, the presence of preservice teacher discomfort may provide us with an entry point for increased empathy and insight about emergent bilinguals. These data also suggest the need to make preservice teachers more at ease with the discomfort of communicating across first languages, and to learn the kinds of scaffolding and other techniques that promote communication regarding academic content and tasks.

Making Content Accessible for Emergent Bilinguals

Eight preservice teachers (both elementary and secondary) explained that they had difficulty making the content accessible, whether through differentiation, finding appropriate materials, or anticipating the extent of their emergent bilinguals' background knowledge. Again, providing our preservice teachers with the ability to reduce the ambiguity of their assignments and tasks could help with this. We could also help our teachers to develop better assessments to identify emergent bilinguals' needs, strengths, extant knowledge, and progress (see Chapter 6 for one approach to developing teachers' ability to know their emergent bilinguals as learners). Such assessments would also help them differentiate and identify additional background knowledge they need to build. Five of our preservice teachers described assessment as an area where they needed more support.

Engaging Emergent Bilinguals

Seven preservice teachers found it challenging to engage their students. These teachers attribute the challenge to students lacking motivation and/or self-efficacy, appearing exhausted, or seeming distracted by issues not connected to the classroom. Five of the seven preservice teachers who described this challenge articulated their concern that additional factors compound the difficulties emergent bilinguals have in learning the content, such as psychosocial issues, students' perceptions of the preservice teachers' background (i.e., the impact of the teachers' race on students' willingness to engage), and their own difficulty in understanding what it's like to be an emergent bilingual.

These data show us that at a programmatic level, our preservice teachers need to better understand the complexities of teaching emergent bilinguals, including the ways in which schools may create cultural mismatches and miscommunication that teachers may not see but that may contribute to teacher perceptions of "lack of engagement" (see Trumbull, Rothstein-Fisch, Greenfield, & Quiroz, 2001; Valdés, 1996). Individual methods instructors have begun to make progress on these areas (see Chapters 6 and 11). Preservice teachers would also benefit from learning more about the kinds of life experience, opportunities, and challenges that emergent bilinguals experience. More opportunities for them to connect to—or experience glimpses of—emergent bilinguals' experiences may further bolster their understanding of emergent bilinguals and how to support them.

What Do Preservice Teachers Recommend We Do Differently?

We invited preservice teachers to tell us what they wished their teacher education courses would do for them to help them with their challenges, and what advice they would give their instructors for improving instructors' teaching around emergent bilinguals in the future. The majority of our preservice teachers' suggestions fell into two broad categories: programmatic improvement and applying their learning.

Suggestions for Programmatic Improvement

Most of the suggestions preservice teachers made regarding how teacher educators could improve our professional practice fall into two main categories: more instruction related to emergent bilinguals (21 suggestions), and opportunities to apply learning about such instruction or see it enacted (14 suggestions).

Of the 21 suggestions asking for more instruction, 13 wanted more strategies that they can use to teach emergent bilinguals. Even before we began our project, we experienced the call for practical and immediately usable strategies as being so common among preservice teachers that it might be considered a professional anthem. Our preservice teachers will see more of these strategies in their masters year—after student teaching—when they take at least one required "diversity" elective course. As we continue seeking ways to infuse teaching into some courses yet untouched in our program, there may be other places where we can more explicitly convey theory or content we deem critical in combination with related practices teachers hunger for. For example, we have succeeded in getting a required course focused on educational linguistics into the current draft of a reformed course sequence for our program.

Several other suggestions offered by teachers can inform our larger program reform and suggest the value of collecting such data. First, 11 interviewees suggest more instructional time dedicated specifically to teaching about emergent bilinguals. Five of these preservice teachers want courses that specifically address teaching second language learners. Again, these student teachers, in our current course configuration, will choose one of several diversity electives. During the school year after this interview, our interviewees will choose from a list of required "diversity" courses. Some will take a course that focuses on emergent bilinguals, but many preservice teachers take a multicultural education course that devotes only one class session to the topic of linguistic diversity. Connected to this point is the suggestion of two preservice teachers that the School of Education require teachers to have second language training. Invariably, those preservice teachers who spoke with some fluency in another language, particularly in Spanish, described this ability as a strength. The teacher education faculty has also authorized an optional Spanish for teachers course, although to date staffing issues have prevented it from being offered.

Suggestions for Applying Their Learning

Fourteen preservice teachers indicated that they want more opportunities to apply or practice what they have learned about the kinds of teaching that support emergent bilinguals' learning. That is, they felt a lot of instruction was too abstract for them to know how to apply effectively in their own classrooms. For some preservice teachers, there should be a greater emphasis on how to apply the theoretical concepts in practice.

Preservice teachers' suggestions for bridging theory and practice fell into two categories: exposing preservice teachers to emergent bilinguals and the experiences of emergent bilinguals, and instructors' articulation of first-hand experiences when teaching emergent bilinguals. To provide an example of what preservice teachers found useful and wanted more of, eight preservice teachers highlighted modeling instruction. Specifically, they recalled participating in language-shock immersion activities, which put preservice teachers into the role of English language learners (ELLs); in these activities, preservice teachers are taught in another language (in one case it was Spanish, and in another it was Swedish) and got a glimpse of what it may be like to be an emergent bilingual. These lessons conclude with a scaffolded learning activity which demonstrated the effectiveness of the SIOP strategies that were the focus of our observations. Preservice teachers described these activities as useful for understanding the challenges and frustrations emergent bilinguals face, as well as how much the use of the SIOP strategies can impact their ability to understand even when language remains a barrier.

Preservice teachers also discussed the possibility of using videos in which expert teachers conducted a lesson for a class of emergent bilinguals. In this way, preservice teachers could be guided through the video while the instructor conducted a play-by-play deconstruction of the pedagogical practices present in the video. Further, preservice teachers mentioned they would appreciate opportunities to practice these techniques. Such practice could take place in the form of in-class mini-lessons, case studies, or problem scenarios, which could, in turn, be critiqued by the class. Finally, three preservice teachers admitted that, given their limited exposure to emergent bilinguals, having opportunities to interact with and learn from with emergent bilinguals would help them to better serve these students.

Summary of Room for Growth

We have found a close congruence between our preservice teachers' self-identified challenges and the suggestions they have for us as we consider program improvements. Preservice teachers want more focused attention on the needs of emergent bilinguals, experiences that enable them to better understand the needs of these students, and diverse opportunities to practice and apply what they have learned before entering student teaching. Our preservice teachers' calls for more strategies are not unexpected, but they dovetail with what our observations show: our current work in university-based courses still leaves preservice teachers with some blind spots as they are developing their practices with emergent bilinguals.

RECOMMENDATIONS

Data Collection in Programs with Limited Resources

Although we have illustrated the value of collecting observational and interview data in this chapter, we recognize that large and small teacher education programs typically service significant numbers of preservice teachers compared with their limited human and financial resources. Based on the value of gaining data about classroom practice and teachers' insights regarding their experiences and challenges, we propose these alternative means of data collection.

Supervisors

First, as faculty undergo training to improve what they know and can do relevant to emergent bilingual instruction, it would be desirable to include university supervisors so they can discuss and support this work in the field. To the extent that university supervisors know what to look for and have observation forms that can capture relevant data, supervisors may be able to collect data that inform a program of problems and progress; during debriefing of their visits to see student teachers, supervisors may also be able to collect brief insights about student teachers' progress and challenges while working with emergent bilinguals also. Using a variety of observers could raise issues of reliability, but it would also help expand the number of people student teachers hear emphasizing these practices. Supervisors are often retired teachers who get limited professional development (Levine, 2011). Programs would benefit from training supervisors regarding effective instruction for emergent bilinguals if they expect such professionals to also collect data; that training would also help supervisors to support student teachers' work implementing such instruction. See Chapter 7 regarding our nascent efforts to help supervisors learn about emergent bilinguals.

Student Teacher Self-Report

Second, student teachers could be required to self-report the frequency of specific practices they have used in their teaching. Retrospective self-reporting will not be as accurate as observation in representing actual practices. Nevertheless, if the same checklist were used over time and required teachers to indicate how many of the listed features of instruction occurred during their first period or class that day, it could create sufficiently comparable data across teachers and cohorts to inform programs about change over time and could generate enough data to do more interesting statistical analyses.

We would be interested to know how cohort year, subject area, placement in urban or suburban districts, and numbers of emergent bilinguals contribute to implementation of whatever kinds of instruction a program promotes, and we wonder whether any of these factors interact in unexpected ways. Finally, systematically looking for practices within student teaching lesson plans may allow programs to glimpse salient features of their preservice teacher practices.

Collect Baseline Data

Another challenge is to be able to see whether teacher educators' infusion of new material leads to changes in teaching practices of our preservice teachers over time. Regardless of what scheme of data collection programs adopt, they would ideally begin all forms of data collection before implementing changes. In our case, doing so would have enabled us to better appraise the outcomes of our efforts.

Be Sensitive When Working with Vulnerable Student Teachers

Because preservice teachers may be reticent to share their teaching practices, it may be difficult to recruit from this population. After two challenging years, we have developed a number of suggestions that may help with recruiting student teachers. First, choose an observer who is well known and well regarded by the majority of preservice teachers. Second, appeal to the mission of the project in a way that emphasizes the opportunity to improve the current program for future preservice teachers, an effort that they could add to their resume. Third, emphasize and guarantee participating preservice teachers the unique opportunity—if they choose this—to receive mentoring support specific to practices that support emergent bilinguals. This emphasis should be coupled with a strong effort to assuage concerns that this is an evaluation of their teaching practices that could be used against them.

CONCLUSION: THE VALUE OF DATA COLLECTION

We believe that the work of preparing teachers for emergent bilinguals will be much more powerful if it is informed by data that reveal what teachers actually do and experience while working in classrooms.

The ultimate aim of adopting a new focus—such as emergent bilinguals—within a teacher education programs is to impact observable practice. This is no simple matter, but falling short of such impact risks playing into the common criticism of teacher education (i.e., that it doesn't prepare preservice teachers to actually teach in real contexts). As teacher educators improve their own practice, such data are likely to reveal a mixed picture of progress and gaps. These data can clarify next steps for entire programs. Chapter 11 will clarify how data from student teachers can also be collected and used by individual instructors. Even the acts of identifying what to assess and making sense of data can prove educative regarding what matters and what counts as effective practice for emergent bilinguals. Finally, such data will support requests for additional program requirements, elective courses, faculty, study-abroad opportunities, professional development, and other resources to improve teacher preparation for work with emergent bilinguals.

APPENDIX

Project Prepare-ELLs Preservice Teacher Post-Observation Interview Protocol

Thank you for inviting me into your room today. It can be hard to have people observe your teaching. I'm going to ask you to talk to me about your lesson today, and will be focusing specifically on how the lesson applies to English language learners. I know that working effectively with emergent bilingual students is an advanced skill, even one that I struggle with, so it is not my intention to judge you according to what you say today. The methods instructors who are involved in this project also recognize that they are just beginning to learn how to help you work with emergent bilingual students effectively, so your candid answers really help their learning about what is working, what they need to improve, as well as what needs you might have that they may not have anticipated. I'm here to help them to learn from you.

I. We'll talk specifically about this lesson in a moment, but I would like to ask you a few more general questions first.
   1. How are you working with English language learners in your classroom?
   2. Did anything in your teacher education coursework help to support your work with emergent bilinguals?
   3. What struggles or dilemmas are you facing in your work with emergent bilinguals?
   4. What do you wish your courses were doing that could help you with these difficulties?
   5. Now that you're in the field, what advice would you have for methods instructors as they prepare to work with other preservice teachers next year?
II. I'd like to ask you a few questions now that are focused specifically on today's lesson.
   6. While designing this lesson, what did you think about that would help emergent bilinguals learn? Please also tell me why you made each of these choices.
   7. How did the lesson go?
      a. If there are some aspects that didn't go as planned ask, why do you think this did not work as you thought it would?
   8. If you had a chance to teach this lesson another time, is there anything you would choose to do differently?
   9. During this lesson, were there any moments when you noticed that emergent bilingual students were able to clarify concepts in their first language?
   10. Is there anything you'd like me to know about your work with emergent bilinguals today that I didn't ask you about?
III. I'd like to ask you a few questions now that give you the opportunity to reflect on your practice up to this point, again in a more general way.
   11. What are three words that describe how you feel about your work with emergent bilinguals?
   12. How confident do you feel about your ability to work effectively with emergent bilinguals?
      a. What, if anything, has made you more or less confident in yourself?
   13. What are your strengths when it comes to working with emergent bilinguals?
      a. Clarify: (In other words, what do you think you're doing well?)

REFERENCES

August, D., & Shanahan, T. (Eds.). (2006). *Developing literacy in second-language learners: Report of the national literacy panel on language-minority children and youth.* Mahwah, NJ: Lawrence Erlbaum Associates.

Ballantyne, J. (2007b). Integration, contextualization and continuity: Three themes for the development of effective music teacher education programmes. *International Journal of Music Education, 25*(2), 119–136. Retrieved from ERIC database.

Bryan, L. A. (2003). Nestedness of beliefs: Examining a prospective elementary teacher's belief system about science teaching and learning. *Journal of Research in Science Teaching, 40*(9), 835–868.

Echevarria, J. & Short, D. (2004). Using Multiple Perspectives in Observations of Diverse Classrooms: The Sheltered Instruction Observation Protocol (SIOP), In H. Waxman, R. Tharp & S. Hilberg (Eds.). *Observational Research in U.S. Classrooms: New Approaches for Understanding Cultural and Linguistic Diversity* (pp. 21–47). Boston: Cambridge University Press.

Echevarria, J., Short, D., & Powers, K. (2006). School reform and standards-based education: A model for English-Language Learners. *Journal of Educational Research, 99*(4), 195–210.

Echevarria, J., Vogt, M. E., & Short, D. (2004). *Making content comprehensible for English learners: The SIOP model* (2nd ed.). Boston, MA: Pearson Allyn & Bacon.

Feiman-Nemser, S. (1990). Teacher preparation: Structural and conceptual alternatives. In W. Robert Houston (Ed.), *Handbook of research on teacher education* (pp. 212–223). New York: Macmillan.

Goldenberg, C., & Coleman, R. (2010). *Promoting academic achievement among English learners: A guide to the research.* Thousand Oaks, CA: Corwin Press.

Grossman, P., Compton, C., Igra, D., Ronfeldt, M., Shahan, E., & Williamson, P. (2009). Teaching practice: A cross-professional perspective. *Teachers College Record, 111*(9).

Howard, E. R., Sugarman, J., & Coburn, C. (2006). *Adapting the Sheltered Instruction Observation Protocol (SIOP) for two-way immersion education: An introduction to the TWIOP.* Washington, DC: Center for Applied Linguistics.

Kaufman, D., & Moss, D. M. (2010). A new look at pre-service teachers' conceptions of classroom management and organization: Uncovering complexity and dissonance. *The Teacher Educator. 45*(2), 118–136.

Levine, T. H. (2011). Features and strategies of supervisor professional community as a means of improving the supervision of preservice teachers. *Teaching and Teacher Education, 27,* 930–941.

MacQueen, K. M., McLellan-Lemal, E., Bartholow, K., & Milstein, B. (2008). Team-based codebook development: Structure, process, and agreement. In G. Guest & K. M. MacQueen, (Eds.), *Handbook for team-based qualitative research* (pp. 119–135) Lanham, MD: Altamira Press.

Merriam, S. B. (2009). *Qualitative research: A guide to design and implementation.* San Francisco, CA: Jossey-Bass.

Saldaña, J. (2009). *The coding manual for qualitative researchers.* Thousand Oaks, CA: Sage.

Short, D., & Echevarria, J. (1999). *The sheltered instruction observation protocol: A tool for teacher-researcher collaboration and professional development.* Educational Practice Report No. 3. Santa Cruz, CA; Washington, DC: Center for Research on Education, Diversity & Excellence. Retrieved March 14, 2014 from http://www.cal.org/crede/pdfs/epr3.pdf

Trumbull, E., Rothstein-Fisch, C., Greenfield, P. M., & Quiroz, B. (2001). *Bridging cultures between home and school: A guide for teachers*. Mahwah, NJ: Lawrence Erlbaum Associates.

Valdés, G. (1996). *Con respeto: Bridging the distances between culturally diverse families and schools: An ethnographic portrait*. New York: Teachers College Press.

van Hover, S. D., & Yeager, E. A. (2003). " 'Making' students better people?" A case study of a beginning history teacher. *International Social Studies Forum, 3*(1), 219–232.

Wideen, M., Mayer-Smith, J., & Moon, B. (1998). A critical analysis of the research on learning to teach: Making the case for an ecological perspective on inquiry. *Review of Educational Research, 68*(2), 130–178.

Yin, R. K. (1994). *Case study research: Design and methods* (2nd ed.). Thousand Oaks, CA: Sage.

Zeichner, K. M., & Tabachnik, B. R. (1981). Are the effects of university teacher education "washed out" by school experience? *Journal of Teacher Education, 32*(3) 7–11.

10 From Professional Learning to Professional Action and Back Again

Rachael Gabriel and Manuela Wagner

THE OVERARCHING CHALLENGE

As Goethe wrote, "knowing is not enough; we must apply" (Goethe, 1858, p 225), and yet the space between learning and doing is often wide. The challenge of moving from professional learning to professional action has often thwarted efforts at professional development and self-directed learning among professionals. In some ways, it is the classic problem of transferring new knowledge, skills, or dispositions into new domains: from collegial discussions to personal and collective action. Research on teacher professional development has often emphasized the need for professional learning to be collaborative, embedded, and aligned with other goals in order to address this problem of transfer from learning to action (Darling-Hammond & Richardson, 2009; Garet, Porter, Desimone, Birman, & Yoon, 2001), but the challenge for teacher educators is perhaps amplified by the solitary nature of our teaching endeavors. Although we have much in common as learners, scholars, and professionals, our sense of subject and disciplinary differences, combined with the ever-increasing demands on the profession, have often led us to walk different paths between what we learn together and what we do with that learning in our classes.

Overarching Question

In this chapter, we describe how teacher educators worked to address the challenge of working in a purposeful professional learning community moving from professional learning to professional action to ensure that our preservice teachers are prepared to engage with emergent bilinguals in schools. The overarching question we address is, "What inspires teacher education faculty to participate in a faculty learning community, and what actions result from their participation?"

Drawing on data gathered across the first two years of Project PREPARE-ELLs, we discuss the ways in which teacher educators have made meaning of their experiences in PREPARE-ELLs and how they have conceptualized the impacts of these experiences. We focus specifically on experiences and processes that participants identify in conversations and written memos regarding what they learned and how it impacted their practice.

METHODS

Using both first-hand accounts from oral interviews and written memos and minutes of PREPARE-ELLs meetings, we consider the role of opportunities for collaboration, student feedback, and individual reflection on the ways in which professional learning impacts professional action. Throughout the chapter, we discuss two different teacher education programs represented by faculty that participated in PREPARE-ELLs: the five-year Integrated Bachelor's/Master's program (IBM), and the one-year Teaching Certificate Program for College Graduates (TCPCG).

Data for the analyses presented in this chapter include: (a) 20 audio recordings and typed minutes of all monthly project PREPARE-ELLs meetings from the first two years of the project, (b) 23 verbatim transcripts of semi-structured interviews with members conducted during the project (interview protocol appears in this chapter's appendix), and (c) 17 end-of-year memos written by individual project members from the first two years of the project. Each faculty participant was asked to write an annual end-of-year memo in response to questions that asked for descriptions of changes in their learning and teaching, reflections on these changes, as well as their experience in project PREPARE-ELLs.

Our analysis began by creating an inventory of changes reported in end-of-year memos and interviews, and noting patterns in the type and reported inspiration for each change. We also considered the program placement and content area of each faculty member when working to identify patterns in the nature of reported changes. Once a pattern was initially identified, we engaged in repeated readings of the transcripts, minutes, and memos to confirm the pattern and identify outlying cases.

While engaging in iterative readings, we were also able explore discussions of intended changes that had not been made, and to consider the circumstances and knowledge that were reported to have resulted in limited changes in practice. From these instances of reported difficulty and resistance, we generated a set of themes related to the ways in which faculty made meaning of the implications of project PREPARE-ELLs for their practice. This set included points of tension as well as patterns of success in initiating and sustaining changes in practice designed to prepare preservice teachers to work with emergent bilinguals.

WHAT INSPIRED PROFESSIONAL LEARNING?

Within teacher education programs, faculty typically do not have shared research interests or abundant time for new projects. In addition, their status as experts can make it hard to ask large groups of faculty to shift into the role of learner. In this section, we identify factors that participants identified as important for inspiring their decision to engage in professional learning with colleagues regarding emergent bilinguals.

Student Data

In some cases, members reported that they were inspired to participate by data that indicated graduating preservice teachers felt underprepared to meet the needs of emergent bilinguals. An exit survey administered by the school of education showed a trend in feedback from graduates and alumni. As one teacher educator noted, "I found that data so compelling from our students [that I felt] morally obligated to do something with this area—that it's worth considering." Others added that they suspected a need for such work even before the data were made available, noting that, "for the last several years I've thought about English language learners as something that was important, and didn't really do much with it." This pre-project, shared point of entry was viewed as important to later changes:

> Let's call it pre-project in that I became utterly convinced of the utility and importance of the work. Most significant in that pre-project period was the data from our own graduates. I don't [want] to dismiss the importance of that buy-in to one's motivation and priority setting to participate in an effort that demands some level of ongoing commitment. I thought that was a necessary and important sort of orientation period.

Mentoring

After the summer institute in 2010 (see Chapter 3), all faculty members were assigned a mentor. In one case, three colleagues formalized a mentorship: one member shared expertise in bilingual education with two other instructors from different areas. This relationship was reported as valuable as the mentor provided subject-related examples that the other two teacher educators felt were missing from the summer workshop. It also set the scene for a "community of practice" (Lave & Wenger, 1991), a model that can be used to describe the general collaboration of PREPARE-ELLs members. One teacher educator's answer to the question of whether she feels like she is part of a learning community describes the "community sentiment" as follows:

> When we talk about practice and collaborating . . . people share pieces, I think that's where you can feel it. That's the intention that people are working to help other people with whatever questions they're bringing to the group. So I think that's important.

That emerging community of practice played a big part in developing and revising common goals for some. Mentors were not reported as important by a majority of faculty, and one teacher educator reported that separate small-group mentoring was not very helpful to him. Issues of fit may account for why some mentors inspired some mentees to deepen and apply their learning while others had less impact.

Peer Accountability

In addition to dyads or smaller groups working with a mentor, some members indicated that the reminder of monthly project PREPARE-ELLs meetings and the accountability of tracking and sharing actions and attempts facilitated a sustained effort that accumulated over time. As one member reported, "For me, I feel like the biggest thing about Project PREPARE-ELLs was pushing me personally and me accepting that I was really gonna . . . try some of this stuff out." Another colleague explained that Project PREPARE-ELLs impact can be summarized as:

> Well, the big picture impact is it's on my radar screen . . . not that I hadn't thought of it before, but I certainly wasn't really doing much about it. It was one of those topics that . . . at some point needs to be addressed.

In addition to connecting colleagues and helping them stay informed about each other's progress, the regularly scheduled Project PREPARE-ELLs meetings continuously punctuated a focused cycle of discussion, reflection, and action. This led to a general sense that these meetings contributed to Project PREPARE-ELLs members' feeling of a collaborative community of practice. As one member shared,

> We now talk about Project PREPARE-ELLs as "we." . . . I notice participants talking about what "we" could do. I can't imagine that sense of joint work, of a group working together, without the regular conversations and shared experiences that monthly meetings allowed.

One colleague wondered whether meeting every two weeks might be even more helpful but pointed out that that would not be possible due to everybody's already heavy work schedule.

Preservice Teachers

Several members reported being inspired to act by the changes in student knowledge and curiosity as a result of their colleagues' efforts. Similarly, members reported being inspired by their preservice teachers to sustain and increase efforts to infuse instruction for emergent bilinguals into their courses. Some systematically solicited feedback about aspects of their instruction in class and in Project PREPARE-ELLs meetings in order to determine what to extend or revise. Others went about collecting data related to their teaching specific to emergent bilinguals to formalize revisions. Others informally noted that PREPARE-ELLs had made them sensitive to the mindsets and beliefs related to emergent bilinguals and cultural diversity that their students displayed. Noticing that there was a need to address students' beliefs about emergent bilinguals often encouraged teacher educators' efforts at professional learning to influence their professional actions.

WHAT PROFESSIONAL ACTIONS WERE TAKEN?

Course-Related Implications of Project PREPARE-ELLs

Course-related changes reported on project surveys and end-of-year memos fell into one of two approaches to course construction: (a) expanding existing routines (e.g., lesson planning) to include specific reference to English language learners (ELL) and sheltered instruction, and 2) the addition of routines and assignments specific to emergent bilinguals.

Expanding or Re-emphasizing Existing Routines

One of the most commonly reported changes in practice included the addition of practices related to sheltered instruction to existing templates and routines. For example, in methods courses that use a lesson planning template, a space for creating language objectives (a feature of the Sheltered Instruction Observation Protocol [SIOP]; see Echevarria, Vogt, & Short, 2004) and an indication to include modeling or sentence frames were added. These changes to existing patterns and routines indicated a larger trend of broadening awareness to explicitly include emergent bilinguals in conceptions about learners and their role in instructional planning. One colleague explained that she found it important to have "a lot more explicit attention to language." This instructor saw a need to be more explicit with explanations and language use in general in response to the potential needs of emergent bilinguals. In subject areas that were already oriented specifically toward issues of language(s) and culture(s) (e.g., English, world language, social studies), the instructors focused on ensuring that their students had the opportunity to reflect on linguistic and cultural diversity more broadly.

Although preservice teachers in these content areas had always been exposed to materials related to emergent bilinguals, it was not always easy for them to understand how they could participate in the effort of advocating for all language learners. This is a good example of how preservice teachers' work can reflect teacher educators' own level of knowledge and awareness: we know such instruction is important but are sometimes unclear how it specifically relates to the content of classes. For example, for preservice world language teachers, it was not immediately clear what their roles could be in facilitating the learning of English. In other words, preservice world language teachers might be too focused on their immediate role in the classroom as a facilitator for students to "learn the content," which in their case is "foreign language and culture(s)," to capitalize on what knowledge, skills,

From Professional Learning to Professional Action and Back Again 179

and depositions make them excellent advocates for language learners in general. Helping them make connections with the content areas (e.g., reading literature on social justice, addressing emergent bilingualism in content areas as well as in world language education, brainstorming ideas of how to help their colleagues understand the process of language acquisition or the role of culture in language learning or for language learners) helped visualize their role in the advocacy for all language learners.

In all cases, teacher educators reported that additions and expansions led to both formal and informal discussions of emergent bilinguals in classes where this may have happened only haphazardly or occasionally in the past. Faculty made explicit connections between actions of advocacy or language development and the fundamental goals of each content area. That in turn facilitated making emergent bilinguals part of the conversation within methods classes and paying attention to language and culture as part of the routine of instructional planning.

Addition of Routines and Assignments Specific to Emergent Bilinguals

In addition to more explicitly including emergent bilingual students in instructional routines and projects, many teacher educators reported adding readings on emergent bilinguals to their course syllabi. These represented an addition to current practice rather than a widening of the perspective of existing assignments. Often the readings were necessarily limited to one to two additional readings per course per semester. The tensions between balancing and expanding previous course content in light of the focus of Project PREPARE-ELLs were highlighted in these cases by frequent references to a lack of time and in questions about when "enough" had been changed (see Chapter 5). It seemed that the extent of explicit connection to course content, rather than the volume of additional elements, was most satisfying to teacher educators.

CONSIDERING FUTURE LEARNING AND ACTION

Three questions emerged as themes within our analyses of reported changes, and we describe each in turn:

1. Should we, as teacher educators, learn about, think about, and act on language and culture in ways that keep them separate or integrate them?
2. What is the developmental trajectory for preservice teachers related to emergent bilinguals, and what should be taught within a one- or three-year program?
3. Are K-12 methods of effective instruction for emergent bilinguals "just good teaching," as some faculty concluded? What does this comment

from our faculty mean, and what is potentially missed—by us and our K-12 pre-service teachers—when we talk this way?

Should We, as Teacher Educators, Learn about, Think about, and Act on Language and Culture in Ways That Keep Them Separate or Integrate Them?

Unsurprisingly, the question of whether and how language and culture are connected in teaching emergent bilinguals came up at several points during PREPARE-ELLs meetings and in interviews. This question was especially salient for teacher educators involved in Project PREPARE-ELLs as they considered "how much was enough," and what role each teacher educator's methods course might play in a coordinated approach to preparing teachers for emergent bilinguals. The challenge was addressed by discussing programmatic decisions about infusing particular content (e.g., the SIOP model) along with awareness and related dispositions across a sequence of courses, rather than attempting to address it all in one course. For example, one PREPARE-ELLs member worked with a small group of faculty that share a single cohort of students to divide elements of the SIOP across a semester's coursework. Four faculty members teaching five courses for elementary preservice teachers divided aspects of awareness and content across a sequence of courses across one semester. Underlying this question, however, was the reflection of what it means to address the needs of emergent bilinguals. Is it about language, culture, or both?

Meeting minutes from early in the first year of PREPARE-ELLs indicate several instances of an ongoing discussion about whether there is a distinction between a focus on the linguistic aspects of instruction and the cultural aspects of instruction, and if so, what to make of it. At one point, the group considered dividing into groups that focused on readings on language *or* culture but bumped up against the idea that they are at once different and inseparable.

Evoking a theoretical perspective, one member said, "It's not that helpful if it is only language tools without cultural understandings." The relationship of culture to issues of equity, and the need to address deficit perspectives, resonated with the group, but actions related to this mission lacked the specificity that characterized the functional linguistics perspective. In that deficit perspectives are often evoked by issues of language, the linguistic aspects of language learning cannot be separated from the cultural ones.

Over the course of meetings, readings, and guest speakers, a continuum of ELL instruction emerged that presented various concepts of language and culture in the teaching of emergent bilinguals. At one end, there was a functional linguistics perspective, supported by readings completed during the reading group phase (e.g., Schleppegrell, 2004), in which faculty members viewed support for emergent bilinguals as awareness of the linguistic structures that characterize academic language in the various disciplines. At the other end was a cultural perspective, in which the work of supporting emergent bilinguals was framed as awareness of diverse funds of knowledge (Gonzalez, Moll, & Amanti, 2005; Valdés, 1996) and culturally responsive pedagogy (Gay, 2010; Ladson-Billings, 2009). Rather than viewing these as distinct areas of pursuit, members collectively constructed a version of emergent bilingual support that required a focus on both language and culture, with various degrees of emphasis on one over the other. The need to focus on language as well as culture is reflected in much of the literature in the field of teacher development (e.g., August & Hakuta, 1997; de Jong & Harper, 2005; Fillmore & Snow, 2002; Ye, Prater, & Steed, 2011).

On this issue, an initial division emerged between methods courses already oriented toward the study on language *and* culture (e.g., literacy, English, world languages) and those previously more oriented toward implications of culture (e.g., social studies, science). A science methods instructor noted at the beginning of the project that when it comes to talking about language and its relationship to STEM fields, "I'm not that guy." In the context of the interview, it was clear that the instructor meant that the activities in Project PREPARE-ELLs were helpful in pointing out the importance of language in all subject areas. However, the focus on discipline-specific language and discourse resonated deeply with math methods instructors, who took up the notion of the "mathematical register" (Pimm, 1987, 1995) as a way to make the language of math and its role in learning explicit to preservice teachers (see Chapter 4). In this way, math teacher educators indicated that making the mathematical register explicit was part of engaging students in the culture of mathematics as a discipline, not only for emergent bilinguals but for all learners. Guest speakers confirmed the notion that the technical aspects of language may have a place in the study of literacy and related areas but are largely too complex and esoteric for uniform integration in all methods classes.

As the English methods instructor noted, issues of culture and equity may spark interest in the technical aspects of language (usage, syntax, and semantics), but such topics should not be viewed as separate within the various courses. Indeed, as the literacy methods instructor noted, this could run contrary to perspectives on literacy learning that argue for contextualized, rather than isolated, grammar instruction and may seem irrelevant to students who have yet to work with emergent bilinguals. After the second year of Project PREPARE-ELLs, however, even those who initially distanced themselves from the language-specific aspects of infusing a focus on emergent bilinguals had found it necessary to address both language and culture:

> Basically, I'm asking students to consider issues of language in a formal way that—I used to address directly the notion of culture so I did have that perspective to build on and I would even say a fairly strong perspective, but I never sort of bridged language specifically to the issues of culture that I was attentive to.

The issue of relevance for preservice teachers seemed more easily addressed by creating awareness of the issues of equity involved in instruction for emergent bilinguals. This social justice orientation provided both the rationale and impetus for changes in course syllabi, routines, activities, and discussions across courses presumably because there had already been a shared focus on social justice focus among the teacher education faculty. It was clear from teacher education faculty meetings that faculty members are deeply concerned with issues of social justice and often expressed the wish to infuse social justice in the curriculum in a coordinated fashion.

In summary, it was the points of connection between issues of language and culture, on the one hand, and instruction for emergent bilinguals and content instruction, on the other, that were eventually viewed as the goal of both professional learning and professional action for teacher educators.

What Is the Developmental Trajectory for Preservice Teachers Related to Emergent Bilinguals, and What Should Be Taught within a One- or Three-Year Program?

Part of the discussion of focus described earlier was related to a larger question about how to sequence and support a trajectory of development over programs of different lengths. A series of discussions during PREPARE-ELLs meetings highlighted the notion that instruction for emergent bilinguals has to be carefully framed and measured incrementally relative to the natural growth curves of the teacher preparation program. For example, one member suggested that instruction for emergent bilinguals might be better absorbed by fifth-year master's candidates than college juniors because the older students have a level of maturity and professionalism that would lend itself to such discussions after their student teaching experiences.

However, there was the notion that reinforcing the issue over course sequences and starting early rather than late might help students grasp the complex issue. An instructor from the one-year TCPCG program concluded that while her students might at times be overwhelmed during methods courses, it was still important to "plant the seed" by continually asking them questions related to emergent bilinguals. She noticed that more of her students reported an interest in working with emergent bilinguals or even pursuing an additional certification during and after their student teaching that occurs right after the methods course. In IBM, because of student feedback that clearly stated that they did not feel prepared to work with emergent bilinguals, exposing the students incrementally over the program and reviewing rather than introducing all material in the final year similarly seemed to be the more effective approach.

Teacher educators also noted a lack of prior experience with cultural and linguistic diversity in their own experiences, which made it difficult to imagine when and how preservice teachers might develop skills and awareness related to emergent bilinguals. Some teacher educators expressed the wish that they would have had more experience teaching ELL students in order to know what was essential and developmentally appropriate to convey to preservice teachers. Some of those with experience questioned exactly how to model the teaching of emergent bilinguals to create the conditions for "approximations of practice" (Grossman et al., 2009). Others noted that student-teaching settings rarely provided explicit models of collaboration with ELL professionals or across teachers attending to issues of cultural and linguistic diversity. Taken together, the lack of experience and exposure may have played a role in general lack of connection between content instruction and ELL-related pedagogies in the past.

We also found that the design of the programs influences the way changes can be introduced. For example, the makeup of faculty teaching preservice teachers also shapes how discussions of important questions can be addressed. The IBM program, in which the courses that could potentially offer content specific to emergent bilinguals are spread out over three years, provides different opportunities and challenges than the one-year program. Specifically, differences in how centralized or dispersed curricular decisions are impact the degree and distribution of changes (within one course or across many). In one case, one teacher educator teaches all content areas because she teaches all general courses for all content areas in the TCPCG program at a satellite campus. Over the course of her participation in PREPARE-ELLs, the instruction of emergent bilinguals became an integral part of the learning and teaching processes, and she addressed it throughout all her courses. During student teaching, her students continued to talk about the strategies they used with emergent bilinguals, and she realized that what they had done really made an impact on them. She decided that she would make similar changes in her teaching in all of her other courses as well. In other cases, decisions about curricular changes in teacher education require more coordination among a number of colleagues.

ARE K-12 METHODS OF EFFECTIVELY TEACHING EMERGENT BILINGUALS "JUST GOOD TEACHING"? WHAT IS POTENTIALLY MISSED WHEN WE ASSUME THIS?

When considering the amount of course additions related to emergent bilinguals, a number of members indicated that Project PREPARE-ELLs had inspired a reinvigorated focus on "just good teaching" or general "best practices" as a way of responding to the specific needs of language learners. For some teacher educators, that meant positioning all students as language learners of one kind or another, whether it is the language of mathematics or the language of ancient primary source documents. One colleague shared, "I always had the sense that . . . the kinds of things we do . . . for SIOP . . . for English language learners using SIOP strategies could be good for all students." This notion is connected with a broader question of how to frame instruction for emergent bilinguals. It is important to note here that these reflections occurred in a group of teacher educators who had spent considerable time discussing the complexity of language and culture in teaching emergent bilinguals. Therefore, we believe that the comments were not meant to undermine the complexity and knowledge required to support emergent bilinguals. Instead, the comments point to the sense of overlap with best practices for emergent bilingual and monolingual learners. This overlap can create a dilemma about whether to frame instruction for emergent bilinguals as unique and specific to emergent bilinguals or as "just good teaching." Each frame has potential consequences for students and implications for practice.

This dilemma is an ongoing source of discussion and reflection, so we feel the need to refer to research here that further complicates but also sheds some light on the complexity of the issue. While it is true that mainstream learners may benefit from teaching practices identified as particularly effective for emergent bilinguals, Harper and de Jong (2009) point out that the "just good teaching" attitude (de Jong & Harper, 2005) can lead to the notion that "ESL specialist teachers are considered redundant and are replaced by mainstream teachers who are minimally prepared to teach ESL" (Harper & de Jong, 2009, p. 138). Indeed, de Jong and Harper (2005) describe a distinct gap between "just good teaching" and teaching effectively for emergent bilinguals in terms of both knowledge and practice. Although associated practices are not limited specifically to emergent bilinguals, the ways in which teachers consider and draw on knowledge of language acquisition, language use, and culture mediates decisions about practices. Thus, a specific set of knowledge is required to create and deliver instruction that will meet the unique needs of emergent bilinguals:

> First, teachers must understand the process of second language acquisition and acculturation. . . . Additionally, teachers must develop an understanding of how bilingual processes are manifested in emergent bilinguals' oral and literacy development, and how they can build on students' L1 resources . . . as well as an awareness of the challenges that emergent bilinguals face in learning academic content through a language they do not yet control (Fillmore & Snow, 1998). From a cultural perspective, teachers need to understand how expectations and opportunities for learning are mediated through culturally based assumptions regarding classroom expectations and literacy that may not be shared by all students. . . . Mainstream teachers need to be able to identify language demands in their content areas and organize their classrooms to support the development of academic language proficiency by integrating their language and content objectives. Crosscultural practices and experiences must inform curriculum planning and implementation. (de Jong and Harper, 2005, p. 110)

As de Jong and Harper (2005) note, it is the thought process involved in planning and implementing instruction with language and culture in mind, not necessarily the presence of specific instructional features, that distinguishes effective ELL instruction from "just good teaching." Moreover, they assert that the need for advocacy to ensure equity for ELL populations also separates effective instruction for emergent bilinguals from "just good teaching." Still, understanding the need for ELL specialists and regular classroom teachers to collaborate in order to successfully teach the growing population of emergent bilinguals, Ye, Prater, and Steed (2011) conclude that careful implementation of professional development in schools that include mainstream and ELL teachers can lead to positive outcomes for emergent bilinguals. Ye and colleagues (2011) draw the following conclusion: "Reflecting on de Jong & Harper's (2005) framework for preparing mainstream teachers for ESL students, we believe that as we move from 'just good teaching' to preparing all students—including ESL students—for academic success, all teachers working with ESL students need to be equipped with not only knowledge of language and culture, but also skills in collaboration, leadership and critical reflection, to engage all educators in the innovative process that leads to change in schools" (p. 15). We believe that the collaboration Ye and colleagues (2005) discuss is a necessary ingredient for teachers who seek to position themselves as advocates and critically reflective leaders for their students. At the same time, we acknowledge that effective teaching of emergent bilinguals involves a separate and specific knowledge base and professional thought process than "just good teaching," and thus deserves separate treatment.

Throughout this chapter, we refer to challenges we encountered in our endeavor of transforming professional learning into professional action. These challenges included a perceived lack of experience with research and practice concerning emergent bilinguals, tension between a cultural and a linguistic focus, clarifying the notion of "just good teaching" in the context of best practices for teaching emergent bilinguals, and unclear trajectories and expectations for preservice teacher development in this area. We now share some recommendations and lessons learned. We know that each context for professional learning and professional action will provide a different set of challenges; however, we hope that faculty groups at a broad range of universities may benefit from some of our experiences.

RECOMMENDATIONS

As a group, project PREPARE-ELLs participants are still engaging with the question of how we can help preservice teachers better understand the complexities of supporting emergent bilinguals academically while also taking into account important cultural considerations. Based on our analysis of meeting minutes, interviews, and end-of-year memos, we have generated a short list of conditions that drive a continuous cycle of learning, action, and reflection that might support others who choose to engage in similar work.

Less Is More: "This Whole Project at Its Core Is an Exercise in Professional Learning and Setting of Priorities"

By the second year, many methods instructors reported that rather than adding more materials and resources related to emergent bilinguals, they learned to teach fewer things with more follow-up or teach fewer things more explicitly. Instructors saw data suggesting that this approach had helped. As shown in Chapter 9, during the first year of implementation, few preservice teachers went beyond writing language objectives to actually using them in classrooms; improvement in their use and an increase in overall implementation of the SIOP features in year two and some improvement from year one to year two led one instructor to remark, "I gotta tell you the realization of no impact . . . is a pretty sad place to be and having some impact in some areas is a much happier place." Project PREPARE-ELLs members started to make more purposeful decisions about what aspects to include in their methods courses. They were more convinced than ever of the importance of the endeavor and were constructively engaged in conversations with each other about efficient ways of creating awareness of the issues at hand and providing tools to address these issues in the classroom. With more than 30 features, methods instructors found it difficult to cover the SIOP comprehensively. As mentioned earlier, instructors found different solutions from sequencing the introduction of the SIOP features between the courses in the TCPCG program to staggering an introduction to priority features in the IBM program. Often the "less is more" mindset appeared in conjunction with the intention to target fewer topics and to do more assessments of topics introduced.

As one colleague stated, "and so it's not so much that I'm teaching different stuff, but I'm teaching stuff differently." Some colleagues spoke about it in terms of consistency: "So every lesson plan had language objectives . . . that the students did." Others made sure to follow up on discussions again to ensure reflection on a topic discussed. That is, the development from "quantity" to "quality" went hand in hand with the realization that the material covered is so complex that it might be more important to make sure students have the opportunity to reflect and instructors have the time to assess what was understood.

Enable Faculty from a Variety of Contexts to Learn and Grow Together

Analyses of interviews and notes of meetings of teacher educators in PREPARE-ELLs suggest several elements that can promote personal and collective action to emerge from collegial learning. Within PREPARE-ELLs, teacher educators were convinced of the validity and urgency of the cause. Data concerning students' perceptions of their readiness to work with emergent bilinguals formed the initial impulse for involvement for many members; such data sustained as well as focused their efforts over time. In our case, evidence from program exit surveys and research initiated by the project and by individual members continued to motivate more learning and more course revision. This offered a shared entry point as well as the impetus for the project co-directors to apply for funding to support the project. Several teacher educators indicated that the incentives provided with that funding (small stipend for participating in the summer workshop, modest summer salary, lunches at meetings) paired with the commitment and leadership of the PREPARE-ELLs co-directors were important factors influencing their sustained involvement in and commitment to PREPARE-ELLs.

In addition to the resources provided through the workshops and in presentations, teacher educators reported that being able to discuss these changes with each other and sharing and working through challenges they encountered in presentations in their meetings with an agreed-on protocol were helpful. Our analysis of the meeting minutes, combined with our own observations from the meetings, led us to believe that the well-guided discussions in which teacher educators confronted the complex issues involved demonstrate that there is no quick and easy solution to providing appropriate resources for emergent bilinguals. However, results as well as experiences reported by teacher educators show that enthusiasm for the program did not dissipate. On the contrary, the group continues to meet, discuss practice, collect and analyze data, and, most important, grow in numbers. We reiterate what participants reported as working as follows:

- small grants to partially compensate faculty for their time;
- protocols that enable active listening, open rapport, and constructive feedback; and
- openness to including faculty members from different disciplines and backgrounds.

Analyze Successes and Challenges

Using data about our state's changing demographics and our students' perceptions of their readiness allowed us to begin our work with a strong sense of needing to change. This shared sense inspired collaboration, learning, and action, which in turn fueled our sense of a continued need for change. This cycle of identifying an area for growth, engaging in development activities, translating these into action, and finding new areas for growth can and does happen organically in a variety of settings. We suggest, however, that this cycle was propelled and supported by the structure of Project PREPARE-ELLs, which allowed it to continue over several academic years despite all the changes in faculty, policy, and circumstance that accompany each new academic year.

The deliberate emphasis on the goal orientation of each meeting—with both short- and long-term goals—as well as the opportunity to connect discussions and actions related to Project PREPARE-ELLs with other scholarly pursuits, such as presentations and publications, allowed teacher educators to make intellectual room for this work and helped us structure and focus it in ways that created deep connections with our varied teaching and research agendas. Indeed the crafting of such artifacts facilitates authors' reflection on their learning and action while also fueling a continued need to learn.

Put simply, this work cannot be separate from or viewed as an addition to the work of being a teacher educator. Rather it must be made central to the activities, goals, and structures that already shape our academic lives.

REFERENCES

August, D., & Hakuta, K. (1997). *Improving schooling for language-minority children*. Washington, DC: National Academy Press.

Darling-Hammond, L., & Richardson, N. (2009). Teacher learning: What matters? *Educational Leadership*, 66 (5), 46–53.

de Jong, E. J., & Harper, C. A. (2005). Preparing mainstream teachers for English language learners: Is being a good teacher good enough? *Teacher Education Quarterly*, 32(2), 101–124.

Echevarria, J., Vogt, M., & Short, D. (2004). *Making content comprehensible for English language learners: The SIOP model* (2nd ed.). Needham Heights, MA: Allyn & Bacon.

Fillmore, L. W., & Snow, C. E. (2002). What teachers need to know about language. In C. A. Adger, C. E. Snow, & D. Christian (Eds.), *What teachers need to know about language* (pp. 7–54). McHenry, IL; Washington, DC: Delta Systems, and Center for Applied Linguistics.

Garet, M. S., Porter, A. C., Desimone, L., Birman, P. F., & Yoon, K. S. (2001). What makes professional development effective? Results from a national sample of teachers. *American Educational Research Journal*, 38(4), 915–945.

Gay, G. (2010). *Culturally responsive teaching: Theory, research, and practice*. New York: Teachers College Press.

Goethe, J. (1854). Goethe's sämmtliche Werke, Band 1. Verlag Cotta.

Gonzalez, N., Moll, L. C., & Amanti, C. (2005). *Funds of knowledge: Theorizing practices in households, communities, and classrooms*. Mahwah, NJ: Lawrence Erlbaum Associates.

Grossman, P., Compton, C., Igra, D., Ronfeldt, M., Shahan, E., & Williamson, P. (2009). Teaching practice: A cross-professional perspective. *Teachers College Record*, 111, pp. 2055–2100.

Harper, C. A., & de Jong, E. J. (2009). Using ESL teachers' expertise to inform mainstream teacher preparation. In C. Rodríguez-Eagle (Ed.), *Achieving literacy success withEnglish language learners: Insights, assessment, and instruction* (pp. 25–42). Worthington, OH: Reading Recovery Council of North America.

Ladson-Billings, G. (2009). *The dreamkeepers: Successful teachers of African American children* (2nd ed.). San Francisco, CA: Jossey-Bass.

Lave, J., & Wenger, E. (1991). *Situated learning: Legitimate peripheral participation.* New York: Cambridge University Press.
Pimm, D. (1987). *Speaking mathematically.* London: Routledge and Kegan Paul.
Pimm, D. (1995). *Symbols and meanings in school mathematics.* London: Routledge and Kegan Paul.
Schleppegrell, M. (2004). *The language of schooling: A functional linguistics perspective.* Mahwah, NJ: Lawrence Erlbaum Associates.
Valdés, G. (1996). *Con respeto: Bridging the distances between culturally diverse families and schools: An ethnographic portrait.* New York: Teachers College Press.
Ye, H., Prater, K., & Steed, T. (2011). Moving beyond "just good teaching": ESL professional =development for all teachers. *Professional Development in Education, 37*(1), 7–18.

APPENDIX

Interview Protocol, Fall 2010 Project PREPARE-ELLs

1. Please describe Project PREPARE-ELLs' impact on what you know about ELLs.
2. Please describe, at present, Project PREPARE-ELLs' impact on your curriculum and instruction.
    - If not answered: What did you get from the summer week?
    - If not answered: How did your coach help you?
3. What are your current obstacles?
4. What additional kinds of knowledge or support for practice would you like?
5. To what extent do you feel like you are part of a learning community, a group engaged in a shared pursuit that includes learning? Is there more we might do to position you and your colleagues to learn together in ways that ultimately improve what you do with preservice teachers?
6. Any additional comments or insights you want to share?

11 Preservice Teachers' Evolving Knowledge and Practice toward Linguistically and Culturally Responsive Pedagogy

Wendy J. Glenn and Mileidis Gort

THE OVERARCHING CHALLENGE

The case study described in this chapter explored what preservice teachers take away from bilingual learner-focused teacher education reform efforts, addressing specifically the challenge of revising a course and other experiences that encourage students to take up the knowledge, dispositions, and practices that instructors seek to promote. Research increasingly addresses the impact of diversity-focused courses and field experiences on pre-professional educators' developing competence in teaching for diversity. Studies focus on the role of multicultural education courses in preservice teachers' conceptual understandings of cultural and racial diversity, including beliefs about other cultures and students of diverse backgrounds and their abilities to engage in culturally responsive teaching (e.g., Brown, 2004; Hill-Jackson, 2007; Milner, 2005, 2006; Thomas & Vanderhaar, 2008). The impact of such courses has been mixed. Some researchers report that preservice teachers enter and exit stand-alone cultural diversity courses relatively unchanged (Banks, 1991; Brown, 2004), whereas others find that students' attitudes and beliefs changed positively as a result of participation (Cho & DeCastro-Ambrosetti, 2005; Milner, 2005, 2006). This suggests that diversity coursework may positively influence preservice teachers' attitudes toward students of diverse backgrounds and their understanding of other cultures; however, research that examines the influence of such courses after the semester ends is extremely limited.

There is a particular dearth of research evaluating the impact of teacher education efforts to prepare teachers to work effectively with the growing numbers of emergent bilingual learners (Cochran-Smith & Zeichner, 2005). One notable exception is Athanases' and colleagues' work investigating the processes, successes, and challenges of preparing teachers to advocate for English language learners (ELLs) (e.g., Athanases & de Oliveira, 2007; 2008; Athanases & Martin, 2006; de Oliveira & Athanases, 2007). This research intimates the critical role of preservice teacher education in providing equitable schooling experiences for emergent bilingual learners.

We investigated two preservice secondary English teachers' evolving knowledge and stances regarding emergent bilingual learners—namely, their perceptions of culturally- and linguistically- diverse students and developing abilities to support the needs of emergent bilingual learners—through an analysis of their methods coursework and student teaching practice. The study reported in this chapter was guided by the following questions: (a) How do preservice English teachers respond to bilingual learner-focused components of a preservice secondary English education methods course? and (b) How do preservice English teachers apply their developing understandings about language and cultural diversity, second language acquisition, and sheltered instruction in their own work with emergent bilinguals? Although the methods course and student teaching experience provided spaces in which preservice teachers built and applied understandings of language and cultural diversity to teaching emergent bilinguals, participants differed in response to these experiences and demonstrated great variability in their abilities to connect their understandings of diversity to teaching emergent bilingual learners. The study illuminates the complexities inherent in preparing preservice teachers to teach culturally and linguistically diverse students well.

REVISED ENGLISH METHODS COURSE

Wendy, an English Education professor and former high school teacher, worked with Mileidis, a Bilingual Education professor and former elementary teacher (both co-authors of this chapter), to reconfigure an existing "Methods of Teaching English" course to reflect bilingual learner scholarship and relevant pedagogy. The course, scheduled during the fall semester prior to student teaching, was populated by seniors in the Integrated Bachelor's/Master's (IBM) English Education certification program. Twelve students, 11 female and one male, were enrolled, and five chose to participate in the study. All self-reported as white, monolingual English speakers whose lived experiences with emergent bilinguals were extremely limited with the exception of a one-semester field placement in a more linguistically diverse urban center during their previous year in the program. Those who did not participate all indicated that their clinic classrooms did not include emergent bilingual students.

Changes to the methods course included the development and implementation of new activities and assignments, as well as revisions to existing activities and assignments. Additions and revisions were grounded in the belief that teacher education students benefit from explicit attention to myths and problematic assumptions held about language diversity, language learning, native languages other than English, and emergent bilinguals and their families (Meskill, 2005), and all were aligned with essential elements of culturally and linguistically responsive instruction, including understanding second language learning processes, the differences between academic and social language, and the roles of the native language and culture in teaching and learning (e.g., Brisk, Horan, & Macdonald, 2007; de Jong & Harper, 2005; Echevarria, Vogt, & Short, 2012; Lucas, Villegas, & Freedson-Gonzalez, 2008; Wong-Fillmore & Snow, 2005).

Across the course, infused content was centered on instructor-generated essential questions intended to raise and address pervasive myths regarding the teaching of emergent bilingual learners, including the following:

1. Who are emergent bilinguals? What experiences do they bring to the classroom?
2. What strategies can English teachers employ to foster the linguistic and social success of emergent bilinguals in the general education classroom?

Two activities and assignments that grew from these overarching questions are relevant to this study.

Activity One: Student Profile Generation and Interview

Early in the semester, all preservice teachers in the methods course generated a student profile of a real or an imagined emergent bilingual. Following explanation of the task, participants drew from their experiences, existing knowledge, and perceptions to consider individually their unique profile: student's name, gender, age, race and ethnicity, socioeconomic background, family and community, previous schooling experiences, home literacy practices, level of linguistic proficiency in the heritage language, and immigration/migration experiences, if applicable. After participants drafted some initial ideas, discussion of the profiles and process was opened to all, and whole-class conversation ensued (see Guiding Questions in Appendix A). Participants then worked independently outside of class to revisit and revise the initial profile in consideration of thoughts shared during the whole-class discussion. Soon after submitting the individual profiles for instructor review, Wendy interviewed each participant with the goal of learning more about the thought processes and assumptions that undergirded the creation of the profile and determining the knowledge and support participants needed as the course continued. Interview questions were differentiated for each participant; in preparation for each meeting, Wendy highlighted aspects of the profiles that seemed to reflect misconceptions about emergent bilinguals and/or their families in each participant's profile and raised these as conversation starters during the interview.

The profile-generating task and interview intended to help participants, through a series of resulting course activities, begin to answer the first set of essential questions: Who are emergent bilinguals? What experiences do they bring to the classroom? Exploration of these questions was designed to expose several common myths about emergent bilinguals (e.g., almost all emergent bilinguals are poor and uneducated; increasing linguistic diversity among students is an urban phenomenon; parents of emergent bilinguals don't value education) and help participants understand the multiple conditions that define and influence bilingual learners' experiences. The activities attempted to help candidates build a richer understanding of (a) the role of native language and the funds of linguistic knowledge that emergent bilingual students bring into the classroom, and (b) the roles of language and culture in teaching and learning and the need for teachers to acknowledge, respect, celebrate, and integrate cultural heritages and languages as legitimate and worthy of inclusion in the school curriculum. All participants indicated that this was the first opportunity they had had prior to and during their teacher training to think critically and carefully about their assumptions relative to emergent bilinguals. Given that these activities provided an initial attempt at deconstruction among beginning teachers who had little experience with emergent bilinguals, success was evaluated by candidates' willingness to question their initial assumptions and any resulting, positive shifts in perspectives or understandings, regardless of where final assumptions existed along the continuum of emergent bilingual myths.

Activity Two: Unit Plan Creation

As students had done in earlier iterations of the course, participants independently designed a two-week unit of instruction to be implemented during student teaching. Units included a rationale for implementing the unit in the middle or high school English classroom, enduring understandings and essential questions, a calendar, daily lesson plans and accompanying materials for each day, daily modifications for two students, and reflection on the resulting product. For the revised methods course assignment, students were asked to consider explicitly second language learning processes and academic and social language differences, two essential elements of culturally and linguistically responsive instruction. To that end, students employed an instructor-modified Sheltered Instruction Observation Protocol (SIOP; Echevarria, Vogt, & Short, 2012) lesson plan in the creation of the lessons each day of the unit (see Appendix B). This process allowed them to explore answers to the second guiding question of the course: What strategies can English teachers employ to foster the linguistic and social success of emergent bilinguals in the classroom?

Wendy generated the revised SIOP lesson plan template to help students attend to particular linguistic and social elements of instruction that, in students' first attempts at unit creation, seemed manageable and of high impact. Students were asked to describe language and content objectives for each lesson; list any supplementary or adapted visuals, models, or technological resources from which they might draw in the implementation of the lesson; describe how they will draw on individual students' prior knowledge, experiences, and learning to introduce and maintain the lesson; describe the instructional grouping choices (individual, small group, whole class) and strategies for modeling or guided practice they might employ in each phase of instruction; and explain how they might differentiate instruction for two students, one with an identified special learning need and one who is an emergent bilingual. For this final element, students utilized the profile generated earlier in the semester to guide their thinking regarding strategies that might best be used to provide necessary differentiation for the emergent bilingual learner.

As with the profile-generating activity, development on this task was evaluated with the recognition that participants are new unit and lesson planners being asked to employ a protocol that extends beyond the knowledge base of what is typically expected among beginning teachers. Levels of competence in the creation of the SIOP-informed unit were considered against a model outcome of a unit that included (a) lessons that attended specifically to students' language development, addressed all elements of language learning (receptive and productive), and encouraged oral and written expression; (b) lessons that provided multiple opportunities for students to draw on their prior knowledge, experiences, and learning as they engaged in writing, thinking, and speaking and employed a variety of instructional practices (mini-lessons, discussions, activities, independent work, etc.), grouping strategies (whole class, small group, pairs, etc.), and assessments (informal and formal); and (c) clear description of appropriate modifications to be employed to meet the academic and social needs of an emergent bilingual learner, including the provision of any modified texts, handouts, assessments, assignment descriptions, and so on.

STUDENT TEACHING

Student Teaching Lesson Plan, Reflection, and Interview

All students in this IBM teacher preparation program, across grade level and certification area, were asked to develop a lesson, enact and videotape the lesson, and reflect on their own and their students' performance during the lesson as part of their student teaching experience during the spring semester of their senior year. The lesson and accompanying teaching performance assignment included five segments (initiation, content delivery, student engagement, assessment, and closure). Students were asked to select approximately one- to two-minute excerpts from each of the lesson segments for subsequent reflection. The reflection on student performance included artifacts of student work and written discussion of how candidates might use this information to inform decisions about student learning and subsequent instructional methods. The self-reflection component encouraged participants to address questions relative to revision. All study participants attended specifically to emergent bilingual student needs in their lesson planning and reflection in an explicit attempt to improve their practice as culturally responsive teachers; this was not a requirement for students across the program.

To better understand preservice teachers' thinking around the videotaped lesson, Wendy interviewed each participant following the conclusion of the student teaching experience, which included the completion of the videotaped lesson assignment. Before and after watching each of the five segments of the video, she posed semi-structured interview questions related to participants' attempts at instruction designed to support emergent bilingual learners (see Appendix C). This conversational, reflective interview was designed to encourage participants to consider the thinking that guided the specific choices and actions made as captured in the videotaped lesson and to allow researchers access to participants' understandings of emergent bilinguals and the pedagogies that might best support their learning.

DATA SOURCES AND ANALYSIS

Data sources informing our analysis, then, consisted of four sets of artifacts and two sets of field notes gathered during the methods course (fall semester) and student teaching experience that followed in the spring. As artifacts, Wendy collected participants' (a) emergent bilingual student profiles (methods course), (b) unit plans with differentiation centered on the profiled student (methods course), (c) videotaped lesson (student teaching), and (d) written lesson plans and reflections on student and personal performance in the videotaped lesson (student teaching). Wendy generated field notes taken from (a) interviews around participants' emergent bilingual learner profiles (methods course), and (b) interviews centered on participants' attention to emergent bilinguals during a process of shared viewing and discussion of the teaching video (student teaching). These multiple data sources allowed for triangulation and enhanced the validity and reliability of the findings (Strauss & Corbin, 1990).

Data analysis involved use of the constant-comparative method (Merriam, 1998; Strauss & Corbin, 1990) to analyze preservice teachers' evolving knowledge and stances regarding emergent bilingual learners, as well as their enactments of these understandings through practice during student teaching. First, we grouped all data by source and compiled them in chronological order for each of the participants. After reading these data multiple times to develop familiarity, we then independently generated annotated comments to provide initial explanation, synthesis, and questioning of participant thinking and behaviors over time. After revisiting, discussing, and revising these annotations over several conversations between the researchers, Wendy drafted cases for each participant that reflected the shared interpretation held by both researchers. Mileidis acted as peer debriefer (Denzin & Lincoln, 1994) in this stage, asking for clarification and offering alternative interpretations of the data.

TWO JOURNEYS

In this section, we describe the journeys of two preservice teachers (both white, U.S. born and raised, monolingual English speakers who do not consider themselves a member of a traditionally underrepresented racial, ethnic, or linguistic group) in exploring and applying their developing understanding of concepts related to the education of emergent bilingual learners. The journeys of these two participants demonstrate the range of candidate development across the larger group of preservice teachers in the study, revealing the disparate location of participants along the continuum of development to reveal the complexity inherent in doing this work and allowing for rich exploration of individual growth over time. The evidence presented here suggests that future teachers, regardless of where they begin the process of learning, can reflect critically on issues of language and culture, language learning, and academic success when provided opportunity and encouragement.

Carissa

As was true for her colleagues, Carissa's conflicting perspectives regarding emergent bilinguals were evidenced early in the methods course in her creation of the student profile. Carissa's fictional subject, 13-year-old Elisa, is an immigrant student from Mexico. Carissa provided this description of the student's background in the following two passages:

> As to her education in the U.S., Elisa's parents are encouraging in that they expect her to succeed in her schooling. She is not forced to practice English at home, but her parents always allow her to, whenever she wants or needs to. However, Elisa's parents expect all other learning to take place in the school setting, and therefore no reading or writing is practiced at home.
>
> Personality-wise, Elisa is a sweet child. She is oftentimes shy and quiet, but she is always willing to try whatever work the teachers give her. She usually will try to complete the assignment without asking questions, but if she is genuinely puzzled, she will ask for help. Due to her parents' encouragement for her to be successful, Elisa expects and wants herself to be successful too.

Reading these two passages back to back reveals the conflicting ways in which Carissa identified her expectations for emergent bilinguals. In the first, she stated that "no reading or writing is practiced at home," suggesting that this is a context devoid of valid or valuable literacy practices. She chose not to address the home literacy practices that Elisa and her family might engage in in the heritage language. In this passage, she also stated that Elisa's parents expect her to succeed in school but also expect the school to be fully responsible for their daughter's education. Learning that takes place in the home environment is not noted or recognized. In contrast, Carissa named Elisa's parents as key support people in her academic development in the school setting and identified Elisa as possessing high standards for herself in the second passage.

This inconsistency of perception was also seen in the ways Carissa attempted to talk critically and accurately about issues of language diversity. In the profile interview, she articulated clearly her view that reading and writing competence in English does not align directly with intelligence among emergent bilinguals: "An ELL [English language learner] might not know how to read or write in English but that doesn't mean he is not intelligent." In the profile, however, she stated the following about Elisa's educational experiences in Mexico:

> Back in her native country, Elisa had none to limited education. Since the time she moved to the States, she has experienced spurts of education, as her family is constantly moving from place to place. Elisa's family moved to the states when she was 10, and since then she has progressed minimally in her learning, as she constantly has to start over in a new school. She is currently in the upper stage of the Beginner level of ELLs. Elisa is proficient at speaking her native language. However, due to her lack of schooling in Mexico, her reading and writing levels are just below intermediate. This affects her ability to pick up the new language in English.

The inclusion of the statement, "none to limited education," suggests a belief that educational knowledge and skill are acquired only through experiences in the school setting. Carissa articulated the struggle Elisa faces given her family's transience due to her father's work and the ways in which this affects her performance in school. She did not identify, however, the strengths (e.g., intelligence and experiences) that Elisa brings with her into the classroom.

Carissa's profile and the interview conversation that followed also revealed conflicting understandings of culture. When reflecting on the profile she created, Carissa explained, "The profile seems stereotypical, but I wanted to look at the norm." In trying to capture what she called "the norm," she created a composite character based on her understandings of Mexicans in general, some of which appear to be grounded in stereotypes. In the profile, for example, she described Elisa's community as

> less supportive about her education. Some of the other children in her community encourage her to put less effort into her schoolwork. Also,

> Elisa hears from some of the other parents that success in school is not necessary (and, in some cases, not even desirable).

This reaffirms the faulty assumption that Mexican parents do little to support their children's success in school and contradicts extensive research evidence that Latino parents value education and, to the extent that they are able, support their children's schooling in various ways (Gaitan, 2004).

Similarly, in the interview, Carissa stated, "In my clinic placement, there are lots of Spanish-speaking students. I don't know if they are Mexican, but it doesn't matter because I don't know enough Spanish anyway." In this statement, she named the students with whom she works as Mexican without identifying any evidence that would support such naming (the majority of bilingual learners in her classroom community were, in reality, Puerto Rican). Additionally, she referred to the Spanish language spoken by her students as the feature that identifies them, reducing culture to a single defining characteristic or practice. Yet when asked, "Does the fact that you don't speak Spanish matter when you consider culture beyond the language spoken by students?", Carissa paused and said, "It would be wrong to clump them all together and assume they're all Mexican," thus demonstrating her potential to rethink what she thought she understood.

The unit that Carissa developed over the duration of the methods course revealed her developing ability to modify instruction to explicitly support the needs of emergent bilinguals. She planned to draw on visual resources by creating picture timelines that provided bilingual learners visual cues for key events in the class novel being read. She also created a handout of contextual information on workers' unions and strikes designed to help students have the necessary understandings of more specific terms and concepts to better understand the choices made by the characters. She built language skill development into each lesson, providing context for and direct application of speaking, writing, and reading strategies for students. And she honored heritage language by planning to encourage emergent bilinguals to compose draft writings in their L1.

Yet in the creation of the unit, Carissa also identified strategies of good teaching as good enough for emergent bilinguals without specific attention to their language and literacy development needs. Carissa named particular practices as examples of modifications for emergent bilinguals rather than identifying them as effective practices for English-proficient students that do not explicitly provide emergent bilingual learners the support they need.

For example, she planned to record student discussion comments in a public place to provide students visual reference for information shared as a class. She provided time in class for individual reading, thus allowing students the opportunity to seek support of a teacher or peer. And she advocated sharing examples of student writing as models. These practices reflect a more generalized attempt to create a space in which learners have access to various supports but fail to explicitly name how these supports would be implemented to meet the unique language and literacy needs of emergent bilinguals. With regard to writing exemplars, for instance, she might have explicitly highlighted genre-specific organizational patterns and transitions and other key words that help the writer meet genre-specific demands.

These same modifications, both those that explicitly addressed the literacy needs of emergent bilinguals and those considered "just good teaching," continued to be evidenced during Carissa's student teaching experience. Carissa's classroom community included several emergent bilinguals, primarily native Spanish speakers, who demonstrated varying levels of English proficiency. With respect to explicit modifications, Carissa implemented the strategies she described in her unit plan, as noted earlier (picture timeline, contextual information handout, language skill instruction, and heritage language valuing). Additionally, she drew on intentional grouping strategies by creating literature response groups in which emergent bilinguals were placed in groups with both proficient English speakers and emergent Spanish-English bilinguals, thus fostering opportunities for effective language modeling and peer translation and communication.

Carissa also continued to identify strategies of good teaching as good enough for bilingual learners rather than providing specific attention to their unique language and literacy needs. In addition to those strategies referenced previously (public recording of comments, time in class for reading and conferencing, and student-generated writing models), Carissa, in the implementation of her unit, identified her provision of a list of questions students answered while they read as an example of an effective bilingual learner modification.

A few of the modifications Carissa implemented during student teaching (and identified as good for emergent bilinguals) were actually not as effective as she believed. Carissa employed explicit strategies that she argued would help her bilingual learners feel more comfortable in the classroom, paralleling her peers' desire to support emergent bilinguals affectively. She chose, for example, to not require students at early stages of English development to read aloud during class, presuming that writing in English would serve as an appropriate alternative to reading aloud for these students:

> For students who were still new at learning the English language, I did give them the option to opt out. Instead of reading out loud, they would have to write me a brief summary during class so I knew whether or not they understood what was going on in the story.

Similarly, she described an activity in which students shared their opinions by standing if they agreed and remaining sitting if they disagreed, arguing that this would lessen any potential anxiety they might feel when asked to participate publically:

> I would ask, "Did Esperanza prick her thumb on a rose?" and have students stand or sit in response. ELLs then wouldn't have to respond verbally, so that would take a lot of pressure off of them.

The strategies Carissa described in these two examples are not responsive to the needs of students at early stages of English development that she identified; the first would likely require skills beyond those that students have developed, and the second demands little of students and does not actually provide evidence of why they might have responded as they did.

Inconsistencies of understanding were also revealed when Carissa attempted to articulate the videotaped lesson objectives she had in mind for all students, more generally, and the bilingual learners in her class, more specifically. Carissa explained that the lesson objectives for all students were developed with emergent bilinguals in mind due to the high number of bilingual learners in the class and the necessity that all students learn these skills:

> I was hoping they could improve their reading and reading comprehension skills through reading the novel and also build their literary analysis. The goals really were directed to ELLs, as, in the entire class, there were so many students who were second language learners. They were ALL in need of this. I didn't necessarily divide the ELLs out as a separate group because so many of them were second language students.

These objectives, however, focus on general goals (improve reading and reading comprehension, build literary analysis) without any language-oriented focus that would distinguish the needs of emergent bilinguals.

In a related homework assignment, Carissa holds all students, emergent bilinguals included, accountable for the same work, reflecting the maintenance of high standards for all:

> At the end of the period, students will be given a homework assignment. In this assignment, students are to write three paragraphs. The first two should summarize the events of the novel so far. Students need to include specific details from the text. These first two paragraphs will show student understanding of the novel so far. The last paragraph in the assignment will be a prediction of what the students think will happen next. This assignment will be due at the beginning of the class period tomorrow.

While it is clear Carissa demands much, she does not provide explicit support for emergent bilinguals in their completion of complex and language-dependent tasks.

At the end of the student teaching experience, Carissa attempted to identify the cultural affiliation of her emergent bilingual students but did so without justification or awareness of who they were as individuals. In describing a student for whom she specifically modified her videotaped lesson, she stated, "Robert is a seventh grader; he is Latino. I don't know what [nationality] he is."

Beth

From the outset of the methods course, Beth demonstrated some skills to talk accurately and critically about emergent bilinguals and where they are in the process of language acquisition. Her emergent bilingual profile centered on a fictional 15-year-old Puerto Rican girl, Noemi. Beth described her as having "strong conversational skills but not academic language," thus suggesting her understanding of the distinction among levels of language proficiency. Additionally, when describing the need to differentiate instruction for Noemi, she pointed to the "complex nature of language," intimating an understanding that language learning demands much of the learner and must be attended to intentionally and with care on behalf of the teacher. In the interview following the creation of the profile, Beth described some essential ways to support language development and acquisition. She reported asking herself while writing the profile, "How can I create social opportunities for Noemi to build her English skills?"

In this same interview, Beth shared what she wanted to learn over the remainder of the methods course in order to best support Noemi. She indicated her desire for Noemi to respect her, stating, "I want to learn how to get Noemi's respect and how to get her to value my opinion." Beth recognized that she plays a role in determining whether Noemi will respect her as her teacher. The focus here is on what she needs to do as an educator to best support Noemi, not what Noemi needs to do to perform. Beth avoids a deficit-based perspective that identifies Noemi as a problem and instead puts an onus of responsibility on herself to find ways to reach her as a student.

Beth's perceptions of Noemi were generally grounded in high expectations and an optimistic vision of emergent bilinguals and their likelihood of success. She explained her thinking around the creation of Noemi's profile: "We hear stories of a lot of kids who seem hopeless. I wanted to focus on a kid whose experience is hopeful." This statement indicates Beth' vision of Noemi as an example of a counter-narrative who offers an alternative to the existing, often negative, vision of emergent bilinguals in the school community. She expressed a desire for Noemi to push herself, to achieve something beyond what the stereotype might suggest she is capable of achieving.

As the conversation continued, however, some inconsistencies emerged in Beth's perceptions. Beth argued, "I want Noemi to be cocky in her choice to work hard to graduate and be different from everyone else in her situation." In contrast to her earlier claims, this statement indicates Beth's assumption that everyone else in this community fails (rather than a false perception that she attempts to undermine through Noemi's story). This suggests a deficit perspective of Noemi's home community at large and positions Noemi as an outlier among low achievers.

Beth was careful to consider her emergent bilinguals' backgrounds, cultures, and experiences and question her own understandings and assumptions. After writing the profile describing Noemi, Beth asked herself whether the persona she created reflects a careful and thoughtful portrayal of an emergent bilingual, particularly with respect to capturing the experiences of the student's mother:

> As I wrote, I questioned the mom. I wondered if she would get a job in America as a secretary. I wondered why Noemi and her family would come to America. I wondered about her home set up; would she really have her own space? I wondered what she might do after high school; is staying home and being a mom such a bad thing?

Beth was willing to admit that her perceptions might be uninformed.

By the end of the methods course, Beth identified and used several EL-responsive practices in her unit plan: modeling of assignments and expectations, provision of questions prior to lesson, vocabulary list with pictures, and structural frames for writing assignments.

A few of her explicit modifications revealed, however, continued need for growth in understanding and skill. For one task, Beth asked Noemi to compose a poetic response to a text rather than a prose response as her peers were directed to complete. The unconventional structure and language use inherent in poetry might prove unnecessarily difficult and counter-productive to an emergent bilingual's English learning. Similarly, as part of an individualized op-ed research and writing assignment, Beth suggested that Noemi tackle a subject related to poverty. Although Noemi did indeed "live" in a low-income community (remember, she is fictional), the decision asked Noemi to speak as a representative of her community. The decision reflected, too, assumptions that Noemi identified with this community and that this community can be defined solely by socioeconomics.

As was true for Carissa in the previous case, Beth's classroom community during student teaching included several emergent bilinguals, primarily native Spanish speakers, who demonstrated varying levels of English proficiency. During this experience, Beth continued to describe some essential ways to support language development and acquisition: "I feel now that vocabulary must be learned in context." Additionally, Beth continued to demonstrate skills to talk accurately and critically about emergent bilinguals and where they are in the process of language acquisition: "My other class with ELLs had mostly bilinguals, not ELLs." Here she distinguished between English-proficient bilinguals and English learners, presenting a nuanced way to refer to students along the bilingual continuum.

Preservice Teachers' Evolving Knowledge and Practice   203

During the student teaching experience, Beth identified and used the same bilingual-responsive practices that appeared in her unit plan (modeling of assignments and expectations, provision of questions prior to lesson, vocabulary list with pictures, and structural frames for writing assignments). Additionally, she drew on intentional grouping strategies and explained clearly how this particular decision was grounded in one emergent bilingual student's need (and desire) for social opportunities to learn English: "I sat Yuri by a Spanish [English] bilingual speaker. I wanted to create a lesson where they could speak all the time because they liked to speak all the time. She did take advantage of having Bebe there. I saw them talking and interacting with each other." Beth considered how to use bilingual teaching strategies to support individual learners rather than considering them a "generic fix."

At the same time, however, Beth did not include language acquisition support as a specific priority in the assessment comments provided to this student. On the sample of student work provided as part of the videotaped lesson, she told Yuri, "You are truly improving" but provided no specific comments to contextualize this generic feedback (i.e., areas in which she showed improvement) or suggestions that would enhance her language development.

At times, Beth conceptualized teaching strategies for emergent bilinguals within a "just good teaching" model. When describing her implementation of an approach to teaching poetry that draws on artistic expression, she explains,

> I was trying to get them to understand imagery and the importance of it in writing, particularly the Shakespearean sonnet, and create a visual representation. They had been doing an incredible amount of writing before this; I wanted to change things up. And I wanted to have them create something to hang up in the room, to display, to have sense of ownership of the classroom. And I wanted them to speak aloud in class and present something to their peers to practice oral expression. For Yuri, drawing was a concrete way of learning the word, "imagery," and it allowed for multiple ways to show ideas. I wanted her to gain a visual understanding of the word, not a dictionary definition. I also chose the poem for the universal theme (love over lust) not particular to any one culture. I wanted to show them that Shakespeare is relatable to their own lives.

Beth articulated her belief that the instructional choices she made for the full class would benefit Yuri. However, she did not describe any strategies she might employ unique to Yuri's language and literacy development.

In the interview following the videotaped lesson, however, Beth offered several additional strategies she would consider for one of her emergent bilingual students given the opportunity to enact the lesson again:

> Some pre-work on the language would have helped Yuri out. We could have identified unfamiliar words from the poem. I would work with her to pick those because how am I to know what she doesn't understand and what she wants to understand? Also, Yuri didn't answer in Spanish, but I didn't say she couldn't. Next time, I would be more explicit about the fact that she could.

These comments reveal Beth's reflective nature and her commitment to continuing to learn and implement various techniques in the attempt to support her students' unique needs. More significantly, they demonstrate her knowledge and valuing of strategies she might employ that are unique to Yuri's needs as an English learner.

Beth's perceptions of the emergent bilingual student with whom she worked in the student teaching classroom were generally grounded in high expectations and an optimistic vision of student success. She described her lesson goals for Yuri in noting, "It was a . . . standards-based lesson. I wanted Yuri to meet the same standards. For her to explain something orally (which she had a tough time with), this was something I felt she could achieve, could push herself toward." When describing the other students in her classes, however, some inconsistencies of perception emerged. Beth described one class as follows: "Students from the other class definitely had a lot to say and could speak, but I would not have done the same lesson with them because of the difference in skill level, ability and age." Her comment appears to reveal somewhat lower expectations of students who are still in the process of learning English. She did not say, "I would include additional modifications to support students' engagement or success with the activity or lesson" or "I would do this in order to specifically support students' developing English vocabulary." Instead, her assumption that she would have had to do a different lesson with that class suggests a deficit perspective of students at beginning stages of English language proficiency.

Similarly, when asked whether the same lesson could be implemented in one of her other, emergent bilingual-rich classrooms, Beth explained: "It could be done for other ELLs, but this was a class with smart students with low motivation." Her comment about students' [low] motivation suggest an inability to recognize that students may not be motivated because school tasks and curricula may not reflect or value their interests, lives, or experiences or because schooling or teaching is not responsive to their particular needs.

Beth continued to be careful to both learn more about her emergent bilinguals' backgrounds, cultures, and experiences and question her own understandings and assumptions. She described, for example, some of the home and school experiences of one of her emergent bilingual students as contextually necessary to make decisions about the kinds of support that would be most valuable to the student in her learning of English:

> Yuri is from the Dominican Republic. During student teaching, she had been in the U.S. for less than a year. She really wanted to write a lot. She was a 17-year-old sophomore. She was in a bilingual class at *** High School. This was a resource supplemental room, but she didn't start until halfway through the spring semester. She was taking other bilingual classes throughout the whole year.

Beth also recognized how learning is culturally influenced:

> I used hand motions with Yuri and in the class because many students in this class come from this tradition of using hand motions to aid them in learning between Spanish and English and to show that there is a definite value in their way of speaking.

Thus, Beth revealed an understanding that physical gesture is a valued communicative behavior in Yuri's culture and used this to both support and honor Yuri as a learner and person.

At the end of student teaching, Beth described herself as "very confident" in her ability to support emergent bilinguals. This confidence, however, resulted not from a belief that she had all of the answers but because she was willing and able to seek out necessary resources. She explicitly acknowledged her sense of self-efficacy: "I feel very confident. I do suffer from a certain over-confidence in my life. My confidence stems from my ability to find resources. I don't ever feel like I am fountain of knowledge." At the same time, Beth also acknowledged her privilege:

> My approach to learning from people is the hardest part for me. My particular brand of talking to adults, in particular, is overwhelming to some people. This enthusiastic friendliness. My approach now is a casual invested curiosity. The awareness of privilege has made it difficult for me to speak to those who don't have this. I was afraid they would see it as barrier, as well, that somehow I can never understand them. "I want to know more about you because you're part of a paper" vs. "You are valuable, and your experiences are crucial to my understanding of the American experience." I see now that this is faulty. In order to get along with one another, we have to understand each other's differences. I hope that people continue to be so receptive when I want to ask them questions about who they are.

Beth grappled with her own identity as a white, middle-class, native English speaker, particularly in the ways this privilege affects her interactions with others. She articulated a desire to seek genuine conversation as a means to learn more about others, not because she had to [because they're "part of a paper"] but because she really wanted to understand 'each other's' differences."

LESSONS LEARNED

To support emergent bilinguals' linguistic and academic development and sociocultural identity, general education teachers must be prepared to differentiate instruction, develop knowledge of strategies and techniques for L2 development, and consider the needs of families and communities. In this study, we examined the emergent bilingual learner-related conceptual and pedagogical development of two preservice secondary English teachers through their participation and performance in an EL-infused methods course and the student teaching experience.

Across multiple data sources, the preservice teachers evidenced varying levels of understanding and enactments of culturally and linguistically responsive pedagogy with regard to emergent bilinguals' language acquisition, academic learning, and bicultural experience, including emergent understandings of several key language-related knowledge and pedagogical competencies mainstream teachers must have to teach emergent bilinguals well (de Jong & Harper, 2005; Lucas, Villegas, & Freedson-Gonzalez, 2008). Findings also revealed the co-existence of persistent and ingrained [mis]conceptions about language, language development, class, and culture, and a complex mixture of low and high expectations and deficit and non-deficit thinking regarding emergent bilinguals and their home communities. Taken together, these findings suggest that scaffolded bilingual learner-focused courses and student teaching experiences provide spaces for preservice teachers to explore, and at times challenge, their knowledge and perceptions of diverse students. Findings also suggest that the development of culturally and linguistically responsive pedagogy involves a journey that does not end at the completion of the preservice education experience.

Participants were conscientious in their work and appeared receptive to learning how to teach so children of all backgrounds can succeed. They evidenced some understanding of bilingual learners' varying proficiencies in each language, as well as differences between the kind of language proficiency that is related to the immediate social context and that is required to navigate most school tasks successfully. For example, Beth addressed the often conflated domains of conversational versus academic language from an informed position when describing emergent bilingual students' developing [English] language. Beth also distinguished between proficient speakers of two languages and students who were developing proficiency in English and spoke another language (i.e., ELLs). These important distinctions serve as the basis for culturally and linguistically responsive instructional planning and teaching, as they help teachers set adequate instructional objectives, select classroom tasks that promote language and content learning, and integrate emergent bilinguals into the academic goals and discourse of the classroom (Harper & de Jong, 2004).

Yet there remained room for additional development in participants' preparation to work effectively with emergent bilinguals, particularly with respect to knowledge of the L2 acquisition process, suggesting a need for more breadth and depth of coverage of this particular topic in these preservice teachers' preparation program. Similarly, descriptions of emergent bilinguals' language abilities and developmental processes were often framed within deficit perspectives; a learner's English ability was used to define her ability to communicate in general and was often equated with limited academic or cognitive ability. Carissa presented an informed counter-narrative, however, by recognizing that limited literacy ability in English does not reflect limited intelligence.

With the exception of a few counter-examples provided by Beth, participants generally were unable or unwilling to distinguish cultural differences within ethnic groups (e.g., Latinas), possessed little or inaccurate knowledge about the cultural backgrounds of their students, and held deficit perspectives with regard to cultural diversity. A recurring pattern highlighted participants' tendency to assume that Spanish-speaking students were either Puerto Rican or Mexican and/or to use broad ethnic categories to describe students' backgrounds, as exemplified in Carissa's description of a student for whom she modified a lesson ("Robert is a seventh grader; he is Latino. I don't know what he was"). Given the changing landscape in U.S. classrooms, preservice teachers needs to be provided scaffolded spaces and experiences wherein to explore their own and their [current and future] students' cultural and linguistic identities.

At the same time, participants clearly and consistently articulated commitments to supporting bilingual learners, particularly in an affective sense. In contrast to their apparent inability or unwillingness to distinguish cultural differences within ethnic groups when describing students' cultural backgrounds, participants articulated a pedagogy of care and concern for students' well-being. For most participants, building relationships with students was identified as the most effective means of promoting learning among emergent bilinguals. Both Carissa and Beth noted the need to know bilingual students as people to build trust and an increased likelihood that learning will occur. Similarly, Carissa modified lessons with the specific purpose of taking pressure off emergent bilinguals to help them feel more comfortable in the classroom.

Preservice teachers who participated in the bilingual learner-infused methods course evidenced emergent understanding of effective grouping strategies to maximize emergent bilinguals' participation and social interaction in the classroom, although some candidates implemented such supports more consistently and intentionally than others. Beth, for example, demonstrated a conscious effort to "create social opportunities for [emergent bilinguals] to build [their] English skills" by thoughtfully grouping emergent bilingual learners with more proficient bilinguals. She recognized that pairing bilingual learners of the same language backgrounds provided opportunities for students to use both the L1 and English for thinking and learning and maximized opportunities for emergent bilinguals to use English with linguistically and academically knowledgeable peers. Carissa also grouped students intentionally in integrated English proficiency literature response groups that included English speakers and English learners. Such structured opportunities for emergent bilinguals to actively engage in the process of negotiating meaning through academic language facilitate rich language input and encourage meaningful interaction, essential components of language learning (Gibbons, 2002; Wong-Fillmore & Snow, 2005).

Findings also revealed various pedagogical tools and practices taken up by participants directly from the revised methods course. A number of participants demonstrated attention to language, particularly second language scaffolding techniques, in their lesson planning and teaching. For example, Beth and Carissa incorporated students' first language to access the curriculum and demonstrate existing knowledge, included pictures of target vocabulary words, drew images to explain concepts, and/or previewed target vocabulary before reading a shared text. Carissa further sheltered instruction for her emergent bilingual students by creating picture timelines of key events in literature assignments and modified supplementary materials to support understanding of critical story concepts. Such lesson modifications provided access to comprehensible input and opportunities for emergent bilinguals to produce meaningful language.

Although candidates learned and employed a number of effective strategies to support emergent bilinguals (e.g., previewing materials and assignments, providing graphic organizers, giving students choice within tasks, providing exemplars of desired products, and varying grouping strategies), most strategies were not specifically focused on scaffolding the language and literacy demands of learning in a second language. Most of these scaffolds involved incorporation of tools, methods, or other supportive frameworks effective with English-speaking students and reflecting "just good teaching" approaches that do not explicitly attend to emergent bilinguals' linguistic needs and cultural experiences.

Further, participants expressed awareness of the need to hold all students to high standards. For some, however, this took the form of undifferentiated assignments and an absence of scaffolded support. Carissa, for example, chose not to alter the project she assigned to her seventh-grade students or her evaluation of the resulting product for the emergent bilinguals in the classroom, articulating her wish to hold all students to the same standard of performance.

In general, the bilingual learner-infused methods course and student teaching experience provided contexts in which preservice teachers could build and apply understandings of language and cultural diversity to teaching emergent bilingual learners. However, these experiences had different impacts on participants as highlighted in the focal cases. Carissa demonstrated knowledge and skill in planning for and enacting modified instruction for emergent bilinguals but drew on "just good teaching" strategies rather than those explicitly focused on language acquisition and development. In contrast, Beth evidenced an enhanced capacity for culturally and linguistically responsive teaching through explicit efforts to respect and capitalize on students' diversity, a reflective/reflexive stance, and an emerging ability to orchestrate multiple supportive scaffolds for emergent bilinguals. Beth's and Carissa's cases reveal different pathways and stages toward culturally and linguistically responsive teaching, suggesting that these preservice teachers' journeys are still "under construction." These findings are quite promising, providing insight into the types of teacher education program content, experiences, and approaches teacher educators might build on in support of their students' culturally and linguistically responsive pedagogical development.

RECOMMENDATIONS

In the current political context, the pre-K-12 ELL population continues to grow while specialized educational programs designed to meet these students' unique language learning needs are diminishing given the push for inclusive education. In response, we must prepare *all* teachers to teach emergent bilingual learners successfully through the development of pedagogical language knowledge (e.g., knowledge about how language works, how it supports learning, how L1 and L2 work together, and how language is modeled and scaffolded for all children; Galguera, 2011). This requires building the capacity of teacher education programs and their pre-K-12 school partners to offer both coursework and clinical experiences to preservice teachers that can provide them with the skills, dispositions, and knowledge they need to work effectively with and advocate for emergent bilingual children from ethnic, cultural, and linguistic backgrounds often different from their own. Our findings illuminate the complexities inherent in this task. Prospective teachers differed in their developing knowledge of the educational needs of culturally and linguistically diverse learners, given similar preservice teacher education course experiences and opportunities to interact with emergent bilinguals in culturally, linguistically, and socioeconomically diverse schools. Further, participants demonstrated a range of developing abilities in lesson planning and applying their understandings of language and culture in their practice in integrated classes that included emergent bilinguals. Such complexity sheds light on the areas where further attention is required in continued curricular restructuring and faculty development across the teacher education program. Specific recommendations include:

- Positioning language as central for learning in academic contexts. The knowledge base for effective teaching has been heavily influenced over the past 25 years by the concept of pedagogical content knowledge, a combination of content knowledge and pedagogical knowledge (Shulman, 1987). This approach, however, overlooks the role of language in learning, the importance of attending to language in learning to teach content well, or the role that language diversity might play in teachers' development of content knowledge (Valdes, 2001).
- Moving away from a "human relations approach" (Akiba, Cockrell, Simmons, Han, & Agarwal, 2010) to learning about diversity, wherein preservice teachers learn about the "other" and focus on ways to accommodate differences that students bring into the classroom rather than learning to inquire about and affirm students' cultural and language diversity as a resource that can be used to inform teacher knowledge and practices to promote student learning. As suggested earlier, positioning language at the center of teaching and learning supports preservice teachers' development of pedagogical language knowledge directly related to disciplinary teaching. Pedagogical language knowledge requires teachers to become critically aware of how students' bilingualism and varied language uses can be deliberately considered in their interpretations of the language demands embedded within the academic disciplines. Teacher education program faculty, field supervisors, and mentor teachers should work together to provide guidance, support, and reflection on the development of preservice teachers' pedagogical language knowledge.
- Infusing bilingual learner-related content across all facets of the teacher education program through ongoing coordination of such content sequenced across time (i.e., the duration of the teacher education program), coursework, and clinical experiences. Efforts to revise coursework and related experiences to support preservice teachers' pedagogical language knowledge would be more powerful if they were supported by more explicit, systematic, and scaffolded experiences that help general education teacher candidates to look *at* rather than *through* the language demands of the classroom (de Jong & Harper, 2011) and to develop the habits of thinking, practices, and dispositions that acknowledge the specific linguistic and cultural needs of emergent bilinguals. In initial preservice teacher education courses, preservice teachers should acquire foundational understanding about how language works, how language supports learning, and how L1 and L2 work together. Later courses should help preservice teachers understand how to model and scaffold disciplinary uses of language (i.e., academic language). This approach may more effectively support the development of preservice teachers' sensitivities, understandings, practices, and inclination to responsibly serve and advocate for emergent bilingual learners.

Understanding the influence of courses and complementary experiences in teacher education that strives to provide learning spaces for preservice teachers to develop culturally and linguistically responsive pedagogy is an ongoing challenge, one that is influenced significantly by instructor/mentor/supervisor knowledge and confidence as well as coordination across program courses and experiences. Participants' struggles to understand and articulate bilingual developmental processes, for example, likely reflected the instructor's own emergent development in this area. This is not surprising considering that the special expertise needed to teach emergent bilinguals well is not generally emphasized in the preparation of teacher educators and other teaching professionals. In response, and in an effort to implement a collective vision of teaching and learning in a multicultural society (Villegas & Lucas, 2002) across the teacher education program, Wendy and her teacher education colleagues continue to engage in professional development designed to fill this gap and foster opportunities for the additional growth of their students in the next iteration of bilingual learner-focused courses and school-based experiences.

REFERENCES

Akiba, M., Cockrell, K. S., Simmons, J. C., Han, S., & Agarwal, G. (2010). Preparing teachers for diversity: Examination of teacher certification and program accreditation standards in the 50 states and Washington, DC. *Equity and Excellence in Education, 43*(4), 446–462.

Athanases, S. Z., & de Oliveira, L. C. (2007). Conviction, confrontation, and risk in new teachers' advocating for equity. *Teaching Education, 18*(2), 123–136.

Athanases, S. Z., & de Oliveira, L. C. (2008). Advocacy for equity in classrooms and beyond: New teachers' challenges and responses. *Teachers College Record, 110*(1), 64–104.

Athanases, S. Z., & Martin, K. J. (2006). Learning to advocate for educational equity in a teacher credential program. *Teaching and Teacher Education, 22*, 627–646.

Banks, J. (1991). A curriculum for empowerment, action, and change. In C. E. Sleeter (Ed.), *Empowerment through multicultural education* (pp. 125–141). Albany: State University of New York Press.

Banks, J. (2001). *Cultural diversity and education: Foundations, curriculum, and teaching* (4th ed.). Boston: Allyn & Bacon.

Brisk, M. E., Horan, D., & Macdonald, E. (2007). A scaffolded approach to learning to write. In L. S. Verplaetse & N. Migliacci (Eds.), *Inclusive pedagogy for English language learners: A handbook of research-informed practices* (pp. 15–32). Mahwah, NJ: Lawrence Erlbaum Associates.

Brown, E. L. (2004). What precipitates change in cultural diversity awareness during a multicultural course? The message or the method? *Journal of Teacher Education, 55*(4), 325–340.

Cho, G., & DeCastro-Ambrosetti, D. (2005). Is ignorance bliss? Pre-service teacher attitudes toward multicultural education. *The High School Journal, 89*(2), 24–28.

Cochran-Smith, M., & Zeichner, K. (Eds.). (2005). *Studying teacher education.* New York: Routledge.

de Jong, E. J., & Harper, C. A. (2005). Preparing mainstream teachers for English language learners: Is being a good teacher good enough? *Teacher Education Quarterly, 32*(2), 101–124.

de Jong, E. J., & Harper, C. A. (2011). "Accommodating diversity": Pre-service teachers' views on effective practices for English language learners. In T. Lucas (Ed.), *Teacher preparation for linguistically diverse classrooms* (pp. 73–90). New York: Routledge.

de Oliveira, L. C., & Athanases, S. Z. (2007). Graduates' reports of advocating for English language learners. *Journal of Teacher Education, 58*(3), 202–215.

Denzin, N., & Lincoln, Y. S. (Eds.). (1994). *Handbook of qualitative research.* Thousand Oaks, CA: Sage.

Echevarria, J., Vogt, M., & Short, D. (2012). *Making content comprehensible for English language learners: The SIOP model* (4th ed.). Needham Heights, MA: Pearson Allyn & Bacon.

Gaitan, C. D. (2004). *Involving Latino families in schools: Raising student achievement through home-school partnerships.* Thousand Oaks, CA: Corwin Press.

Galguera, T. (2011). Participant structures as professional learning tasks and the development of pedagogical of pedagogical langauge knowledge among preservice teachers. *Teacher Education Quarterly, 38*(1), 85–106.

Gibbons, P. (2002). *Scaffolding language, scaffolding learning: Teaching second language learners in the mainstream classroom.* Portsmouth, NH: Heinemann.

Hill-Jackson, V. (2007). Wrestling whiteness: Three stages of shifting multicultural perspectives among White pre-service teachers. *Multicultural Perspectives, 9*(2), 29–35.

Lucas, T., Villegas, A. M., & Freedson-Gonzalez, M. (2008). Linguistically responsive teacher education: Preparing classroom teachers to teach English language learners. *Journal of Teacher Education, 59*, 361–373.

Merriam, S. B. (1998). *Qualitative research and case study applications in education.* San Francisco, CA: Jossey-Bass.

Meskill, C. (2005). Infusing English language learner issues throughout professional educator curricula: The "Training All Teachers" project. *Teachers College Record, 107*, 739–756.

Milner, H. R. (2005). Stability and change in prospective teachers' beliefs and decisions about diversity and learning to teach. *Teaching and Teacher Education, 21*(7), 767–786.

Milner, H. R. (2006). Preservice teachers' learning about cultural and racial diversity: Implications for urban education. *Urban Education, 41*(4), 343–375.

Shulman, L. S. (1987). Knowledge and teaching foundations of the new reform. *Harvard Educational Review, 57*(1), 1–22.

Strauss, A. L., & Corbin, J. (1990). *Basics of qualitative research: Grounded theory procedures and techniques.* Newbury Park, CA: Sage.

Thomas, S., & Vanderhaar, J. (2008). Negotiating resistance to multiculturalism in a teacher education curriculum: A case study. *The Teacher Educator, 43*, 173–197.

Valdes, G. (2001). *Learning and not Learning English: Latino Students in American Schools.* New York: Teachers College Press.

Villegas, A. M., & Lucas, T. (2002). *Educating culturally responsive teachers: A coherent approach.* Albany, NY: State University of New York Press.

Wong-Fillmore, L., & Snow, C. E. (2005). What teachers need to know about language. In C. T. Adger, C. E. Snow, & D. Christian (Eds.), *What teachers need to know about language* (pp. 7–54). Washington, DC: Center for Applied Linguistics.

APPENDIX A

Guiding Questions for Whole-Class Discussion of Emergent Bilingual Student Profiles During Methods Instruction

1. What guided your decision-making process in generating the student profile thus far (experiences, perceptions, readings, etc.)?
2. What about this process is proving challenging?
3. What part of the profile do you feel best captures the student you have in mind?
4. What part of the profile still feels "off"?
5. Consider the components of your own multifaceted identity (i.e., gender, race, culture, education, SES, language, citizenship, etc.). Where in your profile do you see evidence of these identities shaping your understandings of the student you created?

APPENDIX B

SIOP-Infused Daily Lesson Plan Format

Note: Italicized items indicate features of the Sheltered Instruction Observation Protocol (SIOP) designed to evaluate teachers in their ability to support emergent bilinguals. Teacher attention to these features benefits all learners but is essential for emergent bilingual students.

Name: Date(s) of Lesson:

<u>Student Learning Objective(s) and Related Assessment(s)</u>: Identify specific and measurable learning objectives for the lesson. *Include at least one language objective (vocabulary, usage, conventions, etc.).* Describe how you will ask students to demonstrate mastery of objective(s) and how you will use the resulting information to evaluate their understandings. Where appropriate, note how objectives align with the CT Common Core Standards.

<u>Materials/Resources:</u> List the materials you will use during the lesson, *including any supplementary or adapted visuals, models, or technological resources.*

<u>Learning Activities</u>:

Initiation: Describe briefly how you will initiate the lesson.
—How will you set expectations for learning?
—*How will you draw upon individual student's prior knowledge, experiences, and learning?*

—How will you articulate to learners what they will be doing and learning, how they will demonstrate learning, and why this is important?

Lesson Development: Describe how you will develop the lesson.
—What learning activities will students engage in to gain the key content and skills identified in the objective(s)?
—*What instructional grouping (whole class, small groups, pairs, individuals) will you use in each phase of instruction?*
—*What will you do to model or guide practice?*

Closure: Describe briefly how you will close the lesson and help students understand the purpose of the lesson.
—How will you interact with learners to elicit evidence of student understanding of the purpose(s) for learning and mastery of objective(s)?

Individuals Needing Differentiated Instruction: *Differentiate instruction for one emergent bilingual* and one identified Special Needs student. For each student, describe strategies you might employ to modify instruction to meet the needs of each of these learners.

APPENDIX C

Interview Questions Used While Discussing a Videotaped Lesson during Student Teaching

[Before watching the videotaped lesson together]

1. What is some information you can share about the emergent bilingual student(s) with whom you worked in this video?
2. Consider your thoughts going into the lesson. What specific goals did you set out for all students in relation to language, content, and literacy development? How were these similar to or different from those set out for the emergent bilingual student(s)?
3. How did you determine these goals? Why did you choose these versus others, and how did you know these were appropriate for the emergent bilingual learner(s)?

[After viewing the videotaped lesson together]

4. What are your general impressions of what took place?
5. Why did you choose to _____ at this point in the lesson? How was this choice met by the emergent bilingual student(s)? [Repeated where appropriate.]
6. Given the goals you set out for the emergent bilingual learner(s) around language, literacy, and content, how appropriate and effective were

your chosen methods and modifications to help students meet those goals? How do you know? Would you choose to enact this choice if repeating the lesson now?
7. Considering what you know about best practices, what modifications might you consider when working with emergent bilinguals?
8. How confident are you in your ability to support the needs of emergent bilinguals in the classroom setting?
9. What fears, concerns, and gaps in knowledge remain? What more would you like to know?

Part IV
Moving Forward

12 Pathways to Success
Models of Teacher Preparation for Cultural and Linguistic Diversity

David M. Moss, J. Zack, and Susan L. Payne

The work of improving teacher preparation for success in culturally and linguistically diverse classrooms will understandably vary across program models but is presently a well-recognized priority among teacher preparation (Brisk, 2008). We strongly advocate that this timely aim should be viewed as both vital and achievable irrespective of the teacher education program in which preservice candidates are prepared. At the University of Connecticut (UConn), our efforts in this realm have involved teacher education faculty in both our Integrated Bachelor's/Master's (IBM) program as well as faculty in our one-year intensive master's program (Teacher Certification Program for College Graduates [TCPCG]). Drawing on our experiences from our teacher education programs, this chapter will explore the overarching question: Regardless of the constraints of specific program models as well as common programmatic challenges such as accreditation, how can faculty improve teacher preparation for linguistic and cultural diversity?

The chapter will be presented in three sections. The following section will discuss the key tenets of models of teacher education across the U.S. and introduce program elements that are likely "reform points" for considering cultural and linguistic diversity. Within this chapter, reform points are defined as both *opportunities* and *junctures* within teacher education programs that offer significant potential for making programmatic changes. The next section will address select details of the various UConn models as an exemplar for reform, revisiting the notion of reform points in further detail. This section will offer specific examples and commentary regarding the process of fostering change within our teacher education programs, addressing obstacles in our own journey. The final section presents challenges and implications for considering reforms across models of teacher education.

MODELS OF TEACHER EDUCATION IN THE U.S.

There exists a remarkable diversity of program designs within the predominant models of preparing teachers. We distinguish the notion of program design from the broader term of model; within the three overarching models we describe later in this chapter, seemingly endless program designs dictate the finer details of course sequence and other programmatic elements. As scholars and teachers, we have come to recognize that there is no singular pathway to success when it comes to learning, and thus there is no singular "best" program design for the preparation of teachers to succeed with emergent bilinguals. Such varied ways of preparing teachers need not deter reform efforts, in that each and every program has the potential to make significant gains in improving the ways teachers are prepared.

Although there are no universally recognized labels for various models of teacher education in the U.S., for accreditation purposes, programs are often categorized by their duration and/or by any diplomas awarded in conjunction with the resultant certification, also commonly known as licensure. This immediately brings us to our first key reform point for the consideration of preparing candidates to succeed as teachers in classrooms with emergent bilinguals—licensure and accreditation. For our chapter, we link these notions given the fundamentally critical role accreditation has had in teacher education in recent years with respect to program design and the ability to ensure program graduates are credentialed and eligible to teach.

Although accreditation is a popular topic for discussion among almost any gathering of teacher educators, the most common catalyst underpinning such passionate discourse is the need to support each other through such a high-stakes, challenging endeavor. Accreditation has been characterized as "the most fully developed institutionalization of the idea of accountability in higher education" (Wilson & Youngs, 2005, p. 593), yet ironically the gravity of such an accountability model may hinder improvement efforts as opposed to serving as a catalyst for reform. All teacher education programs are held to national and/or state standards, and regrettably the motivation to be innovative—as opposed to conforming—may be severely curtailed in the name of making the grade in mandated programmatic reviews. Although program accreditation is a burden in some respects, we regard it as more of an opportunity to purposefully consider such important notions as data collection for programmatic improvements. As discussed in earlier chapters, such data collection was essential in our efforts to better prepare teacher candidates for success in classrooms with emergent bilingual pupils.

In terms of leveraging the Council for the Accreditation of Educator Preparation (2013) standards as an opportunity for considering programmatic reforms, note that the standards explicitly have aspects of diversity embedded within them:

- Standard 1 emphasizes that "all students" should be the focus of educator preparation and that completers should demonstrate skills and commitment that provide all P-12 students access to rigorous college and career ready standards. Standard 1 endorses the Interstate

Teacher and Support Consortium (InTASC) teacher standards in their entirety, and the performances, knowledge, and dispositions that are extensions of those standards contain literally scores of references to cultural competence, individual differences, creativity and innovation, and working with families and communities.
- Standard 2 on clinical experiences again is cast in terms of preparing candidates to work with "all students" and calls for diversity in clinical experiences.
- Standard 3 on candidate quality insists that providers must undertake positive outreach efforts to recruit a more able and more diverse candidate pool.
- Taken together, the letter and spirit of these new standards encourage teacher education programs, through the process of accreditation, to consider the ways in which they are preparing candidates to teach culturally and linguistically diverse pupils and work effectively with communities in which these students and their families reside.

As we continue our discussion of program reform, we will now briefly delineate three common program models and clarify some terms to help you think about your own program and consider points for reform.

We regard so-called traditional teacher education models as those that exist solely within the context of an undergraduate-only program. This common four-year program model has seemingly countless program designs, but most culminate in some form of practice teaching experience, best known as student teaching. This traditional model sometimes allows for a school-based pre-student teaching experience. Regardless, all requirements for certification are fulfilled within the context of a bachelor's degree. Perhaps the widest variation in program design of this traditional model centers around whether education serves as the major for the degree or if the teacher education element of the undergraduate experience exists as a minor or some equivalent subsidiary designation within the course of study. Andrew (2005) notes that variants of this traditional approach stemming from the normal school model "has produced most of America's public school teachers over the past fifty years" (p. 29).

A second model is the post-baccalaureate program (such as the TCPCG discussed throughout this book). Standing alone beyond the context of an undergraduate program, this program model may or may not lead to a master's degree in conjunction with certification. These programs are frequently designed for career changers in addition to those students who did not pursue teaching as a formal element of their undergraduate experience. Similar to the traditional model, this model typically requires a semester-long student teaching experience. More innovative configurations of this model may require pre- and/or post-teaching practica in schools. Again, the program design variants within this model are as numerous and diverse as the institutions in which they occur.

The third and final model we highlight is the IBM program. At UConn, we transitioned from a traditional undergraduate model to an integrated one, sometimes referred to as an extended model, more than 20 years ago. At our institution, we routinely refer to this model as the "five-year program" because we have extended the time available to us for the preparation of our candidates by adding a required year beyond the bachelor's to allow for school placements and course work *both* prior to and following student teaching (please refer to Chapter 2 in this book for a more detailed discussion of this program design). Andrew (2005) noted the rationale for such extended year models as two-pronged: (a) the more highly regarded professions had evolved to require post-baccalaureate professional training and so should education, and (b) prospective teachers need a strong liberal arts education, a subject field major, challenging professional course work, and clinical practice that goes beyond the traditional single semester. Thus, calls for year-long internships often associated with this model necessitated a repackaging of traditional programs into other than a four-year bachelor's framework. In 1996, the National Commission on Teaching and America's Future launched its first report, *What Matters Most: Teaching for America's Future.* The report's second major recommendation for improving teacher preparation was to develop extended teacher preparation programs that provide a year-long internship in a professional development school (National Commission on Teaching and America's Future, 1996). Consensus among faculty who teach in our integrated program is that our year-long internship in the master's year, after student teaching, is central to whatever success we achieve in the preparation of teachers. It is important to note, however, that research provides conflicting findings regarding the efficacy of different models of teacher education (Cochran-Smith & Zeichner, 2005), and we are not advocating one model over another. Each model has both logical points for reform and inherent challenges in the preparation of teachers for success in classrooms with emergent bilinguals.

Given the vast numbers of teachers in the U.S. prepared through these three models (traditional, post-baccalaureate, integrated/extended year), we have elected not to explicitly address others, including so-called alternate routes to licensure; however, we invite readers who represent such programs to consider our recommendations for reform within their own contexts.

Across the endless program configurations within the various models for the preparation of teachers, there are numerous potential points for reform. We would like to specifically address a key component common to virtually every university-based teacher education program, regardless of model or program design, the methods class(es). This aspect of a program represents a core element of teacher education and thus becomes a likely "reform point" that affords ample opportunities to consider substantial changes to the way teachers are prepared. In fact, it is hard to envision a teacher preparation program without this essential element, and thus it should be considered strategically important as faculty move to enhance their programs to better prepare their candidates to work effectively in culturally and linguistically diverse classrooms. Although teacher education programs often have foundations courses and perhaps even courses that explicitly deal with issues underpinning multicultural education, we have identified the methods courses as a key point for reform because they are likely to help teacher education candidates bridge the theory-practice gap and make actual changes in their practice as beginning teachers. However, as discussed throughout this book, our work was not limited to changes to such methods courses. Within our program, other reform points included the "Introduction to Teaching" course (in this course, we have been experimenting with summits and guest speakers to orient our teacher candidates to various issues underpinning the challenges and policies of teaching emergent bilinguals), Junior Fall Seminar (please refer to Chapter 7 where clinical faculty discuss the "danger of single story"), Student Teaching and Seminar (here we intentionally sought to pair student teachers with mentors and supervisors who could support their emerging planning and instruction in this area), and a diversity course in the fifth and final year of our program (taught by faculty with expertise in the education of linguistically and culturally diverse students).

Early work as a professional learning community allowed us to explore such potential reform points, and in the next section, we will address key details of UConn's teacher education programs. This section will specifically focus on our methods courses along with commentary from a programmatic point of view. We intend that readers will consider the selection of reform points in their own program along with associated mechanisms for leveraging such points into improved instruction for linguistically and culturally diverse students.

A MODEL FOR REFORM

As faculty at UConn, we have endeavored to answer the call for reforming teacher education by constructively responding to external pressures, viewing accreditation as a reform point, and purposefully working as a community of learners to improve our preparation of candidates to work in linguistically and culturally diverse settings. The need for data to support accreditation efforts make it a logical reform point from the perspective of considering assessments that support changes to improve teacher candidate training for work with emergent bilinguals. For example, without the alumni survey data highlighting a gap in their preparation of working with emergent bilinguals, it would have been more challenging to so clearly identify the need for such reforms at the outset of this initiative. Thus, the purposefully cultivated culture of assessment at the Neag School of Education, in support of accreditation and other aims, has served to promote and enhance this effort. As noted in the *Neag School of Education Assessment Plan* (Neag School of Education Assessment Committee, 2012):

> The philosophy embraced by the (Assessment) Office is that each person has ownership in assessment as the School strives for a model of excellence, embracing and promoting a culture characterized by evidence-based decisions. (Assessment is) a collaborative process . . . facilitated by the assessment committee and our various assessment subcommittees. The assessment committee has representation across all levels (students, faculty, staff, administrators) and units.

Therefore, in many ways, Project PREPARE-ELLs has been a living embodiment of our assessment culture. To a large extent, this project was motivated by multiple forms of data, as well as one that has sought to continue to collect and use a broad scope of data to inform our work. Because our assessment culture is pervasive across all programs in the Neag School, our work as a faculty learning community has been able to leverage the mindset of data-driven decision making already unfolding across our teacher education programs. Regardless of your particular program model, as previously outlined in this chapter, the need for data in support of accreditation can and should serve as a catalyst to enhance the scope of your assessment program. For Project PREPARE-ELLs, our data collection was tailored to each of our teacher education programs (integrated and post-baccalaureate); likewise, your program model should dictate the nature of your assessments. For example, the number and duration of school placements will serve to shape the data you will need to inform your faculty regarding selected outcomes. That is, it is important to seek synergy among your program design and any associated programmatic assessments to maximize the potential that such assessments may impact the reform process.

Before we go on to discuss the methods courses through a programmatic lens, we wanted to briefly address an important facet of our various programs, competitive admissions, as another kind of reform point. We have made revisions to our interview questions and required essay to give candidates opportunities to convey their openness to working with diverse learners, and thus we have increased our effort to identify candidates likely to succeed in teaching all kinds of students. Although we do not expect that applicants necessarily bring prior experience working with culturally and linguistically diverse youth, we value such experience and sense that an increasing number of students are choosing to do tutoring or volunteering with more diverse populations since we explicitly began recommending that to prospective candidates. Again, regardless of your program model and whether you have a competitive admissions process for entry into your programs, we have found that communicating our priorities and expectations to future students sets the stage for what they can expect as they begin their work as preservice teachers.

We would now like to programmatically address a key area that Project PREPARE-ELLs has meaningfully impacted through the work of faculty engaged in our learning community: our methods courses. In Chapter 5, the authors noted that significant challenges in the methods courses included preservice teachers' prior knowledge and experiences coupled with a lack of teacher educator knowledge about culturally and linguistically responsive pedagogy. That is, we recognized that the challenge in reforming methods classes lay not merely with what our teacher candidates did or did not believe, but also with the systemic deficiency in knowledge of the faculty charged with teaching these classes. Additionally, we uncovered a lack of communication regarding cultural and linguistic pedagogy among faculty teaching various methods courses. Even given our shared vision and the synergy across programs, we found that as we dug deeper in this one area, there were untapped opportunities to collaborate and coordinate between courses.

Consistent with many program models, methods courses are designed to run seamlessly with seminar courses to help bridge theory and practice and serve to prepare students for success in student teaching and beyond. Thus, we determined that these courses, which strategically occur at a key juncture in our cohort-based program, are at a critical point to promote preservice learning that could actually impact practice. The methods courses are only offered in our plan of study at what we believe to be just the right time in the program—immediately prior to student teaching—to ensure that our preservice candidates "get off on the right foot" with regard to teaching emergent bilinguals. Given this convergence of course content designed to bridge theory and practice with the sequencing of these courses within our plan of study, we focused significant efforts in Project PREPARE-ELLs to modifying and enhancing these courses. Programmatically, we have come to identify this convergence as a "reform point" within our program, and we have come to believe that acting on it is an essential element for success in any reform process. Although various program models and designs will perhaps result in different reform points, the key lesson here is to identify such points as likely high-impact junctures in your program. In our case, methods courses were deemed potentially high impact because of the timing of when they are offered in our program, the potential for students to connect theory with practice given the nature of these courses, and the catalytic potential for faculty to collaborate on content and pedagogy to support the teaching of emergent bilinguals.

From a programmatic point of view, a number of obstacles emerged that needed to be addressed as we began to make program enhancements. One obstacle was the progression of the curriculum as we considered changes to the methods courses. That is, as one modifies one aspect of a program, there are implications for what comes before and after that area of focus. This may be particularly true for traditional undergraduate programs where time for teacher education courses and clinic experiences may already be severely limited. Although changes were largely made within the methods block of courses themselves, we recognized that there are implications across an entire program when reforms are implemented. This consideration of the parts versus the whole from a programmatic standpoint can impose considerable obstacles if not carefully contemplated. For example, we asked ourselves, if significant effort were to be placed in our methods block courses regarding fostering culturally and linguistically meaningful pedagogies, would our school-based cooperating teachers be able to support the implementation of those skills during the subsequent student teaching semester? Faculty expressed some concern that a herculean effort in the methods courses, by both faculty and students, could be for naught if there were not explicit opportunities to impact actual practice down the line.

We did not have all the answers at the outset of this effort, and we still do not, but we forged ahead with purposeful changes to our methods courses, believing that positive change in one aspect of our program would be a catalyst for positive change in others. For instance, the TCPCG has now begun to experiment with providing English as a Second Language (ESL)/sheltered instruction strategies throughout the four semesters of the programs. In the four courses that require teacher candidates to produce lesson plans (general methods, subject-specific methods, student teaching seminar, and multicultural education), they learn strategies to aid emergent bilinguals and are required to explicitly and purposefully weave these into lesson plans. If from the outset we were required to map out all the potential programmatic consequences and needs resulting from making significant changes to the methods courses, we are quite convinced that we would still be merely discussing those implications with little or no action to show for our efforts. Perhaps like many faculty in higher education, we have learned that we are quite adept at contemplating reforms but less accomplished at implementing them.

Thus, a key breakthrough for us was to agree to leap into the great unknown of action, trusting that members of our learning community would support each other and ultimately make informed programmatic changes in the best interest of our students. Although certainly not reckless, it is important to recognize that there was some risk involved in making such substantial changes without fully understanding all the implications across our programs. In the end, what helped empower faculty to make such a commitment to reform was both our mindfulness to our core tenets of our programs and the belief that these reforms embodied the next generation of needed changes. As noted, UConn evolved to an extended year model more than two decades ago, and although many minor adjustments were implemented, there have not been significant programmatic changes in quite some time. In part, many faculty believed that our teacher education programs "worked just fine," and we were cautious not to jettison effective elements. At the same time, certain changes seemed long overdue as the knowledge base for teaching has advanced. As Korthagen, Loughran, and Russell (2006) note:

There has been a remarkable development of the knowledge base for teaching through extensive educational research over the last four decades. Nevertheless, the theory–practice issue seems intractable: telling new teachers what research shows about good teaching and sending them off to practice has failed to change, in any major way, what happens in our schools and universities. (p. 1038)

We have come to believe that aspects of cultural and linguistic diversity are indeed central to the core of a knowledge base within teacher education. This is no small point. Elevating the preparation of preservice teachers to effectively work with emergent bilinguals as *fundamentally* essential within our teacher education program demanded that we act. Thus, whatever risks and uncertainty we faced within programmatic reform became secondary to the pressing need to improve our work in this area.

As a faculty, given our assessment data initially derived from accreditation and now central to our assessment-driven culture, we acknowledged something needed to be done. Grounding our reform efforts in activities that would indeed yield tangible changes to practice was paramount. Merely telling new teachers about research in this area we knew would return unsatisfying results. Recognizing and publicly acknowledging our own deficiencies as teacher educators, identifying potential points for reform and building on the strengths of our programs, leveraging our culture of assessment, and making changes that we believed could immediately impact practice helped us move ahead even if our pathway was beset with uncertainty. Establishing and nurturing a faculty learning community helped make reform both programmatically necessary and doable; indeed, the faculty learning community was a powerful catalyst for action.

PROGRAMMATIC RECOMMENDATIONS

In this final section, as a community of scholars and teachers, we offer recommendations for the consideration of programmatic reform informed by our lived experiences. Before we explicitly offer such recommendations, we'd like to address two challenges common to all models of teacher education. The first is the notion of establishing and acting on priorities, often masked as a dearth of time, and the second is the developmental considerations of when and how we foster certain knowledge, skills, and dispositions with preservice teachers. Recognizing that all teacher education models and program designs have inherent challenges and limitations, we encourage faculty to consider the potential "reform points" of their own programs as we discuss these ideas. Recall that such reform points may be considered as both *opportunities* (such as courses, accreditation, or processes of communication with matriculating and prospective teachers) and *junctures* within teacher education programs that offer significant potential for making programmatic changes. Although this chapter focused mainly on the methods courses as a key reform point for our initiative, as noted, we also directed effort to such areas as a diversity course, an introductory course, and seminars. We strongly encourage you as faculty representing a wide array of program models and designs to identify points of reform specifically targeted to your work in supporting the teaching of emergent bilinguals.

Chapter 5 notes how infusing new material into well-developed courses is a significant challenge. Yet this notion of "time" or more precisely the lack thereof is really an echo of a more systemic issue of the need to both establish and adhere to priorities. Understandably, different program models will have varying pressures when it comes to available time to incorporate changes. For example, an undergraduate program with an education major may have considerably more credits available than one where all the teacher education experiences must be executed within an 18-credit minor. Regardless of the model, we suspect there is not a single program in existence today that doesn't feel pressure to deliver the established curriculum within the confines of the course of study. This is true for us at the Neag School of Education across both our programs. Thus, the notion of establishing priorities and committing to them became a viable means by which to consider making substantial changes, especially because allocating more courses and/or experiences was not an option for us in either program at the outset of the initiative.

Next, we would like to address the age-old teacher education dilemma of when to teach various knowledge, dispositions, and skills within a program. Paradoxically, the soundest solution is to foster key knowledge, dispositions, and skills at all points within a program. For example, addressing issues underpinning the development of a lesson could ideally occur prior to, during, and following the student teaching experience. This would certainly be true for teaching about how to consider specific language objectives within various lessons. Yet such an approach generates considerable programmatic pressures if we were to abdicate the responsibility of setting instructional priorities and attempt to teach *all* aspects of our curriculum at all points within a program, which simply is not realistic. Recalling our earlier notion of establishing and adhering to priorities, we urge faculty to take the necessary time and effort to establish a meaningful shared vision for reform and take into account when and how key knowledge, dispositions, and skills are best taught. For us, such a vision is not a soon-forgotten online mission statement, but a living commitment to an ideal with specific and measurable programmatic aims for identifiable points within our program grounded in the developmental needs of our students. Invoking the leading question from Chapter 9 nicely captures the essence of our mission: Does what we do in our teacher education coursework result in preservice teachers enacting effective practices for emergent bilinguals when they are with K–12 students? This overarching question remains at the core of our work as we act on key programmatic reform points in this ongoing effort.

We now make three programmatic recommendations for you to consider as you initiate and/or sustain a process of reform to support linguistically and culturally diverse teacher education:

1. Take into account the contemporary knowledge base for teacher education. Is your program well aligned with this rapidly evolving framework? Within our teacher education programs, we had previously instituted a diversity course requirement and at one point felt satisfied with our plan of study. Please note we are not advocating for eliminating these focused courses in favor of more programmatic infusion. Yet spurred on by accreditation requirements and compelling research, and following an overwhelming series of data points regarding the preparedness of our graduates, we were motivated to further consider how to more effectually infuse cultural and linguistic diversity as central to the knowledge base within teacher education. We contend that as a formal faculty learning community, exploring the breadth and depth of this swiftly evolving knowledge base for teacher education helped us consider how to best initiate and sustain these changes.
2. Establish and nurture a culture of assessment. This does not happen in a vacuum. Programmatically, such work typically unfolds within the context of certification/ licensure and accreditation, and frustratingly these external influences may serve to hinder improvement efforts as opposed to serve as a catalyst for reform. Thus, assessment efforts must not be seen as merely placating those who represent these external factors, but should be viewed as genuinely serving programmatic needs that are ultimately in the best interest of our candidates. Shifting assessment from the periphery of a program to a driving force within its culture is no easy undertaking. For faculty at the Neag School of Education, one turning point was establishing an Office of Assessment rather than adding all of the significant responsibilities of that ongoing work to the faculty load. Establishing our faculty learning community of Project PREPARE-ELLs as a funded effort that further developed and administered its own data collection and analysis for programmatic improvement goals in conjunction with our Assessment Office yielded additional dividends in being able to establish and act on programmatic priorities.
3. Promote preservice learning likely to directly impact knowledge, dispositions, and ultimately practice. Thus, establish outcomes that will likely make a tangible difference for your preservice teachers and their pupils; focus on changes most likely to yield concrete results. Prior to our work in this area, when considering our routine changes made to syllabi over the normal course of our work as teacher educators, all changes typically aimed to impact practice, even if some of those changes were imagined to emerge at some unspecified point in the developmental progression of our candidates. In contrast, for this effort, we contemplated modest observable changes that we expected to see immediately within the practice teaching of our preservice

candidates. That is, this effort was not merely intended to contribute to the knowledge and dispositions of our students but rather to impact purposefully targeted observable behaviors (Pajares, 1992) supported by explicit, systematic, and scaffolded reflection and experiences.

As we conclude this chapter, we'd like to reinforce for our readers that the establishment and sustainment of our community of learners with a shared vision, although time and labor intensive, was perhaps our most significant catalyst for programmatic reform. In a way it was both a precursor and an outcome of our reform effort as it was a necessary element to begin to move forward and exists as an enduring legacy of our work. It was in this safe place, purposefully built for the consideration of teaching, learning, and research, that as a faculty we faced our systemic deficiency in knowledge with regard to preparing teachers to succeed in classrooms with emergent bilinguals. Without such an honest and transparent beginning to our process, it is unlikely that we would enjoy the successes we have achieved to this point. Even given modest yet impactful changes realized through this unfolding process, we remain convinced that we are not unique, and we encourage you to consider your own pathway to program improvement.

REFERENCES

Andrew, M. D. (2005). Teacher preparation—transition and turmoil. In D. M. Moss, W. J. Glenn, & R. L. Schwab (Eds.), *Portrait of a profession: Teaching and teachers in the 21st Century.* (pp. 27–61). Westport, CT: Greenwood Press.

Brisk, M. E. (2008). Program and faculty transformation: Enhancing teacher preparation. In M. E. Brisk (Ed.), *Language, culture, and community in teacher education* (pp. 249–266). Mahwah, NJ: Lawrence Erlbaum Associates.

Cochran-Smith, M., & Zeichner, K. M. (2005). *Studying teacher education: The report of the AERA panel on research and teacher education.* Mahwah, NJ: Lawrence Erlbaum Associates.

Council for the Accreditation of Educator Preparation. (2013, August 29). *CAEP accreditation standards.* Approved by the CAEP Board of Directors. Washington, DC: Author.

Korthagen, F., Loughran, J., & Russell, T. (2006). Developing fundamental principles for teacher education programs and practices. *Teaching and Teacher Education, 22,* 1020–1041.

National Commission on Teaching and America's Future. (1996). *What matters most: Teaching for America's future.* New York: Author.

Neag School of Education Assessment Committee. (2012). *Neag School of Education Assessment Plan.* Storrs, CT: Author. Retrieved June, 2013, from http://assessment.education.uconn.edu/

Pajares, F.M. (1992). Teachers' beliefs and educational research: Cleaning up a messy construct. *Review of Educational Research, 62*(3), 307–332.

Wilson, S. M., & Youngs, P. (2005). Research on accountability processes in teacher education. In M. Cochran-Smith & K. M. Zeichner (Eds.), *Studying teacher education: The report of the AERA panel on research and teacher education* (pp. 591–644). Mahwah, NJ: Lawrence Erlbaum Associates.

13 Final Recommendations for Initiating a Faculty Learning Community

Elizabeth R. Howard, Thomas H. Levine, and David M. Moss

RECOMMENDATIONS

This chapter closes the book by highlighting five key lessons for those interested in promoting collective faculty learning to improve teacher preparation for emergent bilinguals. We then address some questions or concerns that we anticipate others might have as they consider creating their own version of a collaborative faculty learning community. Our top five recommendations are as follows:

1. *Start simply and simply start.* Eight years ago, one professor at the University of Connecticut (UConn) clearly, kindly, and insistently pointed out to some colleagues that not enough was being done to prepare teachers to succeed with emergent bilinguals. When her urging turned into peer coaching with two colleagues, Dr. Mileidis Gort had no idea that several years later, she would wind up facilitating a book club with six other faculty, much less that even after she left our university, the work would continue to evolve into a learning community fomenting change among 18 faculty members. She just knew that something wasn't right, and she started with the participants and methods that seemed most appropriate given the needs and resources she had at hand. In summary, this book is a testament to the potential and power of starting small but seeking to purposefully collaborate. The insights, dilemmas, practices, and progress we've uncovered would be impossible to imagine if there weren't a larger group working together, but that large group would have been impossible to imagine—or create from scratch—without smaller steps that planted seeds.
2. *When initiating, maintaining, or growing collective faculty development, respond to the unique needs, motivations, resources, and incentives relevant to the individuals and larger organization around you.* We intend for this book to help you think about strategies for recruiting diverse individuals with different agendas, respond to the specific mission and incentives that exist within your institution, and develop a responsive set of plans, expectations, and learning activities

that are appropriate for your particular context (see Chapter 3 for more details). Thus, we can't offer a cookie-cutter model that could be blindly replicated across multiple sites; we see too much advantage in being responsive to individuals and institutional context while identifying your own shared ends. As such, we encourage you to consider how to integrate your efforts as a faculty learning community as seamlessly as possible with your ongoing day-to-day responsibilities. This could include folding the learning community work into various research agendas, committee responsibilities, and/or program structures depending on the mission and priorities of your institution.

3. *Promote sufficiently deep learning about emergent bilinguals so that faculty are empowered to reframe the core content of courses on their own and in synch with others.* Ultimately, as suggested in Chapters 4 through 8, preservice teachers should have the chance to learn about emergent bilinguals not just as a separate or added topic, but in relation to multiple aspects of teaching; this is more likely to happen when professors know enough to weave new material into the important preexisting assignments and content of their courses. Although top-down directives from deans or teacher education directors can get things done, we believe you can foster long-term buy-in and investment by inviting faculty participation in shaping the content and methods of learning. This doesn't mean that the blind lead the blind; such input must co-exist with the guidance or advice of scholars who can point to what must be learned and accomplished to adequately prepare teachers to succeed with emergent bilinguals.

4. *To promote depth of learning about emergent bilinguals, develop activities and routines likely to sustain learning and promote accountability across a long time period.* Vygotsky (1962, 1978), activity theorists (e.g., Engeström, Miettinen, & Punamäki, 1999), and those who write about communities of practice (e.g., Lave & Wenger, 1991) have helped us see how we are often able to think and do things with others that would be impossible if we were acting on our own. It may well be that we acquire and internalize new ways of thinking or acting in the world most easily when we have the chance to develop habits of mind and practice in the company of peers and/or more skilled others. Thus, we encourage you to hasten your own learning by thoughtfully organizing joint routines with colleagues. Whether you commit to monthly readings and discussions, sharing practice, visiting schools and reflecting on these visits, or engaging in co-teaching in a partner school with emergent bilinguals, your commitment to some regular collaborative activity will build greater coherence and accountability into your work. As your group builds some understanding of how to take advantage of their joint activity, you are more likely to feel increased momentum, commitment, and accountability to both peers and a shared mission.

5. *Leverage data.* Assessment data can be a powerful factor in demonstrating a need to prospective participants and to the administrators who can offer financial or administrative support. As suggested in Chapters 9 through 12 of this book, data can also inform participants of progress and gaps in their efforts to prepare teachers for emergent bilinguals. Although data can promote some of the learning we envision among a faculty learning community, with sufficient framing and planning, it also can lead to publishable research, making this work more sustainable in contexts that value publication and impacting the field.

Q&A

To close this chapter and volume, we address questions and concerns that we anticipate some readers might have as they consider moving forward with their own collaborative learning activities. A core goal of this volume is to empower faculty to learn together, and we hope that this list of questions and responses provides some of the needed guidance to help readers do just that.

1. How do we get started?

An important first step is to identify leadership for the project; that leader is potentially you, as you are the one who is reading this book! It is convenient if a leader or co-leader has expertise in the education of emergent bilinguals, but scholars with such expertise could also become involved without taking on a leadership role. We have also found some advantage in having one co-leader with an understanding of learning communities. We can similarly envision how faculty members who study learning theory, professional development, organizational learning, or school reform could use their expertise while designing activities that promote change. Perhaps most important is that a leader possesses an enthusiasm for the project and a willingness to promote that enthusiasm among colleagues. The leader does not have to be a tenured faculty member; in fact, none of the leaders at UConn was tenured at the start of the project.

One of the first essential tasks for the project leader will be to recruit participants for the project. The leader may choose to employ some of the recruitment strategies discussed in Chapter 3, or he or she may find other methods that fit the local context to be more effective. Regardless, at the outset, it is advisable to start small and recruit key members who may be most likely to leverage change and/or who may ultimately influence other faculty members to join the project as well.

Garnering administrative support for the project will be another important task for the project leader. At a minimum, it is important to meet with the department chair and dean to keep them apprised of the presence of the project and to state your beliefs in its importance, drawing on demographic data for the nation and your state (see Chapter 1 for examples) as well as any student evaluation data your teacher education program may have (see Chapter 2 for examples). Aligning the project with a core mission of the university and department is also essential, as it helps to frame the project as advancing established institutional aims rather than creating a new endeavor that will distract or diffuse faculty efforts. If you intend to seek funding for the project, it is useful to write a brief proposal stating the goals of the project, the participants, the planned activities and timeline, and the required budget. This will help to establish credibility for the project and provide a point of departure for dialogue with administrators and other stakeholders in a position to provide resources.

Finally, it's useful to begin the project with an eye to the future in terms of goals that you may hope to accomplish so that you consider the nature and scope of data and documentation you may want to collect over time. In our case, starting with classroom-level data collected by participating faculty was most appropriate and useful during the peer coaching and reading group phases, and it continued to be a powerful form of documentation and data collection even as we progressed to the faculty learning community and added in more program-level data-collection efforts (see chapters in Section III). You may also want to include some forms of data collection related to group process; at a minimum, recording and/or taking notes at meetings can serve this function.

2. How do we achieve buy-in from as many faculty members as possible?

See Chapter 3 for our best ideas about recruitment. One of the advantages of starting small is that it affords the opportunity to try things out, learn about what works in your context, and experience some success that might help entice a next wave of faculty to join. In some settings—especially those with large faculty—it may make sense to allow different tiers of participation, with some committing to a different quantity or pace of learning and curricular change than others. Clinical and tenure-line faculty may also benefit from differentiated expectations appropriate to their respective expertise and roles. Finally, regardless of whether there are tiers of participation, setting shared expectations for participation increases the odds that faculty will see that the work is feasible and will not grow into an unmanageable commitment.

3. I can't imagine this working at my institution. I don't know how I would ever convince most of my colleagues to come together and reflect on our practice on a regular basis.

As Chapter 3 and the opening of this chapter have shown, our work at UConn didn't and likely could not have started with a large, cohesive group.

Even now, within the IBM program, less than half of all teacher education faculty actively participate in Project PREPARE-ELLs, but as noted in Section III, we still have observed measurable differences in preservice teacher outcomes during our time of implementation. Start with any colleagues who are interested and allow your project to grow from there.

4. Our teacher education instructors have neither worked with emergent bilinguals in their professional lives nor learned a great deal related to them in their own education. Realistically, how will they be able to help preservice teachers become adequately prepared to work effectively with emergent bilinguals?

Faculty in our project had the same question, and it is a sincere concern that warrants careful attention. In our experience, faculty with limited prior knowledge and experience related to emergent bilinguals have been able to be successful in preparing preservice teachers by doing the following: (a) taking small, manageable steps in introducing new ideas and content related to emergent bilinguals in courses (see Chapters 4, 5, and 7), (b) taking initiative for our own learning and that of our colleagues through joint learning activities (see Chapter 3), and (c) becoming learners ourselves and modeling that stance for our preservice teachers (see Chapter 6). Working collaboratively and continuously with peer coaches who have expertise in the education of emergent bilinguals is also an excellent way to develop the needed expertise and confidence to help prepare preservice teachers (Chapter 11). Finally, participating in workshops, trainings, conference presentations, and other forms of professional development can be important ways to further your own learning.

5. Our program depends largely on adjunct faculty and/or graduate assistants. Such instructors shift from year to year. How can we expect to have continuity with our project and to effect systemic change under those circumstances?

This situation is challenging but not uncommon. At UConn, while the majority of methods courses are taught by tenure-line faculty, many other courses are taught by adjunct faculty and/or graduate assistants, particularly in the TCPCG. In that program, one strategy that has been found useful in promoting continuity is for the core faculty of the program to make key course changes and provide adjuncts and graduate assistants with existing syllabi and/or lists of essential readings and topics that must be addressed in that course. The core faculty then follow up on those topics in later courses, deepening the conversation with preservice teachers and helping them to achieve greater maturity of understanding. Within the IBM program, a more informal, mentoring approach has been applied to achieve the same aims. One of the co-directors has met with new graduate assistants assigned to the senior-year clinical seminar and with new faculty members in the department, providing them with materials and a brief introduction to key expectations related to emergent bilinguals. Similarly, it is possible to provide specific trainings for support staff, such as a SIOP workshop that we provided to student-teaching supervisors to help them become aware of changing priorities in our program and how they could support those new goals. Finally, it is important to keep in mind that it is possible to effect noticeable change in program outcomes without the participation of every instructor. As noted previously, compelling changes have been noted among graduates of the IBM program despite that less than half of all teacher education faculty participate in Project PREPARE-ELLs.

6. What if we have limited flexibility to change individual courses?

Where a teacher education program prescribes more content or aspects of a course, the kinds of shifts noted in Section II would still help instructors infuse teaching about emergent bilinguals. Consider using a frame for the introduction of issues related to emergent bilinguals (Chapter 4), adapting required assignments or activities to also address emergent bilinguals (Chapter 5), and situating yourself as a learner (Chapter 6). Any of these shifts could be accomplished without major changes to course content. In many cases, it is more a matter of changing stance and focus than one of implementing entirely new course activities and materials.

7. Isn't this the job of the bilingual/ESL faculty? Why do other teacher education faculty need to get involved?

We agree that it is, in part, the responsibility of the bilingual/ESL faculty (assuming they exist at your institution) to provide preservice teachers with sound instruction related to the effective education of emergent bilinguals. However, in a stand-alone diversity course, there is not enough time (particularly if it is not even a full, three-credit course) to explore all of the essential ideas related to ELL education (e.g., demographic information indicating the diversity among the emergent bilingual population, core elements of effective programs, foundations of second language acquisition, literacy challenges and supports, assessment requirements, and effective teaching strategies). Moreover, if the diversity course comes late in the program sequence, as it does in the IBM program at UConn, preservice teachers have already completed methods courses and student teaching, and they have already developed emergent practices and identities as teachers that do not incorporate notions of effective instruction for emergent bilinguals. As a result, we have identified methods courses as a particularly important reform point for addressing emergent bilinguals more programmatically (Chapter 12). Recent research has made clear that there are both subject-specific challenges and pedagogies for working with emergent bilinguals, and this content cannot be addressed in depth by bilingual scholars teaching preservice teachers across subject areas (for a fine review of research on the content areas and emergent bilinguals, see Janzen, 2008; see also volumes in Routledge's Teaching English Language Learners Across the Curriculum series, such as Cruz & Thornton, 2009). In our experience, it is more effective to have the bilingual/ESL faculty work in tandem with other teacher education faculty so that preservice teachers benefit from these ideas throughout their course of study, which includes one or more courses focused on linguistic and cultural diversity.

8. What if we do not have internal expertise from colleagues who specialize in the education of emergent bilinguals?

It is undoubtedly more difficult to navigate unfamiliar material and concepts without guidance from someone who is more knowledgeable about the field. However, faculty groups lacking internal expertise could still come together to read and discuss material related to the education of emergent bilinguals. At the end of Chapter 3, we provide an annotated list of readings that we think might be interesting and useful to others. We also provide a list of websites that have useful resources and information related to emergent bilinguals, and some of these may be more manageable at the outset, such as the many digest and briefs available from the Center for Applied Linguistics or the webinars and/or demographic data available through the National Clearinghouse for English Language Acquisition. It also could be helpful to host a faculty speaker series (perhaps via Skype to reduce costs) with ELL experts at other institutions to allow for greater exchange of ideas and an opportunity to have questions answered from someone who is knowledgeable about the field. Similarly, it may be possible to partner with other institutions in your geographical area that have faculty members with expertise in the education of emergent bilinguals. Finally, we wonder whether relevant personnel in local school districts—such as a director of ELL services or an ELL coach—might be given a stipend to work with faculty, particularly using integrated approaches that incorporate both professional reading and direct experiences with emergent bilinguals in local schools.

9. What if there are only a few emergent bilingual learners in our partner schools?

Even if there are currently limited numbers of emergent bilinguals in the partner schools that work with your institution, there still may be benefits of incorporating more information about emergent bilinguals into your course of study. First, while there may be limited numbers of students who are classified as ELLs, there is still likely to be considerable linguistic and cultural diversity among students in at least some of your partner schools. Moreover, research has documented that sheltered instruction is effective for a variety of learners, including current ELLs, former ELLs, and native English speakers (Echevarria, Richards-Tutor, Canges, & Francis, 2011; Echevarria, Richards-Tutor, Chinn, & Ratleff, 2011; Short, Fidelman, & Louguit, 2012).

10. What if our capacity to collect data is limited? How do we know if our project is effective?

It's important to keep in mind that a key purpose of collecting data is to help you monitor progress toward goals that you set. Determining those goals and being realistic about what data sources might help you document progress toward them is key. In many cases, course-based data (e.g., student work, transcripts from class conversations, and reflective memos written after class) are forms of data that can be integrated most seamlessly into the existing work of university faculty and can also produce compelling information about project impact (see Section II of this book).

11. How is it possible to maintain a project like this over time?

We continually ask ourselves this question as our faculty learning community progresses, and we wonder what may come next for our collaborative work. Some strategies that may be effective in sustaining this type of work include the following: (a) sharing documentable outcomes through publications and presentations to help participating faculty meet expected goals for promotion and tenure; (b) connecting with partner schools to bring the work more clearly into the K–2 context, thus promoting opportunities for reciprocal learning between K–12 teachers and teacher educators; (c) inviting graduates back to discuss their work with emergent bilinguals and how the teacher preparation program enabled them to do so effectively; (d) providing incentives, in terms of both inputs (funding for course releases, summer salary, etc.) and outputs (desired products, such as publications and conference presentations); and (e) engaging in grant writing to pursue external funding to further project activities.

12. The faculty learning community at UConn did not backward map their efforts. Should this type of project be more prescriptive with a clear sense of destination?

Some may reasonably argue that it would be more effective to begin with the aims in mind so that we could have a clear sense of how to get there. However, at the time of onset of the faculty learning community, we didn't know what we didn't know, so it was difficult to narrowly define our own learning objectives and outcomes. In addition, a learning community differs from a professional development initiative, in that the members take it upon themselves to explore areas of interest and allow the individuals and group to shift priorities and interests over time. Having said that, Lucas and Villegas's (2011) *Framework for Preparing Linguistically Responsive Teachers* provides an excellent initial specification of desirable destinations and could aid groups as they consider their current strengths, needs, and priorities, as could work by Nutta, Kouider, and Strebel (2012) or Bunch (2013).

CONCLUSION

We still don't claim to be completely satisfied with our efforts to prepare teachers for cultural and linguistic diversity; however, we are satisfied that we are making good progress. That progress is evident in changes to our courses; our preservice teachers' self-efficacy for teaching emergent bilinguals; the way preservice teachers have begun attending to language in the lessons they write for us and the lessons we've observed them teach; and a shift in some of our research trajectories, which now include attention to cultural and/or linguistic diversity. The work of a faculty learning community has given us a common cause and led us to learn from and look at each other's teacher education practice in a way that is welcome progress compared with our isolation as practitioners of teacher education just a few years ago.

Within our project, there have been differences in implementation across the two teacher education programs. Specifically, the implementation in TCPCG has been more top-down and systemic, whereas the implementation in IBM has been more individually tailored to the interests and goals of each participating faculty member. Closing by highlighting these differences might offer one last aid to those thinking about what faculty development and program revision could look like at their own institution. First, TCPCG is shorter in duration, spanning two summer sessions and an academic year, as opposed to three academic years within the IBM program. As a result, there are fewer course offerings, and it is easier to create a matrix whereby key ideas about emergent bilinguals are taught strategically across the various courses. Second, TCPCG has a smaller number of faculty associated with it and relies more heavily on adjuncts and graduate assistants to teach courses. For this reason, there is both the opportunity and responsibility to ensure quality control by providing more guidance with regard to course syllabi, content, and readings. Third, the research interests of the current leadership in TCPCG at the West Hartford campus focus on multicultural education, so there is an inherent motivation to enhance this aspect of the program.

In the IBM program, by contrast, there are more course offerings spread out over a much longer span of time, and perhaps more important, there is a larger number of tenure-line and clinical faculty, all of whom appreciate the autonomy that is characteristic of work in higher education. As a result, the idea of mapping key ideas across specific courses is less compelling to individual faculty members who have their own interests and goals that they wish to pursue within the project and who will invest more of their identity and mission in this work if they can also shape it. In this context, it has seemed most useful to promote a core knowledge base for all faculty through in-house lectures, workshops with outside experts, and ongoing professional reading, while allowing individual faculty members to navigate their own course modifications as they deem appropriate. One consequence of this approach that we have discussed during monthly meetings is that preservice teachers from different content areas are now entering the fifth-year diversity courses with a much greater sophistication about emergent bilinguals, but also with a much greater degree of heterogeneity in their knowledge base, as faculty members have chosen to focus on different topics in their courses. This approach has left us with more work: We are now going to identify which understandings and practices all students should have coming out of courses shared by our various teacher certification programs and out of program-specific courses. Our current work identifying core practices that we seek to promote across programs may also clarify how the diversity elective courses should deepen or add to the practices we target in earlier courses.

As this discussion makes clear, project-level decisions are highly contextualized and ongoing. Each new level of learning and accomplishment raises further questions about implications for the teacher education program and for the project itself. For those of us involved in the project at UConn, this dynamic, collaborative aspect of the project has been highly engaging and rewarding, prompting many of us to stay involved and continue the work. We hope you will join us!

REFERENCES

Bunch, G. C. (2013). Pedagogical language knowledge: Preparing mainstream teachers for English learners in the new standards era. *Review of Research in Education, 37,* 298–341.

Cruz, B. C., & Thornton, S. J. (2009). *Teaching social studies to English language learners* (Teaching English Language Learners Across the Curriculum series). New York: Routledge.

Echevarria, J., Richards-Tutor, C., Canges, R., & Francis, D. (2011). Using the SIOP model to promote the acquisition of language and science concepts with English learners. *Bilingual Research Journal, 34*(3), 334–351.

Echevarria, J., Richards-Tutor, C., Chinn, V., & Ratleff, P. (2011). Did they get it? The role of fidelity in teaching English learners. *Journal of Adolescent and Adult Literacy, 54*(6), 425–434.

Engeström, Y., Miettinen, R., & Punamäki, R. (1999). *Perspectives on activity theory: Learning in doing: Social, cognitive, and computational perspectives.* Cambridge, UK: Cambridge University Press.

Janzen, J. (2008). Teaching English language learners in the content areas. *Review of Educational Research, 78*(4), 1010–1038.

Lave, J., & Wenger, E. (1991). *Situated learning: Legitimate peripheral participation.* Cambridge, UK: Cambridge University Press.

Lucas, T., & Villegas, A. M. (2011). *Framework for preparing linguistically responsive teachers*. New York: Routledge.

Nutta, J. W., Kouider, M., & Strebel, C. (2012). *Preparing every teacher to reach English learners: A practical guide for teacher educators*. Cambridge, MA: Harvard University Press.

Short, D., Fidelman, C., & Louguit, M. (2012). Developing academic language in English language learners through sheltered instruction. *TESOL Quarterly, 46*(2), 333–360.

Vygotsky, L. S. (1962). *Thought and language*. Cambridge, MA: MIT Press.

Vygotsky, L. S. (1978). Mind in society: The development of higher psychological processes (M. Cole, V. John-Steiner, S. Scribner, & E. Souberman, Eds.). Cambridge, MA: Harvard University Press.

Contributors

Sandra B. Billings is an Assistant Clinical Professor in the Teachers Certification Program for College Graduates (TCPCG) in the Neag School of Education at the University of Connecticut (UConn). Her research interests include multicultural education, especially dealing with sexual orientation and at-risk students, and preservice teacher education. Before coming to UConn, she was the Director of Secondary Certification Programs at Fairfield University, and previous to that, she taught math for 27 years in the Norwalk Public Schools, including 22 years in an alternative high school. In Norwalk she served as Professional Development Facilitator and was involved in Connecticut teacher certification for more than 20 years.

Rebecca D. Eckert is an Assistant Clinical Professor in the Neag School of Education, where she works with preservice teachers as they navigate the joys and challenges of their first classroom experiences. As a Professional Development Center Coordinator for two partner school districts, Rebecca maintains a "foot in both worlds" of academia and public education. Her research interests include talented readers, recruitment and preparation of new teachers, arts in the schools, and public policy and gifted education. She is a former middle-school teacher with experience in geography, history, and theatre arts.

Rachael Gabriel is an Assistant Professor of Reading Education at UConn. A former classroom teacher and literacy specialist, she holds a PhD in Education with a focus on literacy studies and certificates in both quantitative and qualitative research methods. Rachael is an associate of the Center on Education Policy Analysis and the Center on Postsecondary Education and Disability at UConn. Rachael's research focuses on the intersections of literacy, disability studies, and teacher quality. Her current research involves analyzing the role of language in the formulation and implementation of policy, curriculum, and evaluation systems.

Wendy J. Glenn is Associate Professor in the Neag School of Education, where she teaches courses in the theories and methods of teaching literature, writing, and language. Wendy was named a University Teaching Fellow in 2009 and Fulbright Scholar to Norway in 2009–2010. Her research centers on literature and literacies for young adults, particularly in the areas of sociocultural analyses and critical pedagogy. She is the former Literature and Literary Analysis section editor for the *Journal of Literacy Research* and President of the Assembly on Literature for Adolescents of the National Council of Teachers of English.

Eileen M. González is an Assistant Professor in the School of Education at the University of Saint Joseph in West Hartford, Connecticut. Eileen's research builds on the limited but growing body of research on the vocabulary development of Spanish-English bilingual students. She is interested in advancing the field of education by exploring the potential relationship of Spanish vocabulary knowledge to English vocabulary development in order to help the growing population of English language learners (ELLs) in our nation's schools attain academic achievement. A native of Puerto Rico, Eileen herself was an ELL who emigrated from Puerto Rico as a young child.

Mileidis Gort is Associate Professor of Bilingualism and Biliteracy at The Ohio State University. Her research seeks to understand: the nature of emergent bilingualism and biliteracy in early childhood; instructional practices and educational policies that support children's bilingual, biliteracy, and academic development; as well as faculty-initiated reform efforts toward culturally- and linguistically-responsive teacher education. She is co-editor of *Early Biliteracy Development: Exploring Young Learners' Use of Their Linguistic Resources* (Routledge, 2012), a national advisor to Sesame Workshop, and Chair of the American Educational Research Association Bilingual Education Research Special Interest Group.

Robin E. Hands is the Director of School-University Partnerships for the Neag School of Education at UConn. She taught elementary school for 10 years. After receiving her MA in Gifted Education, Robin went on to coordinate an enrichment program and advocate for gifted youth. In 1996, she became a school administrator and continued in that role for 11 years. She holds a PhD in Teacher Education and School Improvement from the University of Massachusetts. She has made professional presentations on issues related to gifted education, learning styles, creativity, twice-exceptionality, school leadership, and teacher preparation.

Elizabeth R. Howard is an Associate Professor of Bilingual Education in the Neag School of Education at UConn, where she teaches graduate courses on linguistic and cultural diversity. Together with Tom Levine, she co-led Project PREPARE-ELLs, the faculty learning community on which this book is based. She has also served as a Principal Investigator of two federally funded research studies focusing on the literacy attainment of Spanish-English bilingual students. Previously, she was a Senior Research Associate with the Center for Applied Linguistics (CAL), where she directed a number of projects related to dual language education and biliteracy development.

Douglas Kaufman is an Associate Professor of Curriculum and Instruction at UConn's Neag School of Education. He is the author and editor of several books and articles that focus on writing, literacy education, and teacher education, and he is the former Co-Lead Editor of the *Journal of Literacy Research*. His research interests include the organization of exemplary literacy classrooms, effective teacher-student relationships in literacy learning, the effect of social talk on literacy development, and the role of the teacher as listener. His current research looks at teachers who write in classrooms with their children.

Thomas H. Levine is an Associate Professor in the Department of Curriculum and Instruction at UConn. His research explores how learning communities among high school teachers and among clinical supervisors influence professional practice. He and Elizabeth R. Howard co-led the faculty learning community described in this book. Tom teaches social studies methods courses for elementary and secondary teachers and a doctoral seminar on teacher education. Before working at UConn, Tom taught high school history and led professional development about groups traditionally left out of curricula. Tom and his wife Jihee are raising twin daughters to be bilingual and bicultural.

Alan S. Marcus is an Associate Professor at the Neag School of Education, University of Connecticut where he runs the secondary history education program. He is a University of Connecticut Teaching Fellow and a former high school social studies teacher. His scholarship focuses on museum education and teaching with film. Alan collaborates with museum educators across the United States, partners with the history education program at the University of Nottingham in England, and runs a study abroad field experience for his pre-service teachers in Europe. He recently co-authored *Teaching History with Museums* (Routledge, 2012) and *Teaching History with Film* (Routledge, 2010).

David M. Moss is an Associate Professor on the faculty of the Neag School of Education at UConn. Specializing in curriculum studies, his research interests are in the areas of culturally responsive teaching, global education, and environmental literacy. His published books include *Reforming Legal Education: Law Schools at the Crossroads* (IAP, 2012), *Critical Essays on Resistance in Education* (Peter Lang, 2010), *Interdisciplinary*

Education in an Age of Assessment (Routledge, 2008), *Portrait of a Profession: Teachers and Teaching in the 21st Century* (Praeger, 2005, 2008), and *Beyond the Boundaries: A Transdisciplinary Approach to Learning and Teaching* (Praeger, 2003).

Susan L. Payne is an Assistant Clinical Professor in the Neag School of Education at UConn. She teaches courses within the Integrated Bachelor's/Master's (IBM) program and works with preservice teachers in Professional Development School Districts. She taught in the Albuquerque Public School District for 15 years.

René Roselle is an Associate Clinical Professor in the Neag School of Education at UConn and the Associate Director of Teacher Education. She is a former high school special education teacher who works in partnership with public schools in Hartford and Windsor, Connecticut. She teaches general education courses across all three cohorts in the IBM program. Her professional interests include preparing resilient teachers, urban schools, mindfulness, and school-university partnerships.

Megan E. Staples is an Associate Professor of Mathematics Education in the Neag School of Education at UConn. Her research focuses on understanding how teachers organize student collaboration, inquiry, and argumentation in secondary mathematics classrooms. Her primary teaching responsibilities are within Neag's secondary mathematics teacher preparation program.

Mary P. Truxaw is an Associate Professor of Mathematics Education in the Department of Curriculum & Instruction in the Neag School of Education at UConn. She teaches mathematics methods classes for elementary preservice teachers, along with other mathematics education and teacher education coursework. Mary's primary research centers on the intersection of mathematics education and language, with growing interest in applying discourse analysis models to linguistically diverse mathematics classrooms. Before earning her PhD, Mary was a public school teacher in Connecticut, New York, and California, where she developed her love for and curiosity about the teaching and learning of mathematics.

Manuela Wagner is an Associate Professor of Foreign Language Education in the Department of Literatures, Cultures, and Languages at UConn, where she teaches courses in teaching methods, Intercultural Competence, Pragmatics, languages and cultures, and German language and culture(s). Her research interests include: advocacy for all language learners; the development and assessment of intercultural competence in education; the use of technology in language education; online education; humor and prosody; humor and education; and communicative development in various contexts. She enjoys collaborating with colleagues in various disciplines in pre-K–12 and taught elementary school Spanish before joining the faculty at UConn.

Megan E. Welsh is an assistant professor in Measurement, Evaluation, and Assessment and a graduate of the PhD program in Educational Psychology at the University of Arizona and of the Master's program in Public Policy program at the University of California, Berkeley. Her research addresses the use of assessment as an educational reform lever, measuring teacher effectiveness, program evaluation, and test validity.

Cory Wright-Maley is an Assistant Professor of Education at St. Mary's University College in Calgary, Canada. His research explores social studies simulations and teachers' efforts to teach more powerfully in the social studies. In addition, he has worked collaboratively to create a simulation that helps preservice teachers to experience what it is like to be an emergent bilingual and how to most effectively help them through the use of strategies such as those suggested by Sheltered Instructional Observational Protocol (SIOP).

j. Zack is the Associate Director of Teacher Education for the Teachers Certification Program for College Graduates (TCPCG). He advises and teaches students across subject areas in the program. He has taught foundations courses, methods courses, multicultural education courses, and student teaching seminars. He has experience infusing teaching about emergent bilingual across courses and coordinating teaching about language and cultural diversity across the TCPCG teacher education program. He has published in *The High School Journal*, coauthored a chapter concerning role plays in *The Status of Social Studies: Views from the Field*, and written the entry on sexual orientation and classroom management in Sage's *Encyclopedia of Classroom Management*.

Index

A
Academic language, 45, 74–75, 180
Academic learning, 5, 117, 206
Accountability, 30–32, 177, 220, 232–233
Accreditation, 152–153, 219–224, 227, 229
Adjunct faculty, 29, 235
Administrative support, 233–234
ANOVA, 148–150
Assessment, 223–224, 227, 229, 233
Assignments, 93–96, 179

B
Bicultural experience, 206
Book clubs, 11, 41–42, 45, 231
Bridging theory and practice—*see* "Theory and Practice"

C
Case studies, 11, 14, 22, 97, 168
Center for Applied Linguistics, 55, 57, 158, 237, 245
Center for Research on Education, Diversity & Excellence (CREDE), 57, 141
Clinical seminars, 12, 22, 25, 127
Coach, 39–40, 44–46, 58–59
Common Core State Standards, 57, 68, 86, 94, 104
Communication across courses, 100
Communication barriers, 164–165
Communities of practice, 27, 232
Competitive admissions, 10, 224
Conceptual frames, 11, 63–64, 75, 77–78
Conceptual models for faculty development, 17, 23–28
Content, making accessible, 76, 165

Content objectives, 93, 161–162
Content requirements, 86
Cooperating Teacher, 83, 123, 128, 132, 226
Council for the Accreditation of Educator Preparation (CAEP), 220
Course/content readings, 26, 41, 96
Critical friends protocol, 50–51
Critical pedagogy, 224
Cultural frame, 76
Culturally responsive pedagogy, 19, 181, 190
Culture of Assessment, 8, 223, 227
Curriculum revision, 24–25, 30, 47, 96

D
Data collection (for program improvement), 47–51, 223–224, 232–233
Demographic frame, 69–79, 73–74
Developmental considerations, 124, 227
Differentiating faculty development, 52
Director of Assessment, 152
Dispositions, 19–20

E
Elementary education, 48, 70, 73–74, 85, 156
Elementary social studies, 70
Engagement, 10, 29, 84, 87, 166, 194, 204
English education, 9, 14, 191
ESL Programs—*see* English as a Second Language, 4, 20, 96, 226
Exit surveys, 122, 139, 152, 187

F
Faculty autonomy, 37

Faculty development, 17–18, 37–38, 231–232
 challenges of, 37–38
 models of, 23–31
Faculty institute (model of faculty professional development), 23–26, 39–42
Faculty learning community, 25–31, 42–54
Faculty research—*see* Research
Features of instruction, 157–161
Fieldwork, 95
First Language, student use of, 164
Foreign language methods, *see* world languages methods course
Frame, 63–64
Functional linguistics, 41, 45–46, 180

G
Graduate assistants, 147, 235–236, 239
Grouping strategies, 72, 194, 199, 203, 207–208

H
Home literacy practices, 192, 197

I
Identity, 205–206
Impact concerns, 124, 127–128, 130, 133
Implementation bridges, 125
Individual mentoring (model of faculty professional development), 23–26, 32
Initiating faculty development, 51–54, 233–234
Inquiry, 27–28, 30–31, 47, 98–99, 114
Institutional incentives, 53
Instructional planning, 178–179, 206
Internet resources, 57–58, 128–129

K
Knowledge base for teacher education, 229
Knowledge, skills, and dispositions, 18–20

L
Language acquisition, 22, 75–76, 183–184, 201–207
Language development—*see* language acquisition
Language development frame, 74–75
Language frame, 68–69, 80, 82, 90

Language objectives, 67, 71, 74, 92–96, 155, 161–162
Lesson plans, 93, 161–169
Licensure, 220, 222, 229
Linguistically responsive pedagogy, 39, 206, 211, 225
Listening (teacher), 105–106, 109–119
Literacy and language arts methods, 70, 87, 181

M
Mathematics methods course, 65–69, 80–84
Mathematics register 65–66
Meeting, 41–46, 50–53, 180–181
Mentors/mentorship, 26, 100, 176, 181
Misconceptions, 19, 123
Multiple perspectives, 102

N
National Clearinghouse for English Language Acquisition, 57, 237
National Commission on Teaching and America's Future, 222, 230
Needs assessment, 52, 152

O
Observations, 157–159, 164, 167–168
Obstacles (to collective faculty professional development) 37–38, 225–226
Obstacles (to preservice teacher enactment of practice), 154
Opportunities to practice, 130, 168

P
Partner schools, 123, 237–238
Pedagogical Content Knowledge, 19, 210
Pedagogy of care, 207
Peer coaching, 39–40, 45–46, 231, 234
Perceptions of emergent bilinguals, 166, 191, 201–202, 204–206
Planning team, 53
Poem, "I'm from", 129
Prescriptive feedback, 128
Presentations (to faculty), 46–47
Presentations (of research by faculty), 188, 238
Preservice teachers
 Background experiences, 7, 87–89, 145, 156
 Perceptions of practice, 162–164
 Program feedback, 166–168

Professional action, 174–175, 178, 182, 185
Professional development—*see* Faculty development
Professional Learning Community (PLC), 174, 223
Professional Practices Observation Tool (UConn), 131
Programmatic improvement, 166, 220, 229
Protocol-guided discussion, 49–51
Pull-in (model of faculty professional development), 23, 25–26, 31

R
Recruitment, 40, 42–45
Reform points, 219, 223, 225, 227–228
Register, 65–69, 80–83, 181
Research (as a feature of a faculty learning community), 29–30, 44, 53

S
Scaffolding, 208
Secondary English, 190–195
Secondary Math, 65–70, 80–84
Self-concerns, 124–125, 128, 130
Self-efficacy, 139–142
Self-perceptions, teachers', 149, 154
Seminar courses, 10, 154, 225
Sentence frames, 92, 178
Sequencing methods courses/materials
Sheltered instruction, 45–46, 56, 107, 133–134
Sheltered Instruction Observation Protocol (SIOP), 19, 46, 158, 160–164, 213–214
Social Justice, 43, 76, 126, 179, 182
Social justice frame, 76
Social studies methods course, 70, 86, 90
Spanish proficiency, support for teachers, 144, 167
Spanish, use of 161, 164
Stages of concern model, 124, 127, 130, 134–135

Student teaching, 8–10, 127–133, 159–166, 194–209
Supervisors, 28, 49, 123, 128, 168–169, 210, 223, 236
Sustaining professional development, 51–54

T
Talk tools, 95
Task concerns, 124, 126–127, 129–130, 133
Teacher as learner, 111–115
Teacher Certification Program for College Graduates (TCPCG), 8–10, 140–151, 221, 226, 235, 239
Teacher listening—*see* Listening (teacher)
Teacher educators' capacity (for preparing preservice teachers for emergent bilinguals), 21, 37
Teaching English Language Learners Self-Efficacy Scale—*see* TELLSES
Teaching practices, 128, 131, 159–164,
TELLSES (Teacher English Language Learners Self-Efficacy Scales), 140–149
Theory and Practice, 129, 167, 225
Time constraints, 86–88, 101–102

U
Universal design frame, 76
University supervisors, 123, 128, 168
Unrelated concerns, 124–125, 129

V
Video Project for student teaching, 133–134
Vision, 18, 20–22, 122
Visuals, use of, 71–72, 90, 163

W
Web resources, 57–58, 128–129
Wisdom of practice, 22
World languages methods course, 88, 94, 178–179

For Product Safety Concerns and Information please contact our EU
representative GPSR@taylorandfrancis.com
Taylor & Francis Verlag GmbH, Kaufingerstraße 24, 80331 München, Germany

www.ingramcontent.com/pod-product-compliance
Lightning Source LLC
Chambersburg PA
CBHW050437240426
43661CB00055B/2415